Additional Praise for
The New Divine Feminine

"*The New Divine Feminine* not only includes the core of various traditions but goes beyond them...Meghan Don skillfully blends with our human nature the various faces of the divine mother as she appears at different times in a seeker's life."

> —Tau Rosamonde, founder and presiding bishop at the Gnostic sanctuary Ecclesia Gnostica Mysteriorum

"Meghan Don is THE VOICE when it comes to how we as humans can integrate the feminine aspect in our lives. *The New Divine Feminine* is a deep and poetic gospel to what is needed in our world today."

> —Lars Muhl, bestselling author of *The O Manuscript* and *The Law of Light*

"[Meghan Don] explores the multiple dimensions of the feminine energy and how its renewal will heal not just women and men but all of the natural world...By internalizing and incorporating into our psyche the true power of the feminine in her many aspects, we can bring about a rebalancing of the world. *The New Divine Feminine* is a great contribution toward this goal."

> —Dena Merriam, founder and convener of Global Peace Initiative of Women and founding member of Contemplative Alliance

"Magical, powerful, embodied are key concepts in this illumined articulation of a new feminine spirituality... [*The New Divine Feminine*] is a remarkable work of creative inspirations and genuine gnostic intuitions...highly recommended!"

> —Lee Irwin, PhD, professor of religious studies at College of Charleston and author of *The Alchemy of Soul: The Art of Spiritual Transformation*

"A deeply wise book...*The New Divine Feminine* is a major contribution to comprehend the multidimensionality and lived experience of the sacred feminine."

> —Annette Knopp, non-duality teacher and shamanic practitioner featured in *Ordinary Women, Extraordinary Wisdom: The Feminine Face of Awakening*

"This book is simply filled with treasures that are rare and precious. I love how Meghan Don interweaves her own story—for me, a radiating sign of lived experience, not just cognitive knowing...Look for [your soul's voice], listen, and it will speak to you."
        —Dr. Marj Britt, founder of Called By Love Institute
        and senior minister emeritus at Unity of Tustin

"In *The New Divine Feminine*, Meghan Don offers readers a dive into the inner richness of the feminine soul. She enables us to reach new levels of self-understanding and awareness of our sacred connection with all life."
        —Dr. Linda Bender, author of *Animal Wisdom:*
        Learning from the Spiritual Lives of Animals

"In her divinely inspired and beautiful book, Meghan Don explores the rise of the divine feminine and what she brings for the healing and evolution of our world...Meghan brings forth a profound understanding and integration that you'll find immensely beneficial and true."
        —Carolyn Rivers, founder and director
        of the Sophia Institute

"I love this book! The importance of reimagining the feminine in her wholeness is impossible to overstate, for it is essential to the evolution of the individual and the expansion of world consciousness...In this timely and compelling work, Meghan Don illuminates the feminine in her many dark and light forms, elegantly articulating the hope of restoration, embodiment, and healing. Meghan is a trustworthy guide on the journey toward ever greater freedom and wholeness."
        —Sharon Martin, PhD, Jungian psychoanalyst

the new
Divine
Feminine

To Linda,

May the Feminine break free
from the bonds + find its
full embodiment in you.

Joy Porter of Winding Road Imagery

About the Author

Meghan Don (Charleston, SC, and Nova Scotia, Canada) is an initiate of the Sophian Lineage and the founder and leading guide of the Gnostic Grace Circle. An award-winning author, spiritual mentor, and retreat presenter, Meghan's work helps to raise the feminine consciousness and confidence in our world. She is the author of *Sacred Companions Sacred Community: Reflections with Clare of Assisi* and *Meditations with Teresa of Avila: A Journey into the Sacred,* which won the Ashton Wylie/New Zealand Book Council Award for best book and author. Visit her online at www.GnosticGrace.com.

Meghan Don

the new
Divine
Feminine

Spiritual Evolution for a Woman's Soul

Llewellyn Publications
Woodbury, Minnesota

FIRST EDITION
First Printing, 2016

Book design by Rebecca Zins
Cover design by Lisa Novak
Cover image: iStockphoto.com/17062724©Vladimir Vladimirov

Cover model used for illustrative purposes only and
may not endorse or represent the book's subject.

Llewellyn Publications is a registered trademark of Llewellyn Worldwide Ltd.

Library of Congress Cataloging-in-Publication Data
Names: Don, Meghan, 1961– author.
Title: The new divine feminine : spiritual evolution for a woman's soul /
    Meghan Don.
Description: FIRST EDITION. | Woodbury : Llewellyn Worldwide, Ltd, 2016. |
    Includes bibliographical references and index.
Identifiers: LCCN 2016013600 (print) | LCCN 2016016875 (ebook) | ISBN
    9780738748610 | ISBN 9780738749167
Subjects: LCSH: Women and religion. | Women—Religious life.
Classification: LCC BL458 .D65 2016 (print) | LCC BL458 (ebook) | DDC
    200.82—dc23
LC record available at https://lccn.loc.gov/2016013600

Llewellyn Worldwide Ltd. does not participate in, endorse, or have any author-ity or responsibility concerning private business transactions between our authors and the public.

All mail addressed to the author is forwarded but the publisher cannot, unless specifically instructed by the author, give out an address or phone number.

Any Internet references contained in this work are current at publication time, but the publisher cannot guarantee that a specific location will continue to be maintained. Please refer to the publisher's website for links to authors' websites and other sources.

Llewellyn Publications
A Division of Llewellyn Worldwide Ltd.
2143 Wooddale Drive
Woodbury, MN 55125-2989

www.llewellyn.com
Printed in the United States of America

To the soul of the world—
to the feminine spirit rising in us all.
May she be heard and seen in her strength
and in the purity and fertility
of the life that she is.

I awakened you under the apple tree.

Song of Songs 8:5 NKJV

And into this life I was born
Already alive
With the One Face seeing through
The many faces
Witnessing the beauty that makes up
This humanity, and also its coarseness.
She, this One Face, has kept me company
As I swirl and slide through seemingly
Unending layers of this earthly living
She never departs from me
Even when my own coarseness seeks its life
Even when death is desired.
There is nothing more loyal in this life and the life hereafter
Than our holy face
She does not know the meaning of separation
She does not know anything other than the fullness of we.

Meghan Don

Contents

Chapter 3: Daughter of the Dark   63

Chapter 4: Our Mother of Light   97

Chapter 5: Our Mother of the Dark   131

Contents

Acknowledgments

Thank you to all at Llewellyn who saw the larger appeal and scope of this book even when my vision was not quite as wide. Thanks to the wonderful team of Amy, Becky, and Kat, and to those in and behind the scenes. Many thanks to Kimberly Walls, my first independent editor, who strengthened the work considerably with her razor-sharp editing eye, always seeking greater clarity for the reader and fine-tuning the initial manuscript. I genuinely enjoyed every question you asked and every suggestion that was made. You are a living example of the feminine intelligence.

My gratitude to Tau Malachi for giving so freely of his time and the Sophian teachings, and for seeing me through some very difficult times and transitions. And to all members of the Sophian community, I thank you for your dedication and all you bring to the world. I pray that the teachings I have received will continue to evolve and go into the world as has been envisioned, to open the mysteries to all the souls who hunger for the greater feminine wisdom.

My gratitude also to all those souls who have been intimately walking with me as their mentor and guide. I love you dearly for your courage and willingness, and also for those times when you have not been so willing. Every single aspect of your journey has contributed to the wisdom shared here. I look forward to walking in ever-greater depth with you all. And thank you to Rev. Janice Billera, who, upon undertaking a personal retreat, asked to know the mysteries of the seven faces of the feminine. It was through your desire and questioning that this book came into its form.

A special thanks to Celia Alvarez for walking through all the trials of spiritual community evolution with me. We are sisters of a strong, interdependent nature, constantly drawing each other along the fertile mother pathway that has yet to be walked. Blessings and thanks to Aimee Cubillo, another renegade sister, who has believed in me from the day we met and has held me to the highest possible vision of myself, even when I was scraping my knees and elbows (and other places) from the friction created between the new and old paradigms. To Suzie Daggett for all the walks and talks, the bed whenever I needed one, numerous rides to the airport, and for allowing me to lie on your lawn and play with your cats; thank you! And thanks to Joy Brisbane, my staunchest supporter for more years than I can remember. Your own journey into your natural feminine strength, simply who you are, has been an inspiration.

Thank you to Mother Earth, who has nourished me on those many contemplative and inspiring walks. And thank you to the many light and dark faces of the daughter, the mother, and the grandmother/ crone, who have revealed to me again and again the inner natural strength, radiant awareness, and capacity of our being. My dearest hope is that many of us will day by day wake up and embody this.

Finally, thanks to Magdalene and Yeshua for consistently shattering old patriarchal paradigms while you were on this earth and for cosmically hanging out with all of us who are called to embark upon the co-creation and embodiment of what you seeded all those many, many years ago.

Introduction

The body, feminine nature, and spiritual mythology—and what role these play in humanity's evolution—have always been a great source of intrigue and contemplation for me. I discovered the ecstatic nature of the body through dance and chant in the Hindu and Sufi religions, a deeply contemplative and mystical nature in the Christian and Jewish traditions, and a great consciousness of mind in Buddhism. However, there was a greater contemporary feminine contribution that was clearly missing; it seemed to be stuck in a mire of unworthiness and a lack of trust and confidence within the women themselves, stopping them from bringing forward new and feminine ways in all of the traditions. Fortunately, this is now slowly changing.

This book was born through many years of seeking to uncover the true empowerment of the feminine soul. It provides a pathway to enter into not only one's own spiritual evolution but also the collective evolution of humanity and this good earth. My own journey has been like an eternal labyrinth: now moving very close to the center, now walking on the outer rim, weaving my way in and out of the land of soul and body and mind. Along the way I have discovered many divine faces of the feminine, and coming into spiritual and earthly intimacy with them has called for courage, determination, receptivity, and a rigorous, loving honesty of self in all possible ways. It is a journey well worth taking, as it reveals the grand jewel of our inner powerful and compassionately loving being.

The Christian mystic women and saints of old who came to me showed me their undeniable strength, courage, and ultimate confidence. I wanted that. I travelled further back in time to the Cathari women and priestesses (a Christian Gnostic branch circa 1100–1300s), who lived in spiritual equality with men and priests. I wanted that too. And even further back, to the time of Magdalene and Yeshua. Time then presented itself to me in a very different way.

It was Easter, and I was on retreat in New Mexico at the Monastery of Christ in the Desert. We rose early in the morning on Sunday, celebrating a fire ritual and welcoming the Risen One. As the abbot was holding the bread and wine high in the air over the altar, asking for it to be blessed, another realm of vision opened to me. What I saw was Yeshua and Magdalene dancing around the altar. This dance was mesmerizing and so very beautiful, as these two souls danced with what I can only describe as a truly honoring unity. I then watched as Yeshua deliberately retreated and allowed Magdalene to come forward. As she did, she began to reveal to me the grandness of her soul, which took on such a vastness and a magnitude that went far beyond this earthly realm, entering into what I can only call cosmic proportions of soul. I witnessed that all of creation was within her, and she was all of creation. She was the matrix in which all of life was transpiring, and even more so—she extended beyond this creation, reaching into all realms and universes. It was truly one of the most expansive visions I have ever seen. She then came close and touched me gently on the shoulder, saying, "It is time to trust in love again."

I knew Magdalene had shown me her expansiveness by way of invitation, she being a way-shower into the true nature of being, sacred womanhood, and what I now understand to be the soul of the world, which is the very feminine creative matrix in which all of life and death unfolds. She was also telling me that only by trusting in love again could I come to know and experience this myself. This vision was a profound experience of soul gratification and affirmation. It left me deeply peaceful, as if a soul awareness within me had been reawakened. It also showed me that the image of this soul of the world—this true sacred womanhood—was alive and well, and that it is here now, not lost in some ancient world. And, most importantly, it is available to all who are willing to enter the great soul realm and trust again. She had spoken a new-old myth for all of our feminine ears and eyes to hear and see.

Part of this new-old myth also includes encountering our sacred nature of darkness. While on a pilgrimage to Italy I found myself before a Black Madonna in a small chapel. Instantaneously I was on my knees in communion with her. She drew from within my soul a very old pain, one I was not even consciously aware of, and she took this and transformed it in the radiant light of her sacred heart. She returned to me the gift of peace, telling me she is here to help heal all of her children, seeking to return them to their rightful spiritual heritage. It was this true spiritual heritage that became my quest, especially in the form of the fulfilled and realized light and dark feminine nature.

The Sophian lineage, where I took up studies and was initiated a few years later, revealed and deepened my knowledge and ultimate gnosis of these experiences. I met the many dark and light faces of the feminine, and it was revealed that the dark faces went far beyond the psychological interpretation of the shadow and were, in fact, where the latent feminine power and wisdom were waiting to resurrect. I have heard the Black Madonna described as the gentle Kali (the Hindu goddess of death and destruction), and while this gentleness is certainly one aspect of the dark mother, there is so much more. There is passion and wildness of spirit, vast wisdom that defies all logic, and life-giving freedom that extends beyond this world and its narrow ways. Equally, the light faces of the feminine have been misrepresented, stripped of their power, and relegated to a wrongful submissiveness.

It is the varied and unique light and dark feminine faces that we explore throughout this book, seeking to bring forth their true power and light in the form of the daughter, mother, and grandmother, or crone. And, most importantly, we look toward the unification of the light and dark faces, for this is where our true nature and strength reside—our inner virgin of pure radiant awareness. When we are able to enter into unification, we not only bring about our own spiritual evolution but also the resurrection of the soul of the world, the feminine soul, in her full creative power.

As we are intricately bound with this soul of the world, she relies upon us to co-create with her in order that we may all evolve, collectively and personally, human and beyond, extending to all the many world systems that exist. A Gnostic text, *Three Forms of First Thought*, offers us a place to view her sacredness and her eternal nature: "I am the movement that is in all, she in whom the realm of all takes its stand...she who exists before all." She is not static or fixed; she is a continual force propelling existence toward its destiny. In *Mysterium Coniunctionis*, Carl Jung writes that the feminine nature relates to the secrets contained in the physical world, and her goal is to seek union with all that exists. This union is the natural ability of the feminine energy and is where her power resides. It is the destiny of both the soul of the world and our own soul; it is she who seeks union with us and we who seek union with her.

In co-creating with the soul of the world, then, we are contributing to the much-needed feminine restoration. Each one of us comes here with our story, our karma, our soul-bleeding, our *tikkune*, which is a Hebrew word for repairing, restoring, or healing. The story of the hemorrhaging woman in Mark 5:25–34 tells us that nothing is able to staunch the flow of her blood—that is, no amount of earthly efforts can stop her life force from leaving her body or the bleeding of her soul's wounds. Only when she encounters the ultimate truth in herself, has faith, and trusts in this truth does her life force take hold in her body and soul. In this instance, then, her healing takes place through her recognition of the truth in Yeshua and having faith. When we can recognize this ultimate reality in another, we are opening the portal to our own true nature. And when we enter into this act of restoring and receive healing on a personal level, we are helping to heal and repair that very wound for the collective good as well. It is often the collective story or myth that can point us toward this place of reparation. We need to unfetter ourselves from stories of long ago and bring a renewed myth-telling for a new consciousness. In this way we are going beyond an individual psychological catharsis and moving into a deeper spiritual healing for the whole of humanity.

As I have worked with my own soul restoration and that of others, the shared themes arising again and again, as stated above, are the feelings of unworthiness and a lack of trust and confidence in self, which I continually trace back to our early stories of creation and soul or, more specifically, the story of Eve and Adam and the biting of that first apple, or what is called the Fall. Somehow deep within the crevices of the feminine soul there lies a feeling of wrongdoing, of no longer trusting her innermost voice, and of pleasure and desire having led her astray. The irony of this is that the Fall story has been completely misrepresented and misunderstood, which has resulted in subjugation rather than liberation. In short, it is a lie in how it has been taught and ingested. No matter what tradition we belong to now, or even if we belong to none at all, and no matter if we are female or male, this myth has had deep psychological and spiritual consequences for our Western culture. It is time for a retelling.

The teachings in this book, though based on the oral tradition of the Sophian Lineage, are given in accordance with my own evolving personal experience as transmitted and revealed directly. I feel blessed to bring them into written form.

We turn now to our spiritual heritage and quest, where we venture into the true story of Eve, the rising of the feminine consciousness, and our quest for the true embodiment of the realized feminine.

1

Our Spiritual Heritage and Quest

The Desire of Eve

Eve, or *Havah* in Hebrew, can be translated as "to be and become life." She can be understood as the daughter (and subsequently the mother) who initiated our life here on earth.

We all know the regular story in Genesis. God tells Eve and Adam they are free to eat of all the trees in the garden—but not of the tree of knowledge of good and evil. The snake shows up and tells Eve, "No, you will not die; in fact, you will acquire great wisdom." Eve saw this to be true, plus she also saw the goodness of the fruit and found it pleasing to her eye. She shared the fruit with Adam, and something happened: they found their eyes opened to the world of duality. They became aware of the feminine and the masculine, and of the polarities within their nature.

Making them tunics of skin—that is, giving them bodies and bringing them into physical form—God sent Adam and Eve into the physical world to begin the journey of remembering their nature of unity.

This was the same unity of nature they had been previously experiencing wandering in the garden with God, but now they were being asked to do this same wandering and remembering in the world of perceived duality. Sound familiar?

Rather than a punishment for disobedience, pride, desire, and all the other interpretations, what really was going on was the great gift of awakened consciousness for humanity. It was the journey of the soul, previously in complete union with the source of creation, now stepping into a unique and distinct skin, or body, and seeking its own conscious union.

And what of the snake? Always personified as the evil one and often portrayed as the feminine temptress, the poor snake has been banished, vilified, and feared. And yet the snake essentially represents the equivalent to the Eastern kundalini energy, or the innate power and life force of the human being. This energy was now unleashed in humanity through Eve and Adam's setting forth on their course of free will, either to become a help or a hindrance to their journey of return. (Some say this snake was Lilith, Adam's first wife, but more of her later.)

For how long have we read this myth as a punishment for doing something wrong—for falling into some wrongful action or place or desire? That some God somewhere doesn't really want our happiness but wants us to suffer our way through this life? And yet, nothing could be further from the truth. Rather than a falling away from God or grace, we can say this whole myth was an activation of our greater inner wisdom, life force, and power. It was also a gift of knowing these forces and qualities consciously within our individual souls rather than through an unconscious unification. I, for one, am glad that Eve took and ate the apple (which was probably a fig or pomegranate, or maybe even an apricot) and that she trusted her inner wisdom to do so. I am pleased that she allowed her vision of goodness, beauty, and pleasure to aid in her decision of true desire, which was clearly joined with an open curiosity, to undertake what she did. And I applaud her for not only wanting to share all of this with her partner, but also for opening the way for the soul of the world to know herself in this physical creation and through all of humanity.

There was no punishment or banishment occurring in this myth. There was, though, a compassionate warning. Adam was told he would have to work hard to receive results; Eve, that she would suffer pain in birthing; and the snake would lose its legs and crawl on its belly. Let us hear this in relation to our inner journey and work. Yes, the inner work does require our determination and perseverance, and we do need to work hard at keeping distractions at bay and maintaining our inner focus. And yes, there are times when it is painful to let go of the old and birth new consciousness. As for crawling on our belly—on this plane we will need to learn to elevate our will and yet be intimately connected with the sacredness of this good earth.

Naturally, there are also external implications to be considered in this myth. If we are still desiring and looking on the outside for our happiness (Eve desiring her husband), if we are still trying so hard to make our living in the world and think we don't deserve anything else (Adam toiling the ground), and if we experience inner conflict about what we are doing here on this earth (the snake offering a greater life-power and the free will to serve either self or all), then we are still bound by this myth. And, of course, the biggest myth of all: if we are denying our feminine voice and are not speaking outwardly, then somehow we are afraid of heeding our inner wife's voice while unconsciously (or perhaps consciously) questioning what form of separatist earthly punishment we may set in motion or have to endure.

Let us instead look anew at Eve's role as an initiator, as one birthing a new consciousness and life for humanity. Let us read her actions as a blessing rather than a curse. And through this, can we stop doubting the feminine voice and guidance and follow her in confidence, knowing that no matter the surface reality or outcome, there is something far larger and greater at play? Can we welcome her back to her natural place of strength and wisdom? Can we call her name in honor and gratitude rather than shame and hiding?

Now, of course, with any myth there are myriad interpretations, and this is one amongst many, but considering the others we have been given, I think it is an important and restoring one. It allows the feminine to rise instead of fall. We will return to this myth and its continuation, with special reference to Lilith, further throughout the book, as that is when we start to bring the dark and the light feminine back into unity.

Embodiment

> Yeshua said, "If the flesh came into being because
> of spirit, it is a marvel. But if spirit came into being
> because of the body, it is a marvel of marvels…"
> Marvin Meyer (translator), The Gospel of Thomas, v. 29

The word *embodiment* has been used a lot in our modern spirituality, and there has been a very necessary movement back into the body intelligence, revealing the true nature of light that is contained therein. With our emphasis on mental consciousness and awareness—the transcendental God, if you will—we have disembodied ourselves from our own earthly ground of being. We have still been acting like the stringent Yahweh supporters of old, thinking or believing that the physical component of life is less than the more spiritual nature of our being.

This belief has led us to disembodiment, separation, and ultimately the denial of the God within all. There is no true enlightenment in this—or, perhaps more accurately, there is a partial enlightenment of mental consciousness only.

We need to learn of the absolute necessity for integrating and living our wisdom and spiritual knowledge upon this earthly plane in this earthly body. We may fly to the regions of spirit and even live there for some lifetimes, learning and understanding more of the spiritual truths; however, it is only when we are able to live them here, upon earth, that they become a reality and we progress and grow in our life. The physical earth in this way becomes the grounding station, if you like, for the evolutionary process of humanity. Far from being inferior or less than, the physical form becomes not only the vehicle of the spirit for the birthing of our (and its) own new consciousness, but also where the spirit of both divine mother and father, daughter and son, are consciously united in the human one, in the physical, mental, and spirit consciousness.

Religious commentaries on our Fall stories and the myths of the world soul have often posited that the physicality of this world—or matter, the body, and the feminine, who represents all of these—needs to be redeemed. I would say there is nothing that needs to be redeemed in any of these; that when we look with the eyes of truth, we will see the light radiating in its full presence, a light that has always been there, will always be there, and is there right now. The physical nature of the world has no problem with its sacredness; it is simply being that sacredness. Our body has no problem with its divinity; it is simply being who it is. And the feminine soul of the world—or matter, which is derived from *mater*, or mother—knows the true nature of all. The only place we find a problem is with our transcendental thoughts and beliefs, believing that none of these physical representations are sacred, thinking there is some kind of deficiency or lack, and believing that some transcendental knowledge is superior to our inner wisdom and knowing. Or, as Reginald Ray says in *Touching Enlightenment: Finding Realization in the Body*:

> We will see that every aspect of our world, our life, and ourselves is and always has been a free, liberated, and completely pure expression of enlightenment. In this sense, we have not redeemed matter, but we have redeemed ourselves from the terrible error of thinking that matter is ultimately not spiritual, that somehow realization is found somewhere else.

We have different aspects of soul, all representing a gradation of understanding; some are more aligned to our earthly nature and others with our heavenly nature. Where they meet is often where the confusion and friction lies—and where the very ground lies for their union. It is this ground that becomes the fertile birthing place: the place where the body, soul, and spirit commune and intermingle, if you will. We have placed much focus on the body and the ego-mind remembering its divine nature, but I don't believe that is the real problem. Try speaking to your soul and telling it that this body and this ego and this world are sacred just as they are, and see what happens. You may just find an enormous relief, quiet, and peace. This understanding paves the way for true union of all aspects of our soul, for without this peacekeeping truce there can be no union. Ultimately what we are speaking of here is self-love, which is the greatest act of embodiment and enlightening peace you can enter into for yourself and this world.

Embodiment begins with feeling, a deep soul feeling. If we listen to this feeling and feel this feeling, we can then speak and act upon what is being revealed and bring it into the world in a true and right way when it is ripe to do so. Janis Joplin captured something of the richness and necessity of this soul feeling when she said that the only reason we're stuck with the myth that only black people have soul is because white people don't let themselves feel things. This ability to feel and to allow communication is the beginning of our sacred relationship with our own selves and the opening to our embodied power. In opening to this power we can then enter into authentic relationship with others, with nature and all of her creatures and creation, and the other cosmic realms and the beings therein. The Gospel of Philip tells us that "authentic beings are who they have always been, and what they engender is authentic: simply becoming who one is." Our authenticity lies in our power to be, our power to be lies in our embodiment, and our embodiment lies in soul feeling, which ultimately becomes not-knowing and knowing all at once, or what we can call *gnosis*.

Our bodies need to become central to our spiritual journey, and increasingly among women it is being shared that the body has begun speaking through its physical pains. These pains are an invitation to us to listen and to feel, usually where we have been unwilling to previously go. We need to make the appropriate space and time to answer these body sensations and what they bring. Great liberation can be found in crying those uncried tears, in feeling that anger that was not allowed expression, in soothing the trauma of days gone by. And in becoming familiar with this, we can then engage in the moment, as much as we are able, so nothing becomes stored for later. As the insightful author Shannon L. Alder says, we must give ourselves permission to communicate what matters to us in every situation, and only then will we have peace, no matter if we are rejected or disapproved of. She also says that we must put a voice to our soul in order to let go of the negative energy of fear and regret. I would add that putting a voice to your soul also expresses the innate power that seeks to rise in you—not in a way that lords it over another but in a way that raises you to your greatest compassionate and loving self, and allows you to bring to the world what you are here to bring.

Embodiment is not just about getting back to the earthly body, however; it is also returning to the light body and allowing the two to become as one. The light body can be understood as our heavenly image and likeness, and our physical body as the earthly image and likeness. In verse 48 of the Gospel of Thomas we read that if two make peace with each other in the one house, they will be able to move a mountain. The one house is our unified being, and the heavenly and earthly bodies are the two. And so what is being said here is that the unity of both brings fullness of strength (expressed through speaking the unified will) and the ability to move any obstacle in life. In verse 22 of the same Gospel we read:

> When you make the two one, and when you make the inside like
> the outside and the outside like the inside, and the above like the

below, and when you make the male and the female one and the same, so that the male be not male nor the female female; and when you fashion eyes in place of an eye, and a hand in place of a hand, and a foot in place of a foot, and a likeness in place of a likeness, then you will enter [the kingdom].

This is a natural extension of verse 48, where the unity of the light and the earthly bodies creates something other, something beyond what we currently know and experience, something that allows us to enter the queendom/kingdom of God here and now, knowing it to be closer to us than our own heartbeat. It is not a disembodied meditative experience but something that moves and breathes and speaks and acts, though in a very different way than this world operates.

My own experiences of this merging of the light and the earthly bodies can only be described as magical and powerful, with the physical body having a great sense of lightness of being. The density of the earthly body disappears and yet the body is still present, though in a much lighter form. These experiences include being able to move very swiftly, with what only can be described as a gliding motion, covering distances in a very short space of time that would normally be impossible for the earthly body alone. Healings have occurred where a person's wholeness of body has been restored as if the physical injury never happened, and one is able to become the very energy that one desires. A particular experience that remains so profoundly with me was becoming the mother body-energy and pouring out blessings upon the earth to all of her children, with such deep compassion and love flowing through the whole of my being. Another was becoming my own innermost bride and feeling the earthly soul and sexual energy merging into one with the heavenly radiant energy, experiencing the fullness of womanhood through a likeness in place of a likeness.

These were all experiences of and through the unified earthly and light bodies, neither one nor the other but both, signifying true embodiment. So let us not stop at our concept of what we think embodiment is but keep moving ever toward that queendom that is near at hand. In the Hebrew language the word hand is equated with the power of God, so let us avail ourselves of this, throwing aside our fears, for this true power is what we all desire because it is ultimately who we are.

I speak of these experiences as a way of saying yes, this is possible. And it must also be said that these experiences happened in very different circumstances: one when there was imminent physical danger from another, one when in the company of love with another, one through loving compassion and necessity for another, and one in dancing alone. There is no one perfect setting or situation but rather the grace of the spirit flowing in accordance with the moment and our own attunement and intimacy with this spirit.

Women are understood to have an advantage when it comes to embodiment as by their very nature they are considered to be closer to their bodies, more available to them. So here we have a turning of the tides: rather than the attunement to the body being an obstacle and a curse, it now becomes a spiritual advantage and a way of advancement. The epigraph at the beginning of this section—"If the flesh came into being because of spirit, it is a marvel. But if spirit came into being because of the body, it is a marvel of marvels..."—gives us much cause for reflection. Where do this earth body and light body wish to take us? What marvels and wonders exist within them that even the spirit can learn from, remembering that even the spirit is evolving also? It feels as if there are many more mysteries than I have spoken of here. What is being spoken and conveyed to us with this bodily attunement is that now is the time for women to trust again, to become the teachers, the protectors of true life, and the providers of spiritual wisdom. It is time for the full realization of the feminine soul. If we can claim the inherent strength that is ours to bring, then this will be so.

Before we can make the male and female one and the same, we must first be able to fully embody both of these energies in their authentic and true nature. I do not feel we have witnessed or experienced the authentic nature of either the masculine or the feminine. When we are able to do this in peace, then all of the judgment stops and unity is possible. With unity comes an even greater power. The Kabbalists, the Jewish mystics of the medieval era, began to bring forward teachings on the union of the immanent and transcendental, or the divine mother and father. They tell us that the inclination of the father and the mother toward each other never ceases. They always dwell together and go out together; they never separate or leave each other. They are together in complete union. Kabbalists honored the Shekinah and began to speak of the interchangeability of the feminine and the masculine energies, now appearing as mother, now as father, now as daughter, now as son. Kabbalistic studies were, and still are, considered an advanced spiritual practice and study, and unfortunately for much of their life were limited to male students only. Women were not considered to have the spiritual or emotional capacity to work with such energies. Perhaps the fear of the feminine nature and power was too much for the male teachers to directly and physically encounter in women students, or perhaps it was simply the ignorance of old religiosity playing out. And so the Shekinah within women, and within men, was still in exile, but she is tenacious, this feminine one, and so she keeps rising. It is to this continual rising that we now turn.

The Second Coming

In her wonderful book *The Dark Mysteries of the Moon,* Demetra George gives an in-depth study of the feminine cosmic cycle, using the phases of the moon and astrological ages as a way to demonstrate the cyclical nature of our history. She speaks of the decline of the age of the Goddess, or the matriarchy, and the rise of the masculine, or patriarchy, and the Sun God. Rather than a deliberate act of repression and annihilation, she understands this as the cosmological ages shifting with the feminine entering into a dark moon phase, or a natural destruction and death phase, where she will regenerate and grow stronger, once more re-emerging when the next cycle arises.

She notes that it was through a feminine constellation that Yeshua appeared. Because he arrived within a masculine age, with the world still monopolized by the masculine warring energy, humanity was unable to receive his message of love and compassion. Understandably, says George, "the feminine principle continued to be dormant in a dark moon phase throughout most of the Piscean Age, while the masculine energy proceeded to ascend unrestricted." Nevertheless, Yeshua sowed the cosmic seeds he was to bring to this earth, and in looking toward another age he spoke of troubled times for the world and how we would see the fully human one coming on the clouds of heaven with power and great glory. (In reference to Matthew 24:30, Son of Man, which is traditionally used, means the fully realized human one.)

For hundreds of years this passage has been interpreted as Yeshua himself literally appearing again; however, this literalism needs addressing, just as all teachings and traditions need to be in a flow of growth. If they remain rigid and fixed, then so do our souls—and our evolution comes to an abrupt halt. In reality our bodies are fluid, our minds are constantly entertaining different concepts and beliefs, and our souls are stretching into the cosmic galaxies, which are always moving and changing. As George points out, we are now entering a 40,000-year lunation cycle of the Goddess, and so our soul and worldviews are changing accordingly. We see this through the rise of ecology awareness, relational modalities coming into the business world, neglected and abused children and women standing up, religious and spiritual paradigms crumbling and being reformed with a feminine face, and the strength and confidence of her voice starting to be heard again through many peoples. We have had the time of single enlightened beings, particularly through the masculine model of mental consciousness, but now is the time for soul consciousness through many beings. This is the Second Coming—the rise of the many through the rise of the feminine in her fullness of power and visibility in the world.

Mother Ann Lee, who became the leader of the Shakers in 1774, began preaching that the Second Coming was to actualize the Christ in feminine form. Those who were following the Shaker way understood Mother Ann as being that very female embodiment of Christ. Unfortunately, she suffered terribly in her body as punishment for such proposed blasphemy, which ultimately led to her death. Around the mid 1850s there arose another who was also considered the feminine Christ or an emanation of Mary Magdalene; her name was Tau Miriam. As she was part of an oral tradition that sought to keep the fullness of the Christian mystical mysteries alive, true to their secret nature, there was nothing written about her. Afraid that she would be placed on a spiritual pedestal, she personally denied all such claims of her supposed emanation and would not allow it to be propagated at all, saying that this would deter others from realizing it in their own selves. At this same time Madame Blavatsky was rising into her leadership role, bringing forward important esoteric and Eastern teachings to the West.

What a fascinating time of the feminine rising. How or what provoked such a thing? As we know, astrological ages have their cusps, or transitional times, so perhaps we can understand it from that perspective as the very early beginnings of the Goddess return. Or, at that time, at least with a small number of people, their consciousness was opening and they were simply ready to receive the fullness of both the feminine and masculine Christ, paving the way for (and of) a very ancient and new path. Of this path we can also say that we now know there were early Christian women teachers, particularly in what are now called the Gnostic communities, through to the time of the Cathars' demise in the 1200s and 1300s and continuing on in underground movements, particularly in Europe. The mystics also arose crying in the dark nights of our spiritual history, holding and developing that spark through their own journeys and bodies—Hildegard of Bingen, Julian of Norwich, Clare of Assisi, and Teresa of Avila, to name a few. These women all spoke of God as Mother and knew greater mystic secrets than they revealed through their writings, but in their time any such thing as the feminine Christ would have been fatal to their very lives and perhaps not even quite admissible to their own selves. They all played an important role, however, in keeping the feminine fire alive, waiting for the time of greater and true recognition.

Sophian legend speaks of Mary Magdalene making a vow to return to this earth in womanly form until the full realization of sacred womanhood was known, and therefore in the more esoteric traditions there was a teaching and belief corresponding to this one woman returning. With time, however, this notion of one turned into many, first being understood as returning through many women and then eventually to returning through many women and men. "You will see the people of the One coming on the clouds of heaven with power and great glory" (another rendition of Matthew 24:30). The clouds are the Shekinah, the divine feminine, joining with the people who know the One, bringing the fulfillment of both heaven and earth through the embodiment of power and glory. Glory speaks of the light body. Power speaks of the return of the feminine, the body of realized matter, allowing for the authentic human being to consciously dwell in the Living Presence of all that she is.

The feminine, in her immanence, represents the many. The masculine, in his transcendence, represents the one. We are now in the time of the many. We are now in the time of the Second Coming. And this Second Coming is not specifically Christian; in fact, it belongs to no tradition at all, for that is where we are heading—spiritual wisdom becoming no lineage at all—and yet still the foundational wisdom of the traditions will be acknowledged and given, but in new form. Much like the cusp times of astrology, we are now in the cusp times of spirituality, with the old breaking down and the new still forming itself. Both are needed, with the old anchoring the ways and practices that bring transformation and the new releasing the old ways that are no longer relevant, bringing forth practices that are more accessible and appropriate for our psyches. This is called spiritual evolution, and it is natural. There is no need for a fight from either side but simply a deeper understanding of frictional cusp times birthing something anew.

The concept of a Second Coming is not isolated to Christianity. It also appears in the major schools of Buddhism with the coming of Maitreya, who is understood to be a future Buddha appearing in this world when the teachings, the *dharma*, have been forgotten by most. There have been Chinese emperors who have claimed the title, the Bahá'ís understand their leader as being Maitreya, and there is even a contemporary male spiritual teacher in California who also lays claim to being this one. And so this Second Coming concept is clearly something that speaks to our natural evolutionary nature, no matter what our tradition. I am delighting in watching the current rise of feminine Buddhist teachers and their communities. Perhaps these communities and the many teachers are all Maitreya!

From Words to Experience

I have but one lamp by which my feet are
guided, and that is the lamp of experience.
Patrick Henry

As with all words, we can read and read but not transform. We must experience and know the reality of what we have read within our own lives. The following chapters in this book bring the journey of this embodiment of power and glory down to earth, dealing with all that arises along the way. In life we move through experiences filled with light, which then draw out the dark within, and then back to light again, and on it goes, and so this book follows this natural pattern accordingly. I draw upon my many studies of, and inner relationships with, the Christian mystics, the varied Gnostic traditions and teachings, my Celtic heritage, and the Kabbalah and Jewish midrashim. The midrashim, based upon sacred texts, are new stories or parables created in order to respond to contemporary human soul needs. These stories are wisdom that is known from the other spiritual realms but is brought back and made relevant for the hearer. Unknowingly, we are living many of those stories that have not been updated for some generations.

Throughout this book I contribute my own modernized midrashim, if you will—something direly needed in our world through the woman's voice, incorporating my own personal experiences and what I see as recurring themes with those whom I mentor and work with in retreats. My aim in conveying these experiences is to provide further meaning and elucidation to the teachings given, with the hope and knowledge that we can all cultivate our own inner experience far beyond what we think we are capable of. All Bible quotations used are from the New Jerusalem Bible unless otherwise indicated with NKJV, meaning they are drawn from the New King James Version. May we joyfully embark upon this journey, one that goes beyond our own personal journey, and know it for what it is: the true transformation of our soul consciousness for the good of all.

How to Engage in the Experience

Prayers

With every chapter there will be a prayer. Please take these up and speak out loud. This gives greater resonance and feeling to the experience. Let the prayer become your own, and add your own words as you feel guided to do.

Chants

You may use the chant as a mantra to repeat over and over or find your own tune and rhythm. Whichever way you choose, continue the chant until the vibration enters every part of your body and mind, losing yourself in the divine energy being transmitted and created. Then let yourself bask in the silence afterwards. If you feel a particular resonance with one but not another, then use the one that speaks to your soul.

All the chants used in this book are either from Hebraic or Aramaic origin. The Hebrew letters are understood to be energies that transmit the very qualities of the divine nature. They are known to open the way to other spiritual realms by way of various combinations of letters and sounds. The meaning of the chant is given after the chant itself. Please see appendix I for a more detailed explanation of the meaning of the Hebrew letters.

Meditations

The meditations are given as suggested guidelines. Use them as a base, and if you are guided in a different way, then please follow where you are led.

Some of the meditations connect with a divine persona. The purpose of having an encounter with a being outside of oneself is to reflect what is already within one's own being. In building a relationship with this outer being, we also build a deeper inner relationship with our own soul and these qualities.

We have swung from the extremes in our world, as we often do. First, the divine was all on the outside; now it is all on the inside. The reality is that it is both, and through engaging in a reciprocal relationship, we all evolve.

Affirmations

When you take up the affirmations, take them up with full faith, knowing the truth of their resonance and meaning resides within you already, and you are merely bringing that truth into consciousness. Bring yourself into full focus and concentration, and let the words resonate throughout your whole being. Keep repeating until you fall into a natural silence. Bask in that silence as long as you are able. If the affirmation naturally changes, then follow what is given.

Journaling

You will be invited to journal your experiences after each meditation. This will give more reflection and integration time and bring greater awareness to your experiences. Do not be in a hurry to move on to the next section, but go out and live in the world what you have just read and experienced.

Interior Stars

At the end of every section you will find an interior star section. More commonly known through Eastern spirituality as chakras, these energy centers can also be called interior stars, as named in the Sophian tradition. There is a brief exploration of these interior stars, aligning them with the divine feminine faces. Each star is paired with a color. As with all systems, there can be slight variations as to how these are represented. I have used the system that equates with my Gnostic training.

Preparing the Ground

A garden requires patient labor and attention.
Plants do not grow merely to satisfy ambitions
or to fulfill good intentions. They thrive
because someone expended effort on them.
Liberty Hyde Bailey

The ground receives the seed lovingly, opening to nurture, feed, protect, and provide all that is required for its growth. And so, too, we must become that very ground of being in order for the seed of our soul to receive all that it needs. This ground of being takes time to cultivate; it requires spaciousness and the willingness to let go of the identity and roles we play in the world, along with all the accompanying thoughts and beliefs.

Entering into and opening to our inherent spacious soul daily allows a natural liberation of our manifold self-identifications to occur, and it is then that we can truly rest in the sacredness and come to know our

23

ground of being. The great Celtic writer John O'Donohue points to this when he says that "behind the façade of your life, there is something beautiful and eternal happening."

Within and through this eternal happening, which is our ground of being, all of life still exists and arises moment to moment, but none of it captures or binds us anymore. With time we develop the capacity to allow all to move fluidly through our being, and we learn how to come into repose and be at peace no matter what is or is not happening. Teresa of Avila spoke of this in her later years, where she no longer felt any attachment to people or to what was occurring in her world, either internally or externally. In her poem "I Am Yours, Born for You," she clearly indicates this freedom. My translation of one of the verses reads:

> Give me death, give me life
> Give health or illness
> Honor or dishonor give me
> Give me war or flood me with peace
> Weakness or fullness of strength
> I say yes to all of these
> What will you have me do?

It no longer mattered to Teresa whether there were external or internal chaotic occurrences; the profound sense of peace remained, and all else simply was.

My own initial experience of this occurred while lying on the floor of a cave deep within a mountain in southern France. Before venturing into the depth of the mountain I knew that something was going to take place; I was feeling a mixture of fear and welcome anticipation. As we ventured deeper and deeper inside the mountain, sometimes crawling on our bellies and squeezing through claustrophobically small spaces, I experienced periodic waves of panic. The final opening we crawled through, which was the smallest of all and induced the most panic, brought us into a magnificent and large internal cave. Lying on my back with arms outstretched I felt the ground of the mother beneath me, and my heart and mind quieted. After some time I began experiencing my own being as that ground. This ground, however, went beyond any ground we know—it was like the eternal ground of being, with no beginning and no end, the eternal happening. And I was equally a part of this eternal happening, which I call the mother-ground of being. I was not separate or distant in any way, and yet, at the same time, I was distinctly aware of my unique being. It was beautifully profound and wonderfully simple. There was nothing to understand or get; it simply was what it was.

Within this mother-ground there seemed to be contained within her nothing at all and yet, at the same time, everything of existence. There was a pregnant spaciousness that had the possibility of giving birth at any moment to anything that was desired, as if it were a great cosmic womb. After some time there arose from within this deep ground of being a thought-desire, and I watched it like a bubble rising in the wind, rising higher and higher until it simply disappeared. And then there rose a fear and the same bubble, the same rising and disappearing. It was quite fascinating to witness. This experience repeated a few times, but in simply watching these thoughts/emotions arising, they were able to move through the different levels of my being and consciousness, and as I did not attach any meaning to them or think they were me, they simply passed on by and literally evaporated. My ground of being was not disturbed or changed in any way by them; I still, simply, was.

This experience laid the bedrock for an ongoing cultivation of such awareness, as even without a cave, and even without such an experience, we can all create our own Mother-cave and come to know our own mother-ground right where we are, for it is who we are. We simply need to enter and be willing to let the soul descend, not to the underworld but to the world that lies beneath and beyond the underworld and all worlds—the ground of All That Is. Many call this the "groundless ground"; however, I feel the words "mother-ground of being," with the inference to the cosmic womb, give a more feminine feel and description. It is here where the seed of our soul will receive its proper nourishment, and a seed properly nourished will have a better chance of growing into what it is destined to be.

I invite you into this ground of being each day, even for a few moments. And yes, you do know this ground; you simply have had your attention elsewhere for a while. Set aside all distractions and come within and experience the eternal happening of your mother-ground, the great cosmic womb, which is within and all around you. Know and experience, then know and accept the peace that you are.

Prayer of the Mother-Ground

> Mother of the ground of my being
> Spacious eternal womb
> May we enter and know you within our own being
> May we enter and know you as our being
> May our small fears dissolve into your breath
> May our small thoughts find their way to you
> May we lay down in your cosmic lap
> May we know the movement of your being
> And the repose of your nature
> May we breathe back into love
> Into our eternal happening.

Chant

> *Eheieh* (ah-hi-yah)
> I am and I am becoming

Meditation: Contacting Your Mother-Ground of Being

Gathering yourself into the quiet of your being, let your breath come into a natural and gentle rhythm. Let yourself deepen and expand. On your next out-breath, let your breath reach out and join with the expansiveness of Sophia, Mother Wisdom. Let your breath rest in the peace and spaciousness here. When needed, take another in-breath and feel this great mother within and all around you. If you like, you may gently say in your mind the name Sophia as you breathe in and out.

Keep repeating as above, finding your own natural rhythm, and continue as long as it feels comfortable.

When it feels time, take up the affirmation "I am the ground of peace; I am pure radiant awareness." Keep repeating this over and over until you naturally fall silent.

When thoughts, desires, or fears arise, simply breathe them out to Sophia, allowing them to dissolve in her, then return to the breath and the affirmation.

When you feel complete, close with the affirmation "I am the ground of peace; I am pure radiant awareness" and add "I am the mother-ground of being." Give thanks to the mother and your own deep soul.

Take up your journal and let the expansiveness of the above chant and meditation experience continue through your reflections.

This is a good meditation practice to become very familiar with, for it is the very foundation of all other meditation practices given in this book. It helps to establish a peacefulness and calmness of being that allows other practices to be experienced in more depth.

2

Daughter of Light

Mary said, "When new life comes to
you, do not cling to the old."
Tau Malachi, The Secret Gospel of
St. Mary Magdalene, verse 156

The sacred daughter has been little known, her energy lying dormant
in many of us, and yet she brings the very vitality and freshness of life.
She awakens us to new ways of being and living, and she is the very
key to our embodied life.

It is time for the daughter to be known and seen and heard. May we
embody her and she us!

Meeting the Daughter of Light

The Daughter of Light, the maiden, the Daughter of Day, daughter Sophia—these are all names given to the exuberant daughter energy within us. She has come to be personified through Mary Magdalene, who is also known as the holy bride, but in reality this daughter-bride lives within each one of us. She is the one who dreams visions of what she and this world are to become; she is the one who holds hope in her breath and spreads it across the earth with every exhale; faith is her middle name, as she knows nothing other. The lightness of her being is infectious, as are her laughter and the suppleness of her light body.

The Daughter of Light knows freedom from societal expectations and roles played for gain. She sees through the falsity of these and wants no part of them. She births through her soul a revolutionary nature as she stands in her own land and cries out for others to join in the play of a new world consciousness. Her energy is boundless and boundary-less, and she is on fire with her visions and cosmic thoughts, which are all wrapped in a natural innocence of awe and wonder at this creation.

This daughter, who lives within us, is the one who brings forward our inspirations, our creative nature, our sensual delights and dreams, always calling us to her land of freedom and play. Do you remember her? Have you ever truly known her? The answers do not really matter, as she is alive and waiting now, truly delighting in the moment.

No matter where we find ourselves chronologically in this life, the Daughter of Light still has her part to play, her gifts to offer. If we deny her because now we are in the latter phases of our life or because of our gender, we deny ourselves the vibrant and inspirational play of our being, and a heaviness and solidness will set in, often in the form of lethargy. We will begin dragging ourselves to those places we formerly loved, with everything taking on the form of effort and manifesting as fatigue. Our senses will become dulled, and a feeling of lifelessness will set in. We may also find it difficult to remember the vision we had for our life and this world. If so, it is time to call on the Daughter of Light.

The daughter delights in roaming through the spaciousness of life. Even if there is no specific vision at hand, she is not disturbed but ventures out into the unknown land of this life, simply opening to what life may offer her. In fact, it is through this venturing that her visions come to be. She is not narrow or solid but fluid and flexible, allowing people, events, teachings, and her own creative and spiritually imaginative world to be in a constant flux of evolution. It is not uncommon for her vision to change, and she does not have a problem with this, as she is busy moving with the pulse of life. It is we who find the change problematical, which we often label as unstable.

This label of instability has been used as a weapon against feminine energy. It has been used as a source of shame and control, but the reality is that no one can control the daughter, and if you try, you may then discover and encounter the dark side of her being, who will fight for her freedom. But again, this does not bother her. It is all part of her play.

Let us call back our daughter of delight, the one who can help us remember joy in our lives, laughter in our bellies, and the rekindling of our deepest desires. She holds these desires for us and waits to give new, expanded ones. Let us not only go back but also forward, stretching into desires we would not even think to own. For this, we need communion; we need to enter her divine playground so we can remember the spaciousness and largeness of our being and not hold back in disbelief.

Let us also follow the daughter back into our bodies, where we can join mind, body, and soul in divine communion through our dance, our lovemaking, our song, and our gardens. The physical needs your soul to honor her too. She (the physical) is the grounding of all the soul mysteries; without her, we remain as disembodied spirits, bound for another world. The daughter reminds us that we are welcome here in this world, and she seeks her embodiment through you. She needs you as much as you need her. May we meet on fertile ground—the ground of our inspirational and creative forces.

Prayer to the Daughter of Light

Daughter of Light
I call to you from the deepest recesses of my soul
I call for you to return to the land of my soul
Where it waits to give birth in this world.
Bring your inspirations, your dreams
Your new ways of being, especially those ones
    that I cannot even imagine.
Why do I hold so tenaciously to the old, solid ways
    when they do not make me happy?
May I trade futility for fertility
And may we together breathe
Into these deadened bodies and hearts
Enlivening them for the adventure that awaits
May we break open all those places
    that have closed and withered.
May we dance freely in the light.

Chant

Ya Ma Kallah Mashiach (ya ma kal-lah ma-shee-ach)
The feminine power of the daughter-bride
The anointed one who fully embodies the light

Meditation

Come into your mother-ground of being, as described in the meditation Contacting Your Mother-Ground of Being from chapter 1, breathing in a natural rhythm and bringing your soul into a quiet and spacious place. Then let your breath stay on the out-breath for a short time, and then breathe in again. Repeat this a few times. Once you feel calm in your soul, ask to feel a desire to engage with and come to know your own feminine presence of the daughter.

Then call upon the Daughter of Light; allow her form to appear to you or simply feel her energetic presence. You may wish to envision the form of Magdalene as a young, vibrant woman wearing red robes and an inner robe of white brilliance. With her olive-colored skin and green eyes, she looks upon you with great love.

Then see her heart shining with a brilliant, shining sun. Let your heart and her heart meet. You may envision a golden thread between your two hearts and your own heart beginning to shine with this same brilliant sun. Begin to exchange your breath and energy with her, she becoming you and you becoming her.

Let your energy be enlivened. Let your daughter awaken.

Ask for Magdalene's, or the outer daughter's, blessing.

When complete, see or feel this outer daughter merge with your inner daughter, becoming as one. Give thanks and spend time grounding this energy by taking it down into your feet.

Now take up your journal and let your experience continue to evolve, then walk in the world as this Daughter of Light.

The Seed Is Planted

She said she wanted to see beautiful things.
I took her to where I planted my seeds.
Darnell Lamont Walker

As we enter the cosmic womb, or the mother-ground, our deeper soul opens to be nourished by this great eternal spaciousness. We must include all aspects of our being and willingly receive what is waiting to be given. In order to receive, we must first perceive that there is this total soul-being nourishment, protection, and infinite flow of blessing. There must be awareness by the daughter that she is her mother's daughter—that is, the divine mother's daughter—and that she is deeply cared for.

How do we cultivate this perception? Firstly, by becoming more present to our life as it is—not as we want it to be, not as we think it should be, but as it actually is. What is repeatedly stirring in our soul? What does our inner voice want to tell us? Are we present enough to hear it or are we too busy trying to make things happen in the world in order to feel good about ourselves and to convince ourselves that we are doing something worthwhile for the world? If so, we must take a step back and come to know our daughter within.

The daughter is the seed. She cannot come into the world until she has ripened accordingly, and she must learn how to perceive the energies around her and discerningly absorb what is good and right for her. If there is too much heat the seed withers, and if there is too much moisture the seed rots, and yet sufficient amounts of each are vital. Do we know the spiritual moisture of the mother's loving-kindness? Can we feel the blessings, expect them, and not rush by them, craving for something other? It is important to perceive, know, and feel the blessing of the mother's love in our life. This will give us the gift of calm and a genuine loving presence in our own person. Can our daughter also discern how much spiritual heat is needed for her to break open and sprout, and can she stay the course or is she running off, avoiding the heat, through a variety of distractions before the process has even had time to transpire?

I have watched myself cry out and rally against the spiritual heat, claiming it is not gentle, not moist, and therefore is not loving, so confined and narrow was my view of what spiritual love looked like. One of my spiritual hot spots is when I am wrongly accused of something. I remember it well as a teenager, when I would rant and rail about the unfairness and take it as a deep soul insult. It also brought up a sense of helplessness when I could not prove that I was innocent. As an adult that hot spot remained, and I watched myself becoming that teenage railing daughter all over again. However, with some spiritual maturity I began to see and feel the gift in the unjust accusations. Instead of feeling them as unfair or as an insult, I started to perceive them as a means of strengthening the soul by having faith in myself and knowing my inner truth, no matter what others thought or said, and not having to prove it. What a valuable teaching!

Looking back, it was often the greatest moments of friction that produced the greatest growth, whether it was between another and myself, myself and the Living Presence, or my own internal soul wrangling (of course, all of them ultimately are the latter). The only thing that can be altered is how I perceive what is happening. If I perceive it as not loving, then it is very painful and all sorts of accusations are laid bare. This lengthens the growth process, as these accusations need to be realized for the projections that they are, and then self-forgiveness needs to be invited and accepted—which, in my experience, is not something that always comes easily or quickly.

Alternatively, if I can understand that this spiritual heat is a timely and necessary thing for my growth, I no longer discern any difference between the heat and the moisture, for I can understand that they both come from the same place of great loving-kindness, and this love would do anything and use anyone for me to know who I am. The question then becomes, are we able to accept the heat and the cool moisture equally?

By taking time to be with our daughter and willingly opening to a deeper level of perception, we can begin to see how at every moment in our lives we have been and are cosmically nourished, watched over, and blessed. But unless we consciously perceive it and know it to be so, then it literally does not exist. We then get busy trying to create all of that nourishment, protection, and blessing for ourselves, but this requires great effort and generally brings small returns compared to the divine gift waiting to be given. We unconsciously bring upon ourselves the pain of Adam and Eve—that is, the pain of working the ground and of giving birth, as was spoken in the Genesis myth when they were sent from the Garden of Eden into this world. Moving beyond the common literal interpretation of ground and understanding it as the mother-ground of our being, we of course do not and cannot work this ground, nor can we give birth from our smaller nature alone, hence our pain and frustration when our attempts fail. Let us instead deepen our perception so that we will know and feel the love that brings all that we need and simultaneously seek to awaken the daughter within. This matter of feeling within the soul is vital; without it, we remain only with head knowledge, and this does not transform our lives. It must become a full-body feeling; through this we are opening the way for the beginning of embodiment.

Prayer of the Sacred Seed

> Mother, as your daughter
> I come asking for your sacred heat and heart to nourish me
> For your sacred coolness and care to moisten me
> May the flame of your love transform all that divides me
>> all that I deny
>> and everything that I fear

May the sacred seed within relish this heat, this moisture,
and burst forth
fearing nothing
Holding onto no form of existence
Lying down in the unfolding Living Presence
The ground of my own being.

Sandalphon is an archangel who walked very closely with Magdalene while on this earth, and she continues to walk very closely with those who seek her assistance. She is known as the shoe angel—that is, she interfaces between heaven and earth, teaching us how to dance between these realities and how to equally accept the moisture and the heat of this dance. She also reveals the feminine mysteries.

She may be envisioned as one wearing the mantle with a thousand eyes looking in all directions, seeing all, and with a rainbow countenance.

Chant

So Da Yo Ma Sandalphon

As you walk through the door of the feminine power, you are
watched over and safely enfolded within the mantle of
Archangel Sandalphon

Meditation

Come into your mother-ground of being, breathe into your belly, and ask to be shown one of your internal hot spots: one of those things in your life that you feel is unfair, unjust, or you are unable to forgive. Ask the Daughter of Light and Sandalphon to reveal to you the blessing contained within this heat.

Then reflect on your life, asking them to show you what blessings have been given, which you may not have recognized at the time. Bow down in thanks to the mother of all creation.

Journal your experiences with the heat and the nourishing moisture of your daughter.

Learning to Receive

While the Giver archetype is celebrated in our culture, the Receiver is almost wholly unknown. The result? Busyness is a virtue.

Amanda Owen

As we begin to cultivate our ability to perceive, we then need to know how to fully receive. Very often we rush past the much-needed energy of the receiving daughter and run straight to the giving mother, busying ourselves in the process, but how can we give if we have not fully received? We have not been taught how to properly receive, and when we do venture into this territory we often skim the surface, not taking the blessing fully into our being and integrating what has been given.

In my own journey, and in watching others as well, I have found that old friend unworthiness rising to obstruct and inhibit my receptivity. There will be subtle or sometimes not-so-subtle energies and voices that will seek to move us away from acknowledging our spiritual experiences. We may know deep within our being they are true, but somehow we only glance sideways at them, and our surface being rises with disbelief—sometimes whispering *oh, I must've imagined that* and at other times simply saying *well, that is interesting*—and, moving on in life, we dismiss it and quickly forget it even happened. We let the experience slip right by us and do not venture into unfolding it in greater depth, nor do we understand how it may become integrated into our daily living, which is what true mysticism is about. Without the integration it merely recedes to the outer edges of our consciousness, and if we do not consciously draw it back in, the blessing remains unfulfilled, which contributes to our lack of fulfillment and that ever-encroaching feeling of soul sadness, which then translates to unworthiness or lack of confidence. And so the circle completes itself and continually spins around this lacking and unworthy orbit.

If, however, we learn how to fully receive, it can cut right through this continuous circle, and we will begin to feel the stirrings of an old known spiritual self-confidence that seems to lie deep in the recesses of our soul. Let us begin now. We are given a dream or an experience in our meditation; it has a different feel and quality to it, and something sparks within us. We must then move beyond the surface mind to understand it. So, coming back into meditation, move into your mother-ground, bringing the experience or dream into the cosmic womb and asking for further elucidation. Too often we ponder only from our smaller surface mind and therefore only receive limited contemplations accordingly. By entering into prayer and our deeper being, we open ourselves to receive the blessing of the mother, as was intended.

Patience is needed here, and also a continual returning. In our quick-fix society we are trained to want an immediate answer and then move on to the next. We have forgotten the true art of contemplation, and we are not skilled at allowing a blessing to unfold over time. Do not be satisfied with the first answer you receive. Keep asking for the deeper layers of meaning to be revealed, and keep returning and keep returning until you have received all the moisture contained within, and then sit with it all. Do not be in a hurry to rush off and make something happen from it, but allow it to settle in your being and your body, allowing it to naturally weave into your life without inserting it anywhere for some perceived gain. Become friends with it; know it well. Know it as well as your lack and unworthiness, and then let them meet. In my experience, when true knowing meets unworthiness, the latter naturally dissolves of its own accord.

Eve was first able to perceive the apple, and then she was able to receive it. Biting into it, she could taste it; eating it, she was able to receive its nourishment and moisture; and through digesting it, her being was opened to knowledge—the knowledge of the world as it is, the world of duality. Her journey then was to navigate in and through this world, coming to learn how to return again and again to the mother-ground of being and how to live in the world of duality as it is, without being bound by it. And so it is with us. Every dream, meditation, and life experience is a blessed apple given so that we too may enter into true knowledge, true knowing of this reality, liberating ourselves and others along the way. What would have happened if Eve only perceived the apple and did not accept or receive or bite or eat or digest it? We can only wonder as to our lives and what we may have missed or are missing. Let us no longer wonder but take up our apple and eat!

Prayer of Receiving

Mother, may you teach me how to receive
How to take all the blessings you wish to give
And honor them, nurture them, feed them
Extracting from them the great love that seeks
To support me at every turn of my life
May I know as daughter
A deeper way of communing in the stillness
Valuing those longer integrating moments
May I not rush into the world
But abide, peacefully contemplating in your arms.

Chant

Ya Ma Kallah Mashiach (ya ma kal-lah ma-shee-ach)
The enlightened feminine nature and power

Meditation

Allowing the surface mind to rest, slip into your mother-ground, taking time to settle and simply be. Then, taking up a dream or experience that has sparked you, ask the daughter in her wisdom to reveal to you the deeper meanings that may lie beneath. Keep asking and asking and keep opening until you see it becoming a viable reality in your everyday life. Know that this may take some time. Allow the answers to reveal themselves in their own way and time. Be patient, watch over what is revealed, and tend it lovingly.

Journal your dreams.

The Daughter of Wings

Dreams are illustrations...from the book
your soul is writing about you.
Marsha Norman

As we allow ourselves to fully receive the energies and love available to us, and as our being begins to trust and know that the mother is constantly conspiring for every event and moment to be in our favor, our dreams and desires begin to grow wings. What we imagine, intend, and desire begins to have a solidity that aligns with all aspects of our soul.

When we are unable to knowingly or consciously receive, our desires remain in the realm of cloudlike wishes and fantasies, having no real solid shape or base, changing as the wind blows, with us running and chasing and trying to desperately grasp onto something that is not real. We may also experience too much solidity, too much gravity, having such a fixed idea of what should happen and how it should look that our poor soul literally has no option but to wait until we are able to release our idea in order to open to another desire in another, more easeful way.

Whether we are chasing clouds or stuck in the earthly mud, they both usually indicate that we are trying to prove that we are somebody, that we have something to offer, that we are worthy in the eyes of the world. In one of the oral legends of Mary Magdalene, Yeshua speaks some heart advice to Magdalene, telling her to seek to become nobody. Here is a teaching giving the liberation we all desire, even though it seems to directly contradict what we are striving toward, which is to be who we are in the world. When we allow ourselves to sink deeply into this teaching, we begin to taste the freedom it offers.

For a moment, imagine what it would be like to have no roles in the world; you are no longer the mother, the wife, the teacher, the businesswoman, the single woman, the husband, the father, the therapist, the woman or man—no role at all. And along with this there are no expectations or demands of you and your actions, not even subtle, unspoken ones; there is nothing to be given, nothing to be gained, and, most importantly, nothing to be proved. There is only a spaciousness of being that has no need or desire to be recognized or filled in any way. Imagine for a moment what it would feel like to have no need of being recognized, to not have to prove your worth.

Our desire to be recognized—to be seen, to be heard—is, of course, our desire to know our own worth and innate power within our soul, yet we look for it in the world through our work roles or from our partners in our love roles or from our teachers in our student roles and so on. If we look closely, we are in a constant mode of trying to prove ourselves to the world, but ultimately we are trying to prove our worth to ourselves. No wonder we feel a deep soul sadness lingering in our beings.

Yet, if we are willing to fall into that space of becoming nobody, we might just find what we are looking for. It can often elicit panic in the mind initially, as the ego rushes to try and grab onto its identity in all the various roles we take up in life, but if we can stay long enough to allow the panic to reside and relax into this grand spaciousness of being, we may even find that we like it! In returning here again and again we also allow room for true dreams and desires to arise, for they are no longer coming from the place of needing to prove but rather from the place of deep soul purpose or mission. It is these dreams and desires that have wings, the ability to truly help the self and others.

It is the daughter who is the great dreamer; she is the one who is filled with a fiery desire deep within the belly. May we aid her in building self-worth and confidence by entering the cosmic womb of our being, where our true desires may be forthcoming and therefore able to be ultimately fulfilled through the fire of the love of all creation and life.

Prayer for the True Being of Your Daughter
> Daughter of my being
> May I no longer feel the need to prove myself or
> To push myself forward, standing as a false warrior
> May I lay all this down in the ground of love and being
> And from this ground
> May true desire rise
> May true dreams come to be known.
> Daughter, may my belly soften
> So I can hear you call my name
> So I can speak the meaning of my name
> Knowing the purpose and way of my life
> As a gift for all.

Chant
> *Adonai Kallah Mashiach* (a-doe-nigh kal-lah ma-shee-ach)
> Beloved, my foundation, daughter-bride, anointed one who
> embodies the light

Meditation
Drop deeply into your breath and connect with your mother-ground. Open to the cosmic womb and bring all of who you are there. Place your worthiness and unworthiness in this womb; place your desire to be recognized, your desire to be seen and heard, all the roles that you play. And then open to your being of no-body. Simply let yourself float and be in this place. If panic arises, simply breathe into and through it; you are still here. Drop deeper and deeper into this no-body, dwelling here as long as you can, and then invite the Daughter of Wings to be born from this place, and welcome her with all that she brings.

Journal what your Daughter of Wings gifts you.

The Fiery Nature of Desire

To burn with desire and keep quiet about it is the
greatest punishment we can bring on ourselves.
Federico García Lorca

If we have no fire in our bellies, we have no will or desire, and our lives become lackluster and filled with effort. From this place we easily fall prey to distractions and addictively seek our feelings of connection on the outside rather than firstly coming within and remembering and knowing the love there. Or, if we do come in, we don't stay there very long. The words in Revelation 2:4 seem to speak to this where it reads "you have left your first love." Our first love, both spiritual and human, is a special fire, a fire that never dies, one that cannot be extinguished with time or apparent loss.

What exactly is this fire? Another cave experience gave me my initiation into this. While wandering on a mountainside I had often climbed in Assisi, Italy, I felt a deep draw to climb farther up the mountain to somewhere I had not been before. I saw an entrance to a small cave, and as I was leaning in, my soul-being was immediately hurled deep within the cave and I found myself traveling very, very quickly, going deeper and deeper into what felt like the very core of the earth, and yet it felt like something more as well. The experience then placed me in the midst of a great eternal fire, a fire beyond what we know or perceive here on earth; it was a fire of pure love, a love that never ceases, a fire that never goes out. I then experienced what I can only describe as a rebirthing from the midst of this fire, from this love, being born anew from the fire of creation. It was a deeply moving and powerful journey, one that I feel I am still unfolding as I live here in this relative reality on earth.

I also, however, have encountered fear of the fire: fear of the intensity of its energy, of its power; fear of what may happen if I continued opening to it. My experiences with Mary Magdalene have been very powerful exchanges, and I could see and experience that this supernatural fire and power I encountered in the cave are what make up her being. It was fine as long as that fire stayed with her and I got to experience it from the outside or as a one-off experience, but when it started to well up within me and I actually became it, soul and body, then that was another thing. It was startling to know such fire and power could literally be embodied here and now, and yet isn't this what the Second Coming is all about? Isn't this what I know to be possible? I was being asked to move beyond words and concepts into a reality of their manifestation. *Gulp!*

And so I sought to go beyond the fear, beyond the concepts, and came with a conscious intention of wanting to truly know this fire and come face-to-face with my inherent fear of its, and my own, power. I was, this time, sitting in my chair at home, taking up a chant that helps to dispel obstacles (see the Stubborn Patterns and Obstructions chant in appendix II), when suddenly I was looking down at my head in my hands (in another realm of reality, of course), and when I looked up I was aware that now I could *really* see. I saw and knew that everything—every tree, every bird, every building, every telephone wire, every soul, even my couch—was comprised of light and fire, with love as its very center. What was there to fear in this? It is who we are. This was a deeply peaceful and calm experience; it simply revealed to me the reality of what is. The choice became clear: did I want to know and live this fire and love within or did I want to live in fear? And so we are all given this choice.

And here is where desire comes in. If we do not desire to know the fire, then we will not. If we do, then we need to feel this desire—feed it and constantly prepare the ground of our soul for this. Yes, we can have random experiences that can burst upon us, much like I described in the first cave experience, and we can also ask and cultivate our souls with deepened meditation, desiring desire if necessary and becoming more available for the mother to send her blessings. It was from this cultivation that the above chair experience emerged.

What we speak of here is a spiritual heat of another kind. Can we and do we desire this? Do we even know that it is possible to desire such a thing or are we still bound to transferring our fire and power onto someone external, whether it is Yeshua, Magdalene, Buddha, Kuan Yin, or our spiritual teachers or partners? Desire is what created our souls and all the worlds and galaxies, and we need it if we are to continue on in our spiritual evolution, for ourselves and all of humanity. We need the fire to burn through spiritual lethargy, to arouse us once more to that first love, to come within and stay within, to consciously be in the present and Presence, without distraction, and to take up our spiritual practice as if our very lives depend upon it—for, in actual fact, they do.

Prayer for True Desire

Daughter of the fire
I invoke you from the deepest source of my belly
May I no longer be afraid of this fire of who I am
May I no longer deny this desire, which makes me who I am
May I come freely, shaking in my soul if necessary
Unbelieving, if that is what is in my body
May I bring it all to this great bonfire* of love
May I feed it and may it burn
Burning the dross into truth
Burning the fear into love
Bringing me back to the true light of being.

** Bon = good in the French language, hence
bringing all to the "good fire," or bonfire.*

Chant

Adonai Kallah Mashiach (a-doe-nigh kal-lah ma-shee-ach)
The embodied light of the feminine one

Meditation: Meeting the Fire of Your Inner Bride

Drawing your breath deep into your belly, find a natural rhythm with your breathing, intending and asking to meet the bride. See or sense her image or energy before you. You may visualize her in a long red robe with long black hair, an olive complexion, and green eyes. Let your breath and her breath converge together, and breathe with her. Then, asking to know your inner bride, visualize or sense a flame of fire within your belly. Let this flame grow brighter and bigger, and let yourself gently burn, burning away all that lethargic energy, all the fear, all that is no longer needed, and asking for and letting your true desires be ignited. You may see or feel yourself dancing as this inner Bride, enjoying the sheer delight of coming alive and being reborn in fire and light, or you may simply enjoy the ecstasy of the living flame. Give thanks to the bride for her communion.

Journal your inner fire.

Daughter of Pleasure

Many of us pursue pleasure with such
breathless haste that we hurry past it.
Søren Kierkegaard

Pleasure is experienced when we are able to enjoy the body and what she desires. It can be through the eating of good food; movement of all its variances in the form of dance, walking, or exercise; laying our bodies on Mother Earth, swimming in her waters, and through our sensual and sexual connections with others. Anywhere the body is feeling into the sacredness of life, pleasure arises.

Our Judaic-Christian heritage has been devastatingly fearful of the body, desire, and pleasure, but the daughter believes in the sacredness of her body and is unafraid of experiencing pleasure. She has not taken on the falsities and fears that have bound the body for so long, and she has much to teach us in re-experiencing true pleasure, for more often than not we have substituted addictive self-narcissistic pleasure for the true sacredness that is available to us.

Can we know pleasure for pleasure's sake? That is, can we enter into a moment of true communion between body and sacred pleasure for no other reason than simply enjoying that communion? Can we come to this communion with the purity of heart and desire without grasping at feeling loved or trying to fill some gap in our life? There is a great difference between *self-serving* and *fulfillment of soul and body*. The former drives us to eat sweets to feel some sweetness in our life, and it steers us toward relationships that are not altogether healthy in order to fill the gap of loneliness. It constantly seeks to fill the self up with some little morsel of pleasure, but it never does get filled—the craving never stops; it continually grows. Ultimately there is no connection with the sacred place within and therefore also no real connection with anything of the outer world.

Fulfillment, on the other hand, comes from a much deeper place of communion. Here there is true relationship with the body and self or the body and other (whoever or whatever that other may be). There is no craving but simple opening, and through this openness comes a sacred communing and a fulfillment that bring both aliveness and peace. Pleasure is not sought but becomes a natural outcome—a gift, if you will, of natural grace. There is nothing more natural on this earth than our bodies, and the daughter knows this well. She does not make a big deal of it, she simply lives it, and in and through it, allowing her soul and spirit to express who they are through her body.

When we are able to come to this place of natural grace in our bodies, we can also take this wisdom to all areas of our life. We can then come to our meditation for its own sake, for its own pleasure, and not seek to get something we want, escape some pain or worry, or fill a gap. Similarly, we can love for the sheer pleasure of loving. We can nap for the sheer pleasure of napping. We can exercise for the sheer pleasure of exercising. In our world we are taught that we do everything for a reason—to get something, to achieve something, to divest ourselves of something—always a reason. Teresa of Avila said, "If you are still looking for a reason, you have not yet allowed yourself to be overwhelmed by love."

We are generally afraid of being overwhelmed, mainly because we have been overwhelmed by fear, but perhaps now we can experiment with being overwhelmed by love. It seems it is the only way to reach into the true pleasure of being and fulfillment because we are then freed from the reason of mind and can begin to play in that playground of the maiden. This playground is also a preparation to open us to even greater delights that the mother wishes to give, bringing happiness of soul and joy of the spirit. This is when ecstasy can start to make its way into our life, but if we are unable to partake of the basic pleasure of our body, then we are limiting ourselves as to how far we can grow and know other dimensional realities and ground them into life. We may experience them in the spiritual realms, but they will be divorced from our everyday lives. Where there is divorce, there is separation. Where there is union, there is embodiment.

There is an understanding that the female has a greater capacity to embody and know enlightened nature due to her natural capacity to enter into a relationship with the body and the world. So let us take up our relationship with our body once more, but let us not stay there thinking this is it. There is more. There is always more.

I watch as the bud of my magnolia tree forms itself and then grows and grows some more, and then one day it simply opens. Perhaps it gets overwhelmed with love and out of sheer pleasure it blooms. May it be so with us.

Prayer for the Sacredness of Pleasure

Daughter of Pleasure
I ask for your presence
I ask for your pleasure
I ask for my own pleasure
May I remember the sacredness
   of this body
May I lay down all addictions
   and all falsities of deeply held belief
May I not be bound by false teachings
   and fears of others
May I not be bound by my own self-cravings
But may I know true fulfillment in the
Communion of body and being
And may I fall headlong into love
Letting myself become overwhelmed
And then begin to bloom all over this world.

Chant

Adonai Kallah Mashiach (a-doe-nigh kal-lah ma-shee-ach)
The foundation of the feminine body living as the light

Meditation

Invoking Magdalene, ask her to dispel any old beliefs that may hinder you knowing the true sacredness of pleasure and communion through your body. Then imagine or sense a deep red rose as a bud in your heart. Feel the bud being filled with love and more love and even more. See the bud and your heart growing as they are being filled with this love, and then feel and watch as the bud becomes completely overwhelmed with this love and magically blooms in its fullness. Let yourself soak in the overwhelming love, the blooming, and see or sense Magdalene dancing all around you in celebration. If inspired, dance with her.

Journal your Daughter of Pleasure.

The Rain of Tears

*Heaven knows we need never be ashamed of
our tears, for they are rain upon the blinding
dust of earth, overlying our hard hearts.*
Charles Dickens

We must let our tears flow freely, whether they are tears of joy, sorrow, pain, or deep empathy and compassion. Some of these tears reside deep in the belly or our womb and others are in the heart, but if we continue to contain them, our desire, our seed, shrivels and has no fertile place to grow. In fact, our tears become the very fertile moisture needed for our growth.

Let us look at joy. Do we enjoy our spiritual life or are we bound in the world of *should* and *have to*? Are we finding ourselves in places and situations where our innate joy and being is feeling inhibited or restrained? Are we holding ourselves in? The daughter invites us to look deeply at these questions and to shake them loose to see the truth of their nature. She also invites us to shake our bodies loose and see what tumbles out. It must be said here, however, there is a difference between joy of the spirit and the surface joy of our lower nature. The former draws one deeper into union with our true being; the latter, even though it may bring a needed sense of fun, ultimately does not affect our inner communion and relationship. It may open the door to the deeper joy, but it is not that joy itself. As Teresa of Avila speaks, "Joy unfolds in the secret of my soul."

Then there is cathartic joy. This is more a psychological phenomenon, where there is a breaking out of old, imposed restrictions. In my experience of working with many souls, there are very few who know true spiritual joy. When I open up the space in my retreats for this, people immediately go to their default of either cathartic or surface joy. It often takes some time to coax and invite people into something deeper that they have yet to taste. Clare of Assisi had tasted this well, as she writes, "No one can give me my joy, and no one can rob me of my joy." It does indeed live within the secret of the soul.

All these types of joy have their place and time; however, it is the joy of the spirit that the mature soul is now called to. To find this, the daughter may need to shake us up a little. In this shaking process we need discernment of a new form. What form of discernment does the daughter bring us? Firstly, she brings spontaneity and fluidity, not rules and rigidity. She does not sit us down with a prescribed formula, no matter how wise-looking it is; rather, she takes us directly into our belly, asking what is the feeling deep within. She asks us to be honest, to be up-close and intimate with ourselves, willing to admit feelings of shame, guilt, failure, strength, knowing, power—false and real—to name a few. She does not ask us to drown in negative feelings or arrogantly declare the positive but simply to acknowledge all of them and bring them into a prayerful place of consideration.

In placing them all at the altar of the mother's heart, we can release what needs to released and bind what needs to be bound—of course using "bind" and "bound" here in the positive sense; that is, binding ourselves to our innate soul qualities that give us our desired and true freedom. This measured honesty is a very simple recipe for coming to know our joy. If we do this on a regular basis and do not allow any emotional accumulation, we will experience the energy of life streaming through us, as there will be no underlying emotive obstruction.

Very early in my life I was branded as the emotional one, so deeply did I feel my own and everyone else's emotions. It has been the greatest curse and the greatest gift, and it has taken some time to be able to live with this in a way that is helpful both to others and myself. I would witness myself again and again returning to immerse myself in and identify with my emotions, reducing who I was to this mass of sometimes seething creatures. It has been a long journey and continues to be so; however, the freedom comes in understanding that my deep-feeling nature is, in fact, a great gift for the world. In being able to honestly look and see, listen and hear my own soul, I can then pray for souls who are also encountering this particular feeling, asking for their liberation and my own. And I know it works. I have been shown that others do benefit, even those I do not know. This opening to and praying for others also frees me from any self-absorption or becoming overly preoccupied with my own inner journey.

Tears of release are the most powerful tears; they are the sweet pain of liberation from long-held grievances; they are the foundation for forgiveness and renewal. They allow us to grieve for what was and for what never was. They cleanse misunderstanding, ignorance, shame, guilt, and fear. They open the way for strength, fluidity, compassion, and joy. If we cannot cry outwardly, let us know our inner tears and let them flood our soul, creating the same cleansing and enlivening movement. In this way we will have a clear discernment of where we are to be and how we are to be, as it will not be our emotions leading us but rather the truth of our way, the truth of our life. Yeshua's words "I am the way, the truth, and the life" (John 14:6) can now take on an added or different meaning. We can read them as learning to maturely follow our own inner way, truth, and life, while always being open to the mother's guidance in all of her infinite ways.

Prayer to the Daughter of Your Soul

Dear daughter of my soul
I come to listen, to feel, to know
So often I have disregarded, avoided, and left you very alone
For this I am sorry
Can we begin again, dear daughter?
Will you speak to me in freedom
Without fear of my judgment or me running away?
I am here, dear soul
Let us sit awhile together

Let us become friends
>let me feel you
>let me cry you
>let me laugh you

And then we will rise together
>as love intended

Then we will live together
>as life intended

Then we will love together
>as we intended

So very long ago.

Chant

Ka-ah-la-la-ah-ha Ma-shee-ach

This chant is Kallah Mashiach elongated, using the sound of "ah," which indicates unity.

Dance as Meditation

Invite the daughter-bride to dance with you and through you. Find your way with this, whether with music, with a rattle, or in a form that you already practice. You may wish to go outdoors in nature and let the elements be your inspiration and accompaniment.

Let your daughter-soul shake loose within you: hear what she says and feel what she feels. Let go and forgive yourself and others. If tears come, let them rain down and cleanse your soul. Let go and enjoy!

Journal your freedom.

Daughter of Respect

When you have self-respect, you have enough.
Gail Sheehy

More than anything else, a daughter needs to learn and know self-respect. From a young age we have been taught how to look up to and respect others, but often with the energy of lack lying underneath; that is, we perceive the one we are looking up to as having something we do not, rather than them teaching and revealing to us what already lies within. We have not been taught the art and skill of how to build our self-respect, and therefore it is resentment or envy that can arise when we encounter others in a position where true respect is warranted.

A daughter must be willing to dive deeply into her being to find this respect, for it lies at a much greater depth than our earthly lives and their accomplishments or lack thereof. It also lies beyond anything that we can recognize and point to and call our self in this world. To know this respect, we are called to reach into our being where gender, our personal stories and lives, our vocations, and even our bodies are not in the picture, so to speak. Let me share an experience with you to clarify.

When I was a teenage daughter I often pondered the nature of God, and the one question that really burned a hole in my soul and mind was who created God? I mean, someone must've, right? When I would contemplate this I would also begin to experience myself growing very, very large, as if my soul were being lifted into the nether regions of the heavens; however, I would grow afraid and then shut the experience, and my expanding self, down. The question remained unanswered, as I was too afraid to go where the answer lay.

In later years I decided to revisit my question. And this time, not being so afraid, my vision opened. Words cannot adequately describe it, but the best I can articulate is that I saw this enormous expanse of light that extended beyond all realms and time. I was given to understand that this expanse, which we call the Creator, had no beginning and no end. It was the Uncreated, if you will. And then I was shown my own soul and how it also was of this same expansive light. It was not born and neither did it die. There was a profound recognition at that time of *oh, there is no death* and *this is the true life*. I saw that this was our being before it begins to wear, or put on, this life—that is, when our gender comes into its specific shape, what our personality will be like, what astrological sign we are born under, what work we will do, and so on. I experienced a deep and profound respect for this, my being without beginning or end, and all beings who are made of the same substance and nonsubstance.

This respect I felt was not based on any one thing, any achievement, or any knowledge. It was not a worldly respect but one of divine origin. This is the true and lasting respect that does not depend upon anything. The worldly notions of respect come and go as our lives rise and fall, and if we are relying on them for our self-respect, then we will be at the mercy of the vicissitudes of time and external events, and we will always find something that we lack in. If, however, we can come to know this being within, then the human angst can finally come to rest, as we are no longer beneath or above others but walking alongside them, even if they do have more knowledge than us. Now our natural respect will flow freely, not from a place of idolization but from a place of soul recognition. This becomes liberating for all involved.

In order for the daughter to know her power, she must know this liberation; otherwise, she will spend her time and energy vying for a respect that she does not own. And as we all know, nobody can give us such a thing; it is only we who can give that to ourselves. So let us begin looking in the right place, and let us visit often to keep reminding ourselves—for, as we also know, we are the forgetful ones.

Let us desire to experience and know our self-respect. We may find a new respect birthed for all of who we are and for the differences of others. Coming from the inside out rather than the outside in, we can now begin to encounter this respect in all aspects of our soul and lives.

This is the pathway of growth for the daughter, and it is what leads to the maturation and liberation of the soul of the world.

Prayer of Remembrance

> I seek my remembrance of a deeper way
> A way where my soul will know its own respectful nature
> I will bow down in honor from where it has come
> > and to where it is going
> I will remember long before time
> > and beyond all space
> I will remember the Creator who is the Uncreated One
> > and I will know that I, too, am one and the same
> For this I surrender all that I am not
> > and open to my splendor of what is.

Chant

Ka-ah-la-la-ah-ha Ma-shee-ach

To be chanted with the intention of respecting yourself as the daughter-bride

Meditation

Centering in your mother-ground, ask to know your inner self-respect. Gently open your being into a greater expansiveness. Then seek to taste or experience who you were before you were birthed in this world and body. Ask to know this, to feel this, and be happy with whatever occurs or does not occur. Keep asking, keep desiring, and keep remembering. The fruit will ripen.

Journal your great soul respect.

The Interior Root Star

Many people who cannot find their true path in life
have simply not yet found their ground…That which
has ground, substance, and validity will find its way
to manifestation. That which has roots will endure.

Anodea Judith, Wheels of Life

Our world seems to be caught between and populated by two opposites: people of the materialistic persuasion, completely attached to the worldly goods and life, and people of the spiritual persuasion, completely detached from the world and what it offers. It is the old dilemma of either/or that we seem to excel at here on earth.

The interior root star is the star of embodiment. It allows us to feel a measure of physical security through our home, bodily nourishment, and health. It gifts us with the benefits of pleasure and joy on this earth, and if these can be experienced in a way of rightful balance, they can open the way for the greater spiritual joys to be entered and known and realized on earth.

The very physical nature of life is paramount with this interior star. Many women experience their emotional pain through the body, and this is, of course, because womanhood is so directly connected to the physical being. However, this is also an indication that there is something out of balance in the interior root star. This is especially so with those who did not experience physical security in their family homes or for those whose bodies have been violated. For both, the pleasure and joy of being a human being on this earth have been seriously compromised. As Anodea Judith, the renowned Western teacher on the chakras, says, "We must make peace with our body so that we can then be at peace in our body." If there is no peace in the body, then we will seek ourselves only in the other spiritual realms, creating a safe, fantastical wonderland of our own false creation, or what can be called a spiritual bypass. With the inability to be who we are on this earthly plane, there is no manifestation, which ultimately means lack will be experienced, and therefore internal stories of ego elevation are needed to compensate for the absence in the earthly life.

What it comes down to for many women is the right to be here, and, I would add, the right to be: the right to be here and receive, and the right to be here and be who you are. Being strongly influenced by and involved in the Eastern ashram and Western monastic way of life, I took great spiritual pride (albeit falsely so) in that I owned nothing. For years I lived in furnished places or bought very minimally and would easily release all of it when I moved. Then there came a time to furnish what, for me, was a large two-bedroom apartment and to buy things. I had never bought so many material things in my life. It was a good grounding exercise of inhabiting the physical plane, and yet at the same time the monastic part of myself was watching with complete disbelief and, may I say, complete wariness as to what was going on.

The final straw came when I bought a cutlery set. My monastic being cried out *no, we are off the path, you have gone too far, stop!* I found it quite amusing that it was the cutlery set that brought forward this ultimate fear. Probably because I often used to say *I don't even own a fork*—and now I owned four of them! Oh no, God forbid such a thing. This is a laughable example as to how we do not allow ourselves to receive on the physical plane but look beneath and see the more serious side of this inability to receive materialistically, as if it is some kind of evil. And so the old beliefs that the structures of money and materialism are against spirituality raise their ugly little heads and we nod right along with them. What we do not realize is that we are condemning the physical and the feminine nature through this compliant nodding, for on what ground do these structures arise? Oh yes, in matter, in *mater*, in the mother's feminine ground.

Naturally there is the other extreme to what we have been speaking of, and that is where the material life is all that is desired, and this can manifest in two ways. First, through those who have no other desires or spiritual inclination at all and just want to find their pleasure and security through the temporal, and secondly, through spiritually inclined people who are so identified with what they don't have that trying to figure out how to survive on this planet takes up much of their prayer time and their energy. Both ways are equally out of balance in the interior root star.

The Daughter of Light teaches us how to find balance with our physical and spiritual nature, with our bodies and souls. She is the one who brings all of our spiritual wisdom to manifestation in this world. The life of Magdalene as Daughter of Light provides us with a vision of spiritual hope. She understood the principles of this interior root star by receiving in full the light of God, and she knew firsthand the words of Yeshua to be true—that is, we are to receive abundance of life in our souls, our minds, and our bodies. If we are able to do this, we can cease the incessant war of duality, release the argument between the physical and the spiritual, and enter into both as one and the same blessing, as one and the same life. This is the queendom/kingdom of God manifested on this good earth. And this most definitely not only has a right to be here and to be, but it is a necessity and a destiny to be manifested and fulfilled in each one of us.

Meditation

Bring yourself into a standing position or sit upright on a chair. Feel your feet firmly on the ground. Breathe into your interior root star, located in the perineum. See it as a shining red star, and then see the energy shoot down into the very center of the earth. Feel yourself grounded and anchored there. Breathe, and feel yourself nourished and supported. Receive this energy into your body, and see your interior root star glowing even brighter. Feel yourself grounded here on earth. Feel your right to receive, your right to be here, your right to be.

Journal your experience. Give thanks and walk with these blessings into the world.

Further Practice

Return to all of your journal entries of the Daughter of Light, read over them, and pray about them. Let the Shekinah show you how to integrate them into your daily life. Anytime you feel your root relationship is out of balance, return to the Daughter of Light chapter and seek your liberation.

Now move on to Daughter of the Dark.

3

Daughter of the Dark

Do not forsake me,
And do not be afraid of my power.
Anne McGuire, Thunder, Perfect Mind

As we engage with our Daughter of Light, we also encounter the Daughter of the Dark. She is our guide into the darkness and into the brilliance of light that stands within and behind this dark, the brilliance of light that lives within us. She is our ally, our protectress, and our liberator. Fear her not, and do not shun her. She comes to liberate.

Both Lilith and Eve have been living in the darkness with the truth of their nature obscured; thus we now seek both of them in the exiled wilderness.

Meeting Lilith

Lilith's epithet was "the beautiful maiden."
She is slender, well-shaped, beautiful
and nude, with wings and owl-feet.
Raphael Patai, The Hebrew Goddess

Lilith is one of the most enigmatic feminine figures to have graced our spiritual heritage. She has been known as a goddess who rules the beasts of night and a she-demon who lures souls to their own wicked depravity. One of the earliest references to Lilith is in Sumerian mythology (ca. 2000 BCE), where it is said in the days of creation she built her house in a willow tree on the bank of the Euphrates, with a dragon nesting in the base of the tree and a zu-bird (a godlike bird) at the crown of the tree.

The Jewish midrashim and Christian Gnostic teachings tell us that Lilith, prior to Eve, was the original divine emanation of the feminine energy, filled with immense power and strength and firmly established in her own being. She was destined to be embodied by the human woman and to live in harmony and in a state of complementarity with the masculine energy, the one whom we call Adam. In my rendition of Genesis 1:27, we can read this: "The mother created humanity in the image of wholeness, in the image of ultimate goodness the human being was created, female and male were brought forth." This original female was Lilith, and the male, Adam.

Through the interactions of Lilith and Adam we come to witness what we experience and know so well in our own lives. In her divine boldness and her naturally explorative and creative nature, Lilith proposed to Adam that they should explore new positions in their lovemaking. She suggested lying side by side, herself being on top, and other explorations, to see what energy may come forth from that loveplay. Adam had always experienced deep awe and wonder and at least a little fear of Lilith's power and divine nature, but now her suggestions were becoming even more frightening, if not outright threatening. Adam was afraid that if he deviated from the original position or allowed Lilith to come on top that she would overpower him, and then he would lose his own power. Silly Adam. Of course not! It would just mean that they would generate more energy and strength between them.

Unfortunately, Lilith could not convince Adam of this combined strength, and he withdrew further into his fear and refused any change or exploration. He was to be on top, and that was that. Lilith did not like that her power was restricted and that it was unable to grow and be expressed. She became restless, frustrated, and then downright angry. This anger grew to such proportions that Lilith could no longer cohabitate with Adam; speaking a divine name of power, she flew off into the wilderness of the desert.

As we know, like attracts like, energies recognize each other and join together; in Lilith's case, it was her anger that was now foremost in her being, not her original grace-filled power. And so, having left the Garden of Paradise, she now found herself in a wilderness that was inhabited by other angry creatures and energies. The book of Isaiah 34:14, interestingly the only direct biblical reference to Lilith, mentions this exile, where it is written that wild cats, hyenas, and satyrs will call to one another, and there Lilith too will lurk, seeking her rest. This was the land of *Sheol*, the realm where the goodness or the word of the Creator is not felt or heard. Her power was still within her, of course, only now it was fuelling the anger, and her anger continued to boil and grow, giving birth to new angels of anger, disappointment, loss, and so many more. Her power was being eaten up and used for creating the angels of the night. Lilith imposed upon herself her own exile, just as we often do, but then turning and pointing the finger at our society, our partners, our teachers, or whoever we may find to rail against, we then fester in this self-imposed exile and breed our own angels of the night.

In this age of the Second Coming it is time for the feminine energy to return to its natural grace and strength and to open to the creative adventures of union with the masculine energy. We need to ask, is this feminine energy on top in our own lives or do we restrict her and diminish her power and force her into the wilderness of our soul? Are we still harboring our anger, our disappointments, and our loss in the wilderness? Yes, we can point to the patriarchy outside of ourselves as being the problem, but remember, we are also the masculine Adam. The question really becomes this: how does our inner Adam fear our inner Lilith?

Let us take a deep breath, dive into this primordial land of our being, and see what is the truth lying beneath. For so many years I had so cleverly disguised and banished Lilith that I did not even know she existed, nor did I know that my inner Adam and Lilith were still at war. And then when I did get a hint of what was perhaps percolating beneath the surface, I immediately pointed to the outer Adam, and we all know where that leads—to a lot of pain and then eventually right back within.

Let us first acknowledge and see where Lilith is residing and also where Adam stands in relationship to her. Please join with me in this prayer.

Prayer to Lilith, Daughter of Night

Lilith, original woman of power and grace
I honor your strength, your wit, your wisdom
You who lay with the original man
Asking your power to be known
Where do you lie now?
What keeps you alive, and on what do you feed?
Speak to me, Lilith, and let me know you
Let me feel you
Let neither Adam nor I fear you any longer
Let your anger and his fear lie down in love together

Let the Creator's plan, the original desire, now unfold
In you, in me, in him
Let there be no more separation.

Chant

La La Lilatu (la la lee-la-tu), *Kali Kallah* (ka-lee kal-lah)
Lilatu is another name of Lilith; Kali Kallah is "dark anointed
daughter-bride"

Meditation

Come into your mother-ground and enter into a gentle and natural breath. Invite the presence of Lilith, or the dark daughter, the anointed one. You may envision her as a young, dark woman with long black hair, adorned with jewels and even a necklace of skulls. She may be dancing wildly or she may just be present in her strength. Open to her and commune with her and accept whatever she wishes to communicate with you. It may come in the form of a vision, a word, a feeling, or even in a dream or in life later on. If you feel fear arising, know this is simply your inner Adam and offer this fear to Lilith, to the dark daughter, letting her take care of it in her own way.

Then feel yourself merge into your own dark, beautiful daughter and begin to establish your relationship as you would with any being, with honor and respect. Know her to be your friend and liberator.

Journal the beauty of your dark daughter.

Daughter of Sacred Anger

She also had seen a vision, but what she saw was
Eve and Lilith and the great divide between them.
Tau Malachi, St. Mary Magdalene:
The Gnostic Tradition of the Holy Bride

As we know, mythologies are not about facts; they are soul stories revealing our own stories and lives. They also are not stagnant; they metamorphose according to what one's soul needs and experiences, with every teller having a different perception, a different rendering that brings forward timeless human truths. It is an expanded revealing of Lilith's story that now continues.

In her anger, Lilith also began to feel a deep sadness overwhelming her, and underneath this sadness was a deep pain and hurt that her power had been denied. There was also a great pain in her heart that she was now separated from Adam. She breathed a long breath, seeing beyond her pain, and speaking another divine name of power she flew back to Adam. But what she found was Adam now making love to another feminine being, the one we call Eve, and this Eve was clearly happy in the safe place and position that Adam desired. There was no speaking Lilith's anger. She was furious with Adam for replacing her so swiftly, and even more furious with Eve for betraying the feminine strength and power. She stormed back into the wilderness and raged even more.

The greatest obstacles I have found to the feminine soul coming fully back into her strength are the repression of feelings—submitting to the many claims of being overly emotional and therefore denying them—or succumbing and being overwhelmed and eaten alive by them. The feelings themselves are, of course, not the problem, but how we choose to work with them is where the empowerment or dis-empowerment lies. The more we feel the feeling, the more energy and power we can engender and use for our advancement and for all souls. For example, anger is the energy of fire. It can burn and consume us, either in a positive or negative way, and it can be fuel to move us into taking the right action. Most of us are deeply afraid of our anger, however, and thereby avoid it at all cost.

I have felt deep anger at men being on top in the world of spirituality and just about everything else in this world, yet when I reached into this anger from another angle, I began to experience the pure or raw quality of anger as a fiery energy. I began to realize that I could choose to use this fiery energy as I desired. I could let the anger consume me in a negative way and rant and rave against the injustice or I could meet it with the positive divine fire and burn away the anger, cleansing my soul and freeing me from all negativity. I could also use that fire to spark my spiritual practices to give greater desire, focus, and concentration. And that fiery presence is one of the best ways to move beyond any feelings of inertia or lack of inspiration in our lives, so by entering into our anger with the intent for transformation, we are, in fact, generating a whole new creative energy.

Through choosing to engage with our anger, or the angel of darkness, in a positive way, it now becomes our ally, a means of entering deeper into our soul and liberating the energy that is bound in a way that can be very hurtful to our souls and to others. With this act of liberation, we enter into it not only for our own souls but also for all who are bound in this way by using the energy generated to pray for others. An example of this was a time when I was experiencing anger arising due to past abusive actions toward me. Underneath this anger I was feeling the helplessness of the young child that I was and the fear that was so sadly and confusingly mixed with the feelings of love toward the family perpetrator. I began to pray to the mother, asking for healing. A feeling of lightness came over my soul, accompanied by a surge of great strength, and then my prayers began to change. I began praying for a father whom I did not know, that he would come to his senses and that his child would be protected. And then I was shown, in what I can only describe as a live spiritual web-cam, a father opening the door to his sleeping child's room. He began to walk into the room but then abruptly stopped, walked back out, closed the door, and walked back down the hallway in shock, saying *what was I thinking?* Another scene was shown of a married man about to enter into an affair but changing his mind at the last moment. All the while I was praying, and I knew instinctively that I was being shown how our prayers for our own healing also extend far beyond to help others if we choose to direct them as such. It was a deeply moving experience, with my Lilith anger transformed into a healing presence for many.

And what of Eve? How often does our anger arise because once again we have submitted where we did not want to? Some old Eve energy within us lowers our eyes to the floor and lies down submissively, either feeling all our power draining out of us or becoming angry later. I have watched this in others and myself. One area in particular where I see this submissive lowering of the eyes is when women are negotiating monetary reimbursement for their work. There is a great struggle in placing a financial value on what they offer to the world, as if it is some kind of sin to even ask to be compensated. I see this as coming from two sources: the first, from the historical and generational work of women as being unpaid caretakers in the family and home, freely giving of their wisdom, intuition, and love. Now that many are taking this wisdom into the world, even with the appropriate worldly credentials, there is unease or, at best, confusion at placing a value on it. And the second source is our spiritual heritage. Shamans, rabbis, and priests have all been traditionally supported by their communities through material gifts or monetary tithes; however, we are now moving forward from these structures and need to find a true and right means of livelihood.

Unfortunately, the Gospels have been interpreted as casting an evil eye over money; over and over we hear how Yeshua drove the moneychangers from the temple, how he told Lazarus to give up all his money and material goods and follow him, and how it was easier for a camel to pass through an eye of the needle than for a rich man to enter heaven. All of his words around money seemed to point to a money versus spirituality mentality, and this runs very deep in our psyche. As always, context means a lot. In the time of Yeshua it was understood that if you were rich, then God favored you, and if you were poor, you were cursed or not in God's favor. Yeshua was dispelling these beliefs and also teaching people the right relationship with money, by not relying on it alone, but also relying on God. Money itself is not the evil, but how we relate to it and use it is of great importance. After all, Yeshua didn't tell Magdalene or the other wealthy women that were with him to give up their money. No—he and his mission, and many with him, were supported by it!

St. Paul, in 1 Corinthians 9:7–14, gives us all the affirmation we need around money and taking our spiritual gifts into the world. He says that if we have sown the seed of spiritual things in another, then we should receive material compensation. He also reminds us that the ministers in the temple get their food from the temple, and those who serve at the altar can claim their material share. In the same way, he said that Yeshua gave the instruction that those who spread the message of the Spirit should also get their living from this. Hallelujah, Paul!

May we no longer lower our submissive Eve eyes when we are negotiating our right livelihood. Let us not be greedy or demanding either but feel what is good and fair in our own hearts. Where Eve's energy and power has been drained in you, let it be replaced with strength and the fire of love, burning away all that keeps you low and small.

In working with both Lilith and Eve, we are cultivating a place in our soul for them to meet once again, but this time in the way of deep respect, recognition, and love. Only when these two are joined can there then be a full communion with Adam. Let us take up this work, which will lead to the full empowerment of the feminine energy, in our souls and in our world.

Prayer for Our Inner Lilith and Eve

> We pray for the energy of the living fire
> To come upon our souls
>> clearing the internal land of long-held anger and loss
>> burning away all the debris of outdated debt and pain
> Come, living flame
> Bring the fire of love and forgiveness
> That we may cultivate the ground of our soul
> Making a place for Lilith and Eve to meet
> Where they may gaze upon one another
>> with love, and know their unity of being
>> in and through our lives.
> May all beings know the unity of their soul.
> Amen.

Chant

> *Aiyah Kali Kallah* (i-yah ka-lee kal-lah), *Kali Mashiach* (ka-lee ma-shee-ach)
> The unifying power of the Dark Daughter, the Anointed One, the Embodied One

Meditation

Coming into your mother-ground, open to the spaciousness and depth of your soul, with the intention of allowing Lilith to dance upon your soul. You may envision her as that young, wild, bejeweled dark maiden in all of her fiery presence, and let her bring the living fire of love into your heart, burning away all anger and drawing forth your natural and divine fiery energy.

You may even see a flame of fire deep in your belly, burning all that needs to be burned and transforming your energy. Then, as you are inspired, use that energy for your good and for the good of all, giving prayers of thanks and uplifting all beings into their innate goodness.

Journal your sacred anger.

Disdain of the Soul

Lilith is the power of Eve, and Eve is the perfection
of Lilith, so that joined they are True Womanhood.

Tau Malachi, The Secret Gospel of
Mary Magdalene, saying 249

When Lilith witnessed Adam in love-play with Eve, her response was one of anger and fury, and as she retreated to the wilderness there came to be born from within her the dark angel of disdain. This energy of disdain was directed toward Eve for her weak submission to Adam, but as it churned within Lilith it grew into something other.

As Lilith was alone in the wilderness with her pain and negativity, the angels of darkness began to feed upon Lilith's anger and started whispering in her ear that not only was Eve the disdained one, but she too, Lilith, in her weakness of fleeing, was also bringing the stain of disdain upon the feminine soul. Lilith's power began to fold in on itself and proceeded to give birth to a self-loathing dismissal of her soul.

When we hold others in disdain and subsequently dismiss them, we can be assured that we are also doing that to our own soul, thereby thieving from others, and ourselves, our innate power of being. I remember oh so clearly when my mother told me I was dismissive. I waved her off with a flick of my hand (oh so dismissively) and said *no, I'm not*. It took many years before I realized just how dismissive I was, and most of all to my own soul power. Sorry, Mom! Sorry, soul!

Let us look at the word *disdain*. This is a strong word of great disrespect. It means, according to the *Oxford Dictionary*, "the feeling that someone or something is unworthy of one's consideration or respect." It also speaks on the outer surface to an intense dislike of oneself or another, and on the inner plane to an inability to recognize the goodness within. How is it that we do not feel our soul is worthy of our consideration? How is that we do not even like our soul? Just ask Lilith, and she will probably provide you with a very good list of what exactly is wrong with your Eve: too submissive, too mild, too meek, too eager to please, unable to say no or yes, too pure, too perfect, smiles too much, too predictable, and is shy in bed. And then ask your Eve, and she will probably provide you with an equally good list of what is wrong with Lilith: too wild, too bold, too outspoken, too fiery, too unpredictable, too sensuous, too curvy, too powerful, too strong, and oh so courageous and outrageous in bed and out.

Lilith is outraged when we falter and fall into Eve, and we're judged by Eve when Lilith starts roaring and rearing up in our soul. How is a gal meant to love herself in and through this? And how do we draw in these energies to use them appropriately in a way that uplifts the soul and does not degrade or find the soul in some ego inflation?

Essentially, there is nothing wrong with Eve and there is nothing wrong with Lilith; it is how their energies are known and expressed that become key. Eve, in her fullness of power, is the essence of true humility. In using the energy of submission in a right way—that is, submitting to her inner soul and not to some false god who wants to dominate her—Eve can open the way for true knowledge and wisdom to be received and known. Lilith can then take this knowledge and wisdom and, through her fiery energy and action, embody it and realize it in the world. Together, Eve and Lilith come into the fullness of sacred womanhood, bearing spiritual self-worth and spiritual self-confidence. Our true spiritual pride is reborn when we have the ability to bow low before the One and to stand tall within ourselves.

Prayer of Welcome

Eve, I welcome you back into my soul
Let all the lies of weakness and shame
    and false perfection become as if they never existed
For in the One they never have
Let your true humility rise in my soul
So that it may bow down in honest reverence
In a deep abiding love opening the way
    for my true soul knowledge

Come, Eve, come
It is time to return.

Lilith, I welcome you back into my soul
Let all the lies about your wildness and
    all the fear of your power be gone
May you now resurrect in a way
    that breeds true strength of soul
    that gives birth to true power and spiritual
    knowledge in our bodies and in our souls
Come, Lilith, come
It is time to return.

Chant

Aiyah Kali Kallah (i-yah ka-lee kal-lah), *Kali Mashiach* (ka-lee
ma-shee-ach)
The power of unification through the embodied daughter

Meditation

Breathe into your mother-ground, coming with the intention of knowing Eve's true energy. Invite and welcome her from within your soul, and allow to rise all that she wishes to share. If false weakness and false submission rise, place them in the womb of the mother-ground, asking for their healing and their truth to be revealed. Let Eve have a new face, a new body, a new way of being in your soul.

Breathe into your mother-ground, coming with the intention of knowing the true energy of Lilith. Invite and welcome her from within your soul, and allow all that she wishes to share to rise. If anger, arrogance, disdain, or dismissal arise, place them in the womb of the mother-ground, asking for their healing and their truth to be revealed. Let Lilith have a new face, a new body, a new way of being in your soul.

Ask the bride, bearing her unified nature of Eve and Lilith, to bless you. Take this blessing in and become this very same unification.

Journal your experiences.

The Subtle Face of Jealousy

I am the one upon whom you have thought
and whom you have scorned.
Anne McGuire, *Thunder, Perfect Mind*

Whenever we open the way into our soul, one never knows what will happen or what will appear. This is the great adventure-challenge we are called to in our spiritual life, and so we must draw on the strength of our inner Lilith to meet it all and not collapse into the false weakness of Eve. We do have a great inner strength and all we need within, including the ability to pray to the mother.

Returning to our story, let us go back and take a snapshot of the moment when Lilith witnessed Adam and Eve in their love-play. At this same time Eve, unable to meet Adam's eye, was gazing into the distance and saw this great and wonderful and terrifying being coming toward her. She was at once horrified and yet deeply drawn to this being who she thought was a woman but was not sure, so different was she to her own self. Eve looked down and within and did not understand what she was feeling; it was as if something was jolted into life within her, but she did not know what. She felt intrigued and yet repulsed at this terrifying vision. She had heard about she-demons and was afraid of them and afraid she had just seen one. She clung tighter to Adam. This being Eve saw was, of course, Lilith.

Meanwhile, Lilith, in her fury, also felt a strange sensation within herself, something she had not known. This sensation grew and gave birth and found its name: jealousy. As Lilith kept seeing the vision of Eve and Adam, jealousy grew rapidly and had its own family. In the darkness of night they would wander, seeping into soul dreams, arousing the energy of their name in those they visited. They especially liked to visit Eve as she dreamed night after night of that terrifyingly beautiful vision that she had beheld. Every morning, comparing herself to that one, Eve would feel less and less sure of herself and would lie down even when she was not asked to. Lilith, on the other hand, spent her mornings counting the ways of how much better she was than this Eve and how much more she had to offer. The family of jealousy was very successful in spreading their genes.

Jealousy is an insidious and sometimes very subtle energy that we all encounter. Whenever we are comparing ourselves to another, this is the secret and sly way of jealousy wrapping itself around our soul. In our comparisons we become like Eve, feeling less and less confident about ourselves and always placing the other above or before us. Then Lilith enters and counteracts this by trying to bolster us from this place of lack of confidence, which of course never works and is merely trying to convince us that we are as good as the other. What a mess!

Here we have Lilith and Eve working together in a disempowering way, and this is often what happens when we try to awaken and empower ourselves from the source of lack. It simply doesn't work and ends up with a lot of *I am woman, I am powerful* statements that get us nowhere. We need to look deeper; we need to be willing to dive beneath the façade of jealousy, which masks all of our insecurities. We need to reach deep within our soul to our natural splendor and thus be able to appreciate the splendor of others.

The key word here is natural. Eve is naturally mild of nature, which speaks of tenderness and patience. Lilith is naturally powerful and sensuous, which tells us she has the ability to physically relate to this world, uplifting the soul of the world in and through her body and senses. Eve can return us to a natural purity of soul, as she demonstrated with her open curiosity in the Garden of Eden and her willingness to take the first bite. Lilith can return us to a natural power of soul, where she courageously does not lie down at the expense of her own soul for anybody. Some of these states we will excel at more than others, and some we will be drawn to, while others will exasperate us; hence, we know where our work lies. What draws you is a natural gift, and what terrifies or repulses or irritates you is also a gift, albeit an undeveloped one. Let both Lilith and Eve start developing within.

Prayer for Power and Purity

> Lilith, sometimes your power terrifies me
> I want to run and hide and become Eve hidden behind
> > the fig leaf where no one can see me or hear me
> > because—well—what do I have to offer?
> The world has been a harsh place, Lilith
> I don't know how to navigate it from the truth of my soul
> It has never really listened
> It has never known the truth of woman
> > and...I have never really listened
> I have never known the truth of woman
> Let this stop now
> Let there be a turning within me
> Let there be a turning within you and Eve
> May the naturalness of power and purity
> > be born
> > be known
> > understood
> And lived in our world and all worlds
> I love you, Lilith. I love you, Eve.

Chant

> *Ma-Ah-Shah Ma-Ah-Shah Ma-Ah-Shah Shekinah Ha-Mashiach*
> (sheck-ee-nah ha-ma-shee-ach)

This is a wonderful and powerful chant of the Red Maiden, who cuts through all falsity, obstinacy, wrongful pride, and fear. She may be envisioned as a wild young woman with ruby red heart energy extending out to you, long black hair, and a sword that cuts through all that needs to be let go of. She also carries a blessing bowl from which she pours her blessing upon you from the necessary release. She is akin to the dakini energy of Tibetan Buddhism.

Meditation

Breathe deeply into your mother-ground, coming into the spaciousness of your being. Invite the Red Maiden to show you those things that repel, frighten, or irritate. Let the Red Maiden cut them away, and let her power transform them into their true state. Let her pour her blessings upon you from her blessing bowl.

Then let her show you the natural splendor of your soul, allowing those things that are natural gifts be revealed. Acknowledge them and give thanks for them.

Place all of who you are in the womb of your mother-ground, and feel the Red Maiden pouring her blessing upon you.

Journal all that was revealed.

The Unsure Eye

The thought of truth drove me;
I walked to it and didn't wander off.
Songs of Solomon, Song 17, The Gnostic Bible

We read that Eve was unable to meet Adam's eye during their love-making. What was it that Eve was unable to meet or look into, and what did she gain by gazing into the distance?

If we are unable to engage with another and look them in the eye, it can sometimes mean an insecurity or nervousness of self, an inability or unwillingness to reveal the honest truth of our soul. If we were to meet another's gaze and they were truly loving us, then what would we do? Perhaps all our vulnerabilities would come crashing into the moment and we would feel ashamed or embarrassed or overwhelmed. Best just to glance over here.

Or perhaps we are afraid that if we did look too deeply, we would actually see the other, not as loving us but loving themselves for what they can gain in the moment. Then we would feel another type of vulnerability, feelings of disappointment and loss. We don't want to know these either. Best glance over there.

Our vulnerabilities are the gifts that we bring into the world for our own healing and for the healing of the soul of the world. They are not something to be stashed away where only our best friend sees them, but they are to be prayed for and shared with those who also feel that same vulnerable spot in their soul. There is no shame and no time limit or expiry date of where and when they should dissolve and disappear. There are some vulnerabilities that will be with us throughout our lives, but rather than treating them as the enemy, we would do well to welcome them and compassionately love them like a friend. Perhaps this is one angle Yeshua was aiming at when he said "love your enemies"? In compassionately loving these vulnerabilities, we may find that they become less and less bothersome, that they are simply there like a younger sibling—sometimes irritating but not affecting us in any dire way.

Generally, however, we do not like our vulnerabilities because, in our eyes, they seem to erode our feelings of confidence and power and feeling good about ourselves, and so we become like Eve and gaze off into the distance. However, true power and confidence do not erode, and Lilith will come by and visit us again and again, deflating all sense of false power and reminding us of true soul power. She will come in any form it takes until we genuinely engage and know the power within each vulnerable moment. These moments are doorways into a greater expansion of the inner strength of our Lilith soul and a release of the shame and hiding of our Eve soul.

At crucial vulnerable moments I have watched myself gaze off into the distance, turn the conversation, use humor to change the energy, sit silently when words were needed, or prematurely get up and leave (whether it be in the company of another human being or divine beings in my meditation). I missed or deliberately avoided an opening of soul between another and myself, between the Beloved and myself. I rejected a deep soul intimacy, the very life that my soul yearned for. Lilith screeched and danced all over me in these moments. Eve closed her eyes and sighed. And why did I do this? We are like an eternal well of reasons—we can always find one, but it's better to not even go there. Underneath every reason is always the same sensation of fear, no matter how we mask it. Instead, let's simply stop avoiding these beautiful soul moments and enter them fully, bringing all of Lilith's strength and all of Eve's shame with us, to the Beloved, to another, and to ourselves.

Do we know of Lilith's vulnerable strength? It was when she asked again and again to try new positions and places in her love-play with Adam. She was asking for a vulnerability of newness, a release of control by both of them, and ultimately an action of true spiritual adventure into the unknown. How vulnerable this is, how strong and how exciting! May we know such vulnerable strength.

Prayer for Vulnerable Strength

> Lilith, fly toward me now
> Show me your terrifying beauty
> Your desire and strength
> To fall into the dark of the night sky
> Show me it here—within
> Don't let me turn aside
>> or around
>> or fidget
>> or leave
> Come, Lilith, show me the way.

> Eve, there is no shame
> You too can come
>> and tremble and shake and cry
>> if you need to
> There is room here
> In this inn
> Come, Eve, let's go
> Come, Eve, let go.

Chant

> *Ma-Ah-Shah Ma-Ah-Shah Ma-Ah-Shah Shekinah Ha-Mashiach*
> (sheck-ee-nah ha-ma-shee-ach)
> The power of the feminine fire, the spirit of liberating wisdom

Meditation

Coming into your breath and the spaciousness of your mother-ground, invite the dark daughter-bride, Kali Kallah, into your space and into your heart. You may envision her with long black hair and green, piercing eyes, dressed in a flowing black robe with an inner robe of white brilliance. Begin to breathe with her, letting her energy infuse your being. Let her dance on your soul and open those places that

remain closed and afraid. Bring your fear of surrender, your vulnerabilities, and let them go out on your breath to her. In their place breathe
in her breath of strength and power. Keep doing this, letting your vulnerable and powerful energy mingle together and become as one.

When complete, give thanks and walk in the world in this surren-
dered place of spiritual adventure.

Journal the power of your vulnerabilities.

The One Who Gazes

And that which you see outside of you, you see
within you. It is manifest and it is your garment.
Anne McGuire, *Thunder, Perfect Mind*

Gazing is known to be a very prophetic action. It goes beyond looking with the physical eye or inquiring with the rational mind. Gazing is a skill of the inner soul in which we open and allow ourselves to be taken into the dimensions of existence that lie beyond our earthly realm. In returning from our gazing, we are then asked to integrate what we have seen into our earthly life, to make it visible and wear it like a garment of the soul.

With every negative experience there are things we learn from its implications, and more often than not there are also positive outcomes and gifts given. Here we look at the positive aspect of Eve's gazing. As we previously read, when Eve was entering into her lovemaking with Adam she was gazing into the distance, and it was through this gazing that she witnessed the great form of Lilith. Though not consciously aware at the time, what Eve saw was the power of her own soul that she did not know even existed. This initial ability of gazing by Eve was the initiatory step toward the liberation and redemption of the feminine soul of the world. In Eve seeing Lilith and Lilith seeing Eve, the journey of reuniting both the Daughter of Light and the Daughter of the Dark began. This journey of reuniting continues in each one of us to this day and beyond, and it will continue until there is a full resurrection, claiming, and daily living of this union.

Gazing becomes a way for us to see not only who we are in this moment, but also who we are becoming. It is an act of faith, which then becomes knowledge, experienced through every mystical sighting. First, we must have the faith that we can gaze into the one we are becoming, and then we must have the desire and skill to travel there and see and encounter the mystical sighting. In bringing back this sighting, this recognition, we are then asked to make it knowledge, or realize it, through our everyday living. Recognition, then realization; if we return and fall back into the disempowered self, then our mystical sighting slips away and does not become an embodied reality, no matter how much we huff and puff and protest and try to prove we are what we saw. We must become what we see and not just bring back the sighting report. Of course, this embodiment takes time and can often be like two steps forward and three back, but if you glance back to your life a few years or even a few months ago and can see how differently you are living in the world, then you know you are steadily moving into your becoming.

This, in fact, has been a great source of my own personal exasperation. I would have all these great mystical sightings but would slip, again and again, back into my old disempowered ways. Why is this so? Somehow the faith was there to enter the gazing journey, but then the mystical sightings would slip out of my grasp when I returned to daily living. The recognition just did not make it to realization, and subsequently even the faith to make the mystical sightings would disappear. What a terribly painful cycle, and one that I endured over and over until I realized the great role of distraction in this cycle.

When returning from one of our mystical sightings or deep meditations, or often even right in the middle of them, a distracted thought may come to mind. It may be something from our life, diverting our attention, or it may be a questioning of what we were just sighting or being shown. A seed of doubt arises, or even a very visual and audible accusation of our spiritual nature and gazing ability. I have heard and seen many such things but have come to know them for what they are: spirits of distraction, who often team up with other spirits, particularly ones of judgment, seeking to divert us from embodying the wisdom or sight just given and attempting to abort the realization of our empowerment.

One vivid example was when I was falling very deeply and ecstatically into chant with my sacred rattle and there came, ever so clearly into my mind, a male religious figure shouting at me that what I was doing was heresy. It was so loud and real that I immediately stopped my chanting and opened my eyes to make sure he wasn't in my living room. Fortunately, he was not, but what a poignant moment it was, as I had been feeling myself falling into such a deep place of ecstatic surrender when these spirits of distraction and judgment entered and, doing their job, shattered the moment.

We often blame ourselves for these moments, judging ourselves for judging! Obviously this has definite negative connotations toward our soul, and yet this is just another form of the spirits of distraction and judgment seeking to draw us away from our empowerment. The more vivid and obvious spirits are easier to deal with, but the more subtle voices of distraction are the ones that can trick us, as we tend to hear them as our own voices in our minds and therefore believe them to be true. Saying 237 in *The Secret Gospel of St. Mary Magdalene* tells us that "words have no meaning apart from the mother spirit," so if we are hearing words of blame, shame, or anything inducing fear or doubt, know these do not come from the mother and are therefore not true, no matter whose voice is speaking.

A rendition of the passage of Mark 8:22–26 gives us a beautiful example of what we have been speaking. A daughter who was blind to the greater spiritual realities is brought to Yeshua for healing. Taking her by the hand, he leads her away from the village—that is, away from her friends and her life as she knows it. He then spits on his hands and lays them over her eyes, awakening her gently to a new sight and reality. She begins to see another world, but not clearly. He then lays his hands with the healing power of light directly onto her eyes, and with this she sees everything plainly and distinctly: she sees the spiritual reality in and behind this earthly reality. He tells her to not go back to the village; that is, don't go back to your old ways of being or become distracted by all the various entertainments you call your life.

Let us not go back to our village of distractions but have faith in our mystical sightings, asking how to embody and live them, and asking for the power and grace of Yeshua and the bride to guide and watch over us.

Prayer for Mystical Sight

I come into my mystical gazing
Into my sight within
I lay down all thoughts of myself and being
And open to who I am in the becoming
Feeling, seeing, sensing
    and believing
I come with faith
I leave with knowledge
Drawing my being and becoming
    into one
I return to earth
In peace, in calm
In knowing.

Chant

Adonai (a-doe-nigh), *Da-ha da-ha, Da-har-ee-el*

This is the chant for Archangel Dahariel. She/he is known as an angelic helper. Dahariel comes to those who call upon her/him to help increase faith. She/he may appear in any manner of form or feeling, all according to what each is able to receive.

Meditation

Choose an object to gaze upon: the flame of a candle, a crystal sphere, or even the horizon where sea and sky or mountain and sky meet. Bring yourself into the mother-ground, gently and rhythmically breathing. Have your eyes partially open with a gentle, soft gaze, focusing your attention on your chosen object or place. Intentionally open to your mystical gaze. Using chant, breath, or simply being, let yourself fall into a peace-filled openness of soul, not doing anything. If thoughts come to distract, smile at them and refocus. If they are stubborn, take up the chant and pray to Dahariel to assist you.

Stay with the mystical gaze as long as you feel. Do not get up too soon. Give it time to work into your soul and sight. Be happy with whatever comes. All is good.

Further Meditation

Read through the passage of Mark 8:22–26, then bring the story alive with your imagination with the rendition given below.

You are in your home village or town, walking with your friends, being distracted here and there by all the stores, things on sale, and conversations of no real importance. And then there comes a presence before you, one you have not encountered before. It is the presence of truth in the form of Magdalene. She takes you by the hand and leads you away from your friends, from your village, from everything familiar and known to you. You become afraid as she takes you out into a desert land. What is going to happen?

She then spits on her hands and lays them over your eyes. You feel like a healing balm is soaking into your whole being, with a gentle light spreading within and all around you. You feel a new vision begin to open to you, but it is a little hazy. It is as if you are about to see something new and wonderful but cannot quite grasp it. She then lays her hands on your eyes again, and with this there is a great light flooding your soul. You see! You see beyond the ways of this world; you see a whole other reality open before you. You see the pure land of being. Magdalene gently whispers to you, "Now go home; don't go back to the village."

Journal your experiences.

The Prodigal Daughter

Peace be with you. Receive my peace.
Be careful that no one leads you astray
with "Come over here!" or "Go there!"
Jean-Yves Leloup, The Gospel of Mary Magdalene

More needs to be said about this spirit of distraction, as it is so prevalent in our world at this time and can be very subtle, so our inner vigilance needs to be on the alert. As with all spirits, there are many faces.

Often our spiritual pathway is one of a circuitous nature. Sometimes it is spirit-led and at other times we are merely chasing another wind of so-called opportunity. How do we know when we are following the spirit or when we are chasing something other? We may experience all kinds of twists and turns in our journey but still not find ourselves with any deeper connection, and we simply move from one place or distraction to another, believing it is the spirit guiding us.

It may feel like we are communing deeper with our soul, but are we? If we are constantly absorbed in my path, my experience, and not finding ourselves drawn deeper and deeper into the Beloved's arms, with a deeper peace in our soul and with less of a fixation on self, then we have fallen prey to a very subtle and clever spirit. And so we will continue spinning around and around, experiencing a sense of false liberation over and over but never really knowing the deep peace that is ours to know.

Another example is when we may experience a slight irritation in our soul, and without giving it too much investigative thought we shift our attention ever so slightly, which then takes us in a direction away from the irritation. A deeper sense of unease then starts to be felt, and we move further away. A strange feeling, like something gnawing at our soul, starts to creep in, and we keep moving and entertaining ourselves with all sorts of stories on the Internet or in life. We start to feel a loneliness and isolation and spend even more time distracting ourselves and trying to feel connected. Then we look and see how our meditation and prayer have slipped or lost their energy and passion, or we resist and don't want to do it, and on it goes.

Oh, what happened to the mystical gazing? What happened to the connection with the Beloved, my own soul, and others in a real and genuine way, and not simply in a fill-the-gap-in-my-heart way? How did I get here? You simply fell off the spiritual wagon, became as prey to the spirit of distraction, and became the prodigal daughter, understanding "prodigal" to mean using our resources (energy and time) recklessly and wastefully. How did all that Internet gazing (or wherever one ended up) really transform your soul? It may have made you feel better for a while and certainly there may have been moments of connection, but our souls are capable of so much more. We need to ask ourselves if we really wish to know this soul peace and capacity or if we are happy in our underlying discontent. It is this very discontent that is asking to be revealed in our initial soul irritation, but when we overlook it, our soul also gets overlooked. A deeper consideration and listening to that initial stirring will reveal a different path to follow, one where the true spirit will be leading you, and one that will be filled with the fruit of deep peace.

Another common cry I hear with those I work with is that their very life is a distraction—their work, their spouse, or whatever else is currently filling their lives—and yet this life and all it holds is the very ground for our spiritual advancement. In this instance we can say the liberation is in the distraction; that is, by bringing our love and prayer to our husbands, work, or whatever is calling us in life, we can help uplift the situation to a greater level of consciousness and ask for it to be liberated. By doing this we will become more energized rather than what we perceive as the distraction taking our energy or focus away from what is important. Let us pray for discernment to know the truth in every situation.

Prayer of Return

Mother, here I am

The prodigal daughter returned

I look down at my feet, ashamed

For it seemed I was so close to you

But now I look and I am so far away

Something tells me I should know better

Than to waste what I have been given

But sometimes it is so hard here, Mother

    sometimes I forget to listen

    sometimes I forget to come to you

    and to lean into your heart

Can I come back now?

Can I come home to you?

Sometimes a daughter just needs

To come home to her mother.

Chant

Amma Elohim (ah-ma el-oh-heem)

Amma and Elohim are divine names attributed to the mother;

    Elohim in particular speaks to the many, or the vast womb

    that contains all of life

Meditation

Feel into what lies underneath all your distractions. What are you running from? What are you afraid of? Are you simply frittering away time and energy because you lack focus and concentration or do you lack desire and passion for your own soul intimacy?

Are you fooling yourself into a surface spirituality but are unwilling to go deeper? If needed, feel the loneliness, isolation, and disconnection that may lie deeply in your being. Now see yourself as the prodigal daughter returning. See the divine mother before you, waiting. Then see her inviting you to come. Step forward and, bringing all that lies within your heart, walk closer and closer to the loving mother. See and feel her welcoming you, lean into her heart, and let yourself be received and loved. Let all dissolve in her presence.

Ask her for a blessing and the strength to know the truth of your distraction, and let her lead you back into the true life.

Journal your return.

The Interior Navel Star

Like the moon's pull on the tides, our desires
and passions can move great oceans of energy.
Anodea Judith, Wheels of Life

Even though it's called the navel star, the location in our body is a little lower, midway between the navel and the groin. It is associated with the womb, the sexual organs, and the moon, and correspondingly with procreation, sexuality, and desire. How appropriate for our Daughter of the Dark in the form of Lilith!

This interior star demands that our desires come into movement and into manifestation. If we do not follow and act on our desires, they will eventually wither and die, and we will literally become as the barren womb, not giving birth to any new creation. We need not be afraid of the depth of our feelings that birth our desires but understand them as inner cosmic catalysts revealing change, growth, and evolution. When our desires are elevated beyond survival, we enter another arena where the Shekinah can begin to dance in her creative power through us and as us.

Desire is not bad. Desire does not lead to a life of debauchery unless, of course, we let it lead us there. Remember Lilith's desire to be on top; this was her way of attempting to open to new ways of experiencing intimacy with another, to join in unity for spiritual adventure, and to bring a renewed relationship between the feminine and masculine. And remember Eve's desire of wanting to know a greater consciousness for humanity. Both were engaging in a forward vision and movement, a flow of energy and change, attempting to create a renewed consciousness. This is the ultimate task of desire. We need to seek out this true desire, which is usually buried underneath many superficial ones. We then need to know that this desire is possible and lay to rest, through not believing, all those little demon voices of not being good enough that shout out to us from our wilderness.

A lovely story about my mom speaks to this. Her means of clearing her mind of any trouble or worry, or what she called her meditation, was to go and play the slot machines in a casino. She spoke of completely losing herself while doing this. We are all such wonderfully unique beings, are we not? Anyway, she began winning jackpots, one after another, and in fact so many that it was becoming increasingly uncanny. I asked her, *What is happening, how are you doing this?* She replied that she just woke up one morning and decided she deserved it! I must also add that every time she won, she would take friends and family out to dinner straightaway, and I often received a hundred dollars in the mail.

Let us move from the whole money aspect to the notion of deserving. This is very closely linked with our previous interior root star and the right to be. Simply put, you deserve your desires to come into being because you are a child of the mother. That is it. No other reason, and no reason why they cannot. We would do well to look more closely at this. Do we believe that we deserve our desires or do we keep raging in the wilderness like Lilith, birthing all sorts of negative creations? The choice is always ours.

Fluidity is also a navel star attribute that we need to develop if we wish for our desires to unfold, learning to flow with the universal life-energy and not against it. As the wise Cistercian monk and writer Thomas Merton said, the way the Beloved has laid open for us is an easy way compared to the hard way of our own. Fluidity is being able to both feel and release our desires in one great balancing action. When our desires arise we tend to hang on so tightly to them that we do not allow them or their creative fluidity to change and manifest. It is an intricate balance of maintaining the energy and letting it flow at the same time, another example of not either/or but both/and. The small mind finds this difficult to grasp, but if you reach into your womb-feeling, it will understand. Ask to experience this.

There are some individuals, and many women, who are too fluid. Being naturally empathic and feeling other people's feelings, they lose the very ground of their own being. This can be especially so with those individuals who have been forcefully overpowered by another, in body or emotionally. However, if properly worked with, this can be a great gift of compassionate understanding for another. What is needed in this case is to work with the interior root star to gain more solidity and gravitas.

We will be speaking more throughout this book of the projections onto women's sexuality, so suffice it to say here that sexuality is a great life force, with the potential for giving great fulfillment on every level of our being. Unfortunately, it has been denied, denigrated, and hidden, as the less noble side of this great creative act has taken precedence in our world. And, equally, pleasure has also found its home in the dark backstreets of our world. The cries of Lilith (and Magdalene) as being the temptress are long overdue for a new song, and only we can sing this. Even if the action of sexuality is not valid for us, the desire, energy, and pleasure of the body associated with this force still remain, and we can stir and utilize them in ways that will enhance our growth and not inhibit it. To enjoy our body is not a sin. It can open the doorway to many wonderful experiences in and of the spirit, and it can open the way to a deep feeling of a long-neglected self-love. In loving our feminine nature, we will then open the way to enter our sacred womanhood. Whether it is through dance, yoga, massage, aromatherapy, or swimming in a natural pool in the moonlight, find what gives pleasure, invigorates, and draws you closer to the Shekinah. In drawing closer to her, she will draw closer to us!

Meditation

Focus on your interior navel star. See it as a glowing orange star. Feel the light of this star getting brighter and brighter, filling your whole abdomen, womb, hips, and sexual organs. Feel its natural fluid nature and let desire arise. Then focus this desire onto a spiritual desire for yourself, whether it is the gift of wisdom, joy, or something you wish to manifest in the world. Dedicate this desire to the mother and for the good of all, and let it be ignited by the light of the interior star. Know that, as a child of the mother, you do deserve this to come to be. Open to the creative fluidity and ask to be shown how to birth this desire in all of its goodness.

You may also add this prayer: "If this desire is not for my good, then please let it dissolve, and may another arise that is in alignment with my holy soul."

Journal what feelings and desires arose.

Further Practice

Return to your journal entries of the Daughter of the Dark. Contemplate and feel them; see them coming alive in your life. Anytime you feel your navel relationship is out of balance, return to the Daughter of the Dark chapter and take up the relevant practices and prayers.

When ready, move on to Our Mother of Light.

4

Our Mother of Light

> I am she who cries out, and I am cast upon the face
> of the earth…I am the one whose image is multiple.
> *Anne McGuire, Thunder, Perfect Mind*

The mother has many forms and faces, which she shows us through all traditions. An expanded view of the mother as she appears to us and is experienced by us, and not as she has been presented to us by the Western tradition, is long overdue. Her light has been dimmed and her darkness covered over. In this chapter we focus on the light. May she be allowed to shine in her brightness, revealing herself in our own consciousness. May we let her shine through us, as us.

The Woman of Light

*Now a great sign appeared in heaven: a woman
robed with the sun, standing on the moon, and on
her head a crown of twelve stars. She was pregnant
and in labor, crying aloud in the pangs of childbirth.*
Revelation 12:1–2

The woman spoken of in the above passage from the book of Revelation is known in Christian mystical teachings as the Woman of Light. Her appearance is understood as a great sign. It is a sign of faith in the birthing of a new humanity, a sign of great hope that such an evolutionary birth does not cease, and a sign of great love that all of creation has been brought into existence for this very birthing to occur.

This Woman of Light stands upon the moon, the feminine nature being her very foundation, support, and strength. The moon's rays radiate from her feet, shining upward, forming her outer robe, so to speak. And the sun, representing the masculine nature in its pure form, is her inner robe, shining forth in all of its glory. Joined together, the moonlight and the sunlight give birth to an even greater light. In the Tree of Life, the daughter is associated with the moon, feet, and throat, and the son is associated with the sun and the torso of the body. In joining with the son/sun, the daughter becomes the mother, and the birthing of another energy, another consciousness, occurs.

In the continuation of the above quotation from Revelation, it speaks of a male child being birthed and a great beast/demon waiting to devour the child and to steal its light—that is, it wants to devour the light that the child brings and use it for its own means and power. The Woman of Light, however, is given a pair of eagle wings and escapes all attempts at the subjugation of herself and her child. The light lives on to liberate humanity, hence the faith, hope, and love being enacted. We can understand this as occurring in both an individual and worldly context, with the great beast representing our own inner demon that wants our own way and willfulness to be enforced or the collective conscious acting out all repressions and fears through violent means. In certain Gnostic traditions it is spoken that at this time in our world-evolution it is a female child or the feminine energy that is birthing, and thus we are witnessing many of the atrocities against the feminine nature coming into the full light. The demon of darkness and repression rages, and yet the Woman of Light is there to help us anytime we seek to call upon her and take refuge and sanctuary under her eagle wings.

When the feminine has come into the fullness of her being, we will then witness a true uniting of the child being birthed into humanity. This child will be the authentic human being, the one who knows neither division between male and female nor division between human and divine. This is the fully human one that Magdalene speaks about in *The Gospel of Mary Magdalene*. This is the one who is available to us all once we have loved and integrated our feminine and masculine energies, and our human nature, back into unification with our divinity.

This Woman of Light also wears upon her head a garland of twelve stars. This has different connotations, relating to the twelve tribes of Israel and the twelve disciples, both understood to have brought new energies to our earth from other star systems and consequently bringing forth different levels of consciousness, or the spiritual evolution of humanity. These twelve stars also relate to the twelve astrological signs and gateways that we are born through as we make our way onto this earth, each of us bringing forward a predominant energy as our entry dictates. During our different lifetimes we will enter through each of these twelve gateways or zodiac signs, with the aim of purifying the attributes of these signs and, consequently, our own nature, thus furthering the evolution of humanity.

Essentially, the Woman of Light is one who is crowned in the full glory, the one who is shining with a light that is greater than the moon and the sun. She is the one birthing us into a greater reality and existence. In *The Secret Gospel of St. Mary Magdalene*, it is written:

> Mary said, "If you know the Woman of Light, you will know your
> Mother and be reborn of the Mother Spirit as a child of Light.
> Because the Light is bornless, you will have eternal life."

Our light being or light body is our heavenly nature or soul, that place of soul which remains with us throughout our life and death journey. It is not born and it does not die. It is the one that remembers and travels through all dimensions of time and space as we encounter the Beloved in our dreams, prayers, and meditations. We would do well to come to know this one that lives within and around us, so that when we let go of this husk, in the form of our body and personality, we will not be at a loss but will feel comfortably familiar with the light body we will be left with.

This is what the Woman of Light desires for us—to become more and more aware of our multidimensionality and our different soul aspects, aware that we too can be clothed with the radiance of the sun and stand upon the brilliance of the moon. This awareness comes through experience, which is born through our desire to know our light body and our consistency with our prayer and meditation. As every mother knows, birthing can be both an ordeal and an overwhelmingly blissful experience. So it is with our spiritual birthing.

Sometimes we need to restrict ourselves, or who we are not, to become who we are—something akin to traveling down the narrow birth canal. It can be painful and constricting, and we can wrestle and kick, but if we can stay the course, the opening will appear and the birth will happen. As with any birth, it is then necessary for the proper care to be taken straightaway so that the new energy may have time to strengthen and find its place and not be usurped by the old energy wanting to have its life back or the demon waiting to devour the newly awakened light. When we take up our prayers and spiritual heart songs or chanting of divine names, and also have a commitment to our path and meditation, then we can be assured that the Woman of Light will be there as our sanctuary and protector of new life, giving us eagles' wings to make our flight home.

Prayer to the Woman of Light

Woman of Light

We pray to you in all of your splendor and
    your brightness of soul

May we come to our birthing
    with grace, with openness, with desire

Letting complacency fall aside

And with old energies willing to die

Let our heavenly soul be known
    within and all around us

For this is our saving grace

Our soul known in you

Our soul born in you

Praise to you, Mother

Our Woman of Light

Teach me how to fly with

Your eagle wings.

Chant

Ha Isha Ha Elyona Amma Israel (ha eesha ha el-ee-oh-na ah-ma
    is-ray-el)

Woman of Light, mother of all humanity (Israel is understood
    here to mean the family or community of the Creator—
    that is, not a country but all of the human family)

Meditation

If this can be done under the starry night sky, then do so. If not, imagine yourself sitting out in that great cosmic womb. Relax and breathe here for some time. Then see or sense the Woman of Light arising upon the moon, shining with the radiance of the sun and wearing a crown of stars. See her pregnant and smiling her blessing upon you. Allow yourself to be lifted into her arms, into her womb, and feel the light filling you. Take in this light and let it gift you what it will, whether it be healing, peace, or whatever your soul needs in that moment.

Then let yourself be birthed from the womb of this mother, bringing back with you all that was given. Give thanks and watch over your renewed being, praying that it grows and strengthens daily.

Further Meditation

Contemplate your zodiac sign and its different attributes. Bring forward an attribute that you wish to magnify and another that you wish to purify. Pray to the Woman of Light for her purification and magnification of these qualities, and pray that the very gateway of this zodiac sign be both purified and magnified in ways that will help humanity evolve. As you go about in the world, see how these qualities and your zodiac gateway may serve instead of bind you.

Journal all that was revealed.

Mother of God

O greening branch, you stand in your nobility
like the rising dawn. Rejoice now and exult...
and hold out your hand to raise us up.
Hildegard of Bingen

The divine mother is at once in this physical world and beyond in the transcendent realms. We witness this with earthly mothers, especially during a pregnancy, where they have an otherworldly glow to them. It is like they are accessing a direct connection to the divine mother and the feelings and nature of this great love. Their thoughts are consequently elevated, and even though they are experiencing a full-body physical experience and being very much in this world, there becomes now an otherworldly knowing and wisdom as well. Welcome to the Mother of God.

Principally, this title, if we can call it that, has been associated with Mother Mary, who we shall call Mother Miriam, as per her name in Hebrew. It is important we acknowledge that she was a very spiritually accomplished and advanced soul, and not a neophyte in spiritual matters, as she is often portrayed. This is obvious when we read that archangels were able to visit and communicate with her, and she was readily able to enter into conversation with them and not become overwhelmed by their energy or light. Furthermore, both her soul and body became a sacred chamber, witnessing and allowing a great and holy soul to grow within her and be nourished by her. Mother Miriam's ability to bow down in true humility before the One allowed her to see her own light within and thus to be able to recognize it in others, whether it be the archangels; her husband, Joseph; or her son, Jesus/ Yeshua. Unfortunately, her true humility has often been turned into a false humility, where the bowing down was not accompanied by a raising up or a standing tall in the knowledge and sight she gained therein.

As mother, she was given great gifts of understanding and wisdom, which she shared and put into action with her son. We see this particularly with opening the way for Yeshua to begin his mission in John 2: 1–11, where she tells him there is no wine at the wedding, indicating that is was time for him to show who he was to the world. Yeshua actually then challenges her wisdom and literally says, "It is not time, woman, what does your concern have to do with me? My hour has not yet come." Mother Miriam stood tall in her wisdom, however, and overriding her son's wisdom, she told the servants to do what he told them to. And so Yeshua's mission began.

When the word *woman* is used in our contemporary culture, it is usually delivered in a derogatory way. When it is used in the scriptures, however, the meaning is the exact opposite: it is an acknowledgement of the wisdom and knowledge of the feminine soul and energy, though, of course, there were many in that ancient cultural milieu who could not as yet believe or admit such a thing. And we see Yeshua questioning his mother's authority, even while honoring it at the same time. Perhaps he was apprehensive about bringing his mission out into the world, which would be completely understandable. It must not be easy being a bearer of light of such magnitude.

We can understand the gifts of Mother Miriam in this way. She had the knowledge of what needed to be done, with Yeshua publicly initiating his spiritual power; she had the understanding of how it needed to be done, through alchemically turning the natural substance of water into a superior wine, imbuing it with a spiritual quality that would open and increase the consciousness of the human heart; and she had the wisdom of knowing when to do it. Mother Miriam had an obvious and very deep connection to the Holy One in being able to access such wisdom, for what she set into motion at this time was a great and momentous spiritual movement.

Her ability to access such spiritual knowledge is what true humility is about—simply being open to the Holy One's guidance and wisdom.

She also had an equally obvious ability to stand tall in the knowledge and understanding she had been given, with a definite inner strength and self-confidence in being able to deliver it and override her very spiritually adept son. Here was a woman who truly was a woman— that is, one fully embodying her feminine soul power and not afraid to use and be it. This is a far cry from the meek and mild Mother Mary with lowered eyes, which is how she has been portrayed over the centuries. May we all rise into becoming this same mother of inner strength, both in the world and also gazing into and accessing the wisdom of the worlds beyond.

Prayer: Re-Created Version of the Hail Mary
Hail, Miriam
Full of grace
Adonai is with you
Blessed are you among women
And blessed is the fruit of your womb
Yeshua Mashiach
Holy Miriam, *Imma Gadol**
Pray for us now
And at the hour of our death
Amen.

* Imma Gadol (ee-ma ga-dole) = Great Mother

Chant
Amma Ah Imma (ah-ma ah ee-ma)
Mother of Unity (*Amma* is the Aramaic spelling of "mother"; *Imma* is the Hebrew spelling of "mother" and indicates feminine unity)

Meditation
Coming into your mother-ground, have the intention of connecting with Mother Miriam. Feel a beautiful spiritual sun rising in and behind your heart, and invite the mother's presence. Let her appear to you as

she wills or you may simply feel or be aware of her presence. Let there be an exchange between her sacred heart and your heart, breathing in her loving energy. Ask for her blessings, and open to receive her wisdom, understanding, and knowledge. When complete, let the mother merge into you, and feel your own mother energy becoming activated and grounded in your being. Give thanks, and let the mother's wisdom guide you.

Journal your wisdom, understanding, and knowledge.

Sophia Stellarum: Wisdom of the Stars

Rejoice, lightning that lights up our souls!
Rejoice, star that causes the sun to appear!
Rejoice, radiant blaze of grace!

Hymn to the Virgin

Many of Mother Mary's images, surroundings, and meditations incorporate stars. We have already seen her as the Woman of Light with the crown of stars; Our Lady of Guadalupe has stars upon her robe; vaulted ceilings in chapels have her surrounded by the starry night sky; and meditations on the mother and the cosmic womb speak to all of these images. This repeated reference to the stars tells us something of our cosmic mother and her extension beyond this earthly time and space into other dimensions.

Our origins also extend into these other dimensions. With every new galaxy born there are countless others completing their cycle, and the physical substance of their demise is recycled, if you will, becoming the substance of other world systems bursting forth into new life. In essence, these bodies that we inhabit are made up of stardust, and they too will be recycled in time into other world systems coming into creation. Our souls also come to be affiliated with specific star systems—places we may have inhabited during our many life cycles, learning ways of being and wisdom far beyond our own here on earth. All great spiritual masters are known to have inhabited other world systems, learning and integrating their wisdom, ultimately to bring it to earth to help in its liberation.

We each have a star home with a very specific energy that is ours to bring forth as a gift to this world. Often when we resonate with another in a deep way, it is because we are literally star-crossed—that is, we have crossed one another's path before, in another or this star system, and recognize a synchronistic alignment in fulfilling our soul purpose here. Whether conscious of this or not, or even if you believe it or not, what is important is to know that we all have the ability to reach into and access greater forms of wisdom than our current human condition would have us believe. We can cross over from our human self to our cosmic self and open to experiential possibilities of greater cosmic proportions. In this way we travel into the realm of the mother, or the wisdom of the stars.

With the mother as our guide, there is no need to fear what may happen or that you may get lost, which is only too common with many. Underneath this fear is, I believe, a primal memory of our birthing into this world. An experience revealed to me the very nature of this birthing. I was in another realm, and knowing the birth into this world was about to happen, I found myself tumbling and falling down through many light realms. I came into and through the astral plane, the realm closest to earth, and as I left this plane a feeling of panic set in. It was a panic induced by a very intense feeling of separation. I was now tumbling into a realm and a density of form that can only be described as being clothed in darkness—the realm we call earth. The feeling of separation and panic remained with me as I came back into my living-room chair awareness with quite a heavy soul-thump back into earthly consciousness, I might add. It was a very vivid experience, but what I was given to understand is that this feeling of separation is from where much of our earthly fear arises. Oddly, we hang onto the solidity of earth even more, seeking our security. Yet, if we trust Sophia Stellarum, our mother of the stars, we can once more venture into the realms we once knew or wish to know now, approaching it as a great adventure rather than something to be feared.

There is also another aspect to this. If we reach beneath our fear and can openly admit that yes, there will come a day when this world system will complete its cycle, just as yes, there will come a day when I complete my cycle in this body, then we are more able to fully engage with the day at hand. We will not have some blasé attitude that life is forever. The life of the eternal soul lives forever, yes, but not this physical world and body. Let us make peace with this and keep open to our awakening in every moment, dropping our fear and resolving to gain greater access to our cosmic being. It will help us in our future soul travels, and it will open the way for others to follow. Also, it is helpful to know that this wisdom of the stars is of a gentle and merciful nature, so we need not be fearful of our expansion. Let us trust in Sophia Stellarum.

The starry night sky of the mother beckons, and the great transformation of the soul of the world and all souls contained therein cry out to be realized. May we each play our destined role and be unafraid to look and see, to listen and hear.

Prayer to Sophia Stellarum
> Mother of the starry night
> We look up into you
> Feeling you as the great cosmic womb
> Surrounding and enveloping us
> May we release all fear
> Of ancient past and future time
> Being here now in this soul, in this body
> May we remember the glories from
> > where we have come
> And be willing to the glories of
> > where we will go
> May we know the unknown as our friend
> May we know the unknown as you
> Our great cosmic mother of the stars.

Chant
> *Ha Isha Ha Elyona Amma Israel* (ha eesha ha el-ee-oh-na ah-ma
> > is-ray-el)
> Woman of light, mother of all humanity

Meditation

Come out into the physical night sky, with many stars if possible. If not, imagine your own image of a starry heaven overhead. Breathe into your body and the above chant and ask for the presence of the great cosmic mother of the stars. Feel yourself enveloped and relax into this great womb. Let any fear arise and give it to the mother. Know you are held safely in her. Open yourself to travel into this night sky, into this great womb, and see where you are taken. Breathe and know you are loved in all dimensions.

Journal your travels with Sophia Stellarum.

Mother of Humanity

God has been like a mother to me.
Clare of Assisi

Our mother in her transcendent aspect has appeared in various forms upon this earth perhaps as long as the human one has existed, her appearance changing in accordance with belief, ability of consciousness to perceive, and the needs of the time. She has been known as Our Lady of Hope, Our Lady of the Sea, the Blue Lady, Our Lady of Lourdes, and all the many names she has been given according to the geographical location of a visitation. Often, for the knowing mystic, she is simply called mother. These visitations and visions become a meeting place of the mother's transcendence and immanence, as her sacred heart is pierced again and again by the growing pains of her human children, and she appears out of her deep compassion to encourage and guide.

In Luke 2:25–35 we read of Simeon, a holy man, who clearly had a very deep relationship with the divine presence. *Ruach Ha-Khodesh*, the Holy Spirit, had conveyed to Simeon that before he died he would see the light of the spirit in the Anointed One. As Mother Miriam and Joseph were in the Jerusalem temple with the baby Yeshua, Simeon recognized Yeshua as this One, and, taking him in his arms, he spoke prophetic words about Yeshua's life. He then looked into Mother Miriam's eyes and spoke that her son would experience great resistance, and that her own soul would be pierced with a sword in order that the thoughts of many hearts might be revealed.

We have all had those moments of feeling as if our heart and soul have been pierced with a sword. Those moments can be paralyzing, and sometimes the numbing effect stays for some time while we try to understand and accept what just occurred. These moments reveal much about our lives and where we are going. Often our direction can be radically changed, and we find ourselves seemingly cast adrift.

Depending upon the circumstance, there can be much anger, confusion, fear, loss, and ultimately a deep pain and hurt in the soul and heart. Until we reach into the deep pain, we remain bound to whatever revealing moment has come our way. The larger the revealing, often the more time is needed to feel into every nuance and repercussion. These times can also prove to be the most liberating, and when we are able to reorient ourselves, we can find a freedom that we secretly desired but did not know how to find.

Our mother's sacred heart knows our pain, and in her own pain being revealed, she opens the way for our revealing and healing. I have experienced many times where deep pain rises, and in giving it to the mother she takes it and transforms it, giving back to me the gift of deep peace. There can also be other instances where the piercing of the heart can be an ecstatic experience, much like the one that Teresa of Avila and other mystics have experienced, where we are taken out of time and place and are filled with an experience of a painfully sweet, ecstatic, divine love. The revealing in this case is an awareness of our unity with a greater divine love so overwhelmingly loving in its nature that it hurts our small heart. This can also be a numbing experience from the human functioning point of view, as we are taken completely out of ourselves and directly into a revelatory state of being. We cease to be who we normally are, walking and talking in the world, and are brought into another realm of experience. The sacred heart of the mother reveals all that is needed in the moment; she is the one who is masterful at revealing what is concealed. We can say the oneness of the Father is concealed, and it is the mother who reveals this oneness through the plurality of our lives and experiences here on earth and beyond.

With the piercing of Mother Miriam's human heart and the subsequent pain and glory of her life, she began—and continues to participate in—a great and ongoing mission for humanity. That mission was and is to constantly transform our pain and separation into the glory and unity, and to reveal the true light for and of humanity. As Evelyn Underhill, the great mystic writer, so beautifully writes:

> To be a mystic is simply to participate here and now in that real and eternal life; in the fullest, deepest sense which is possible...It is to share, as a free and conscious [being]...in the joyous travail of the Universe: its mighty onward sweep through pain and glory towards its home in God.

May we, with the mother, fully participate in this mighty onward sweep, and may our very lives be the revealing of the concealed divinity.

Prayer to Our Mother of the Sacred Heart

Mother, we thank you for opening the way
For our souls to become known
You were willing to the fullness of human life
And human transcendence both
One without the other leaves us
    in a spiritual or earthly limbo
Desiring our power
    but never knowing it
Avoiding our pain
    and yet never being free of it
May we be willing to both
And come to the fullness of our revealing
With open hearts
We place all in your sacred heart
And surrender to your love.

Chant

Amma Ah Imma (ah-ma ah ee-ma)
Mother of Unity

Meditation

If possible, do this meditation outdoors in a place that is sacred to you. Come with the intention of freeing your energy, opening your heart to receive the peace and freedom of the mother, and tasting the expanded energy of your own innate mother. Breathe into your mother-ground and simply be. If you have a particular visionary image of the mother that you relate to, then invoke this form and invite her presence; otherwise, simply be in the energy of the natural presence. Allow any deep pain, known or unknown, to arise in your heart. Give it to the mother and accept what she gives you in return.

Now open your energy to the mother's transcendent energy and breathe it into your soul. Let her fill your soul and body deeply. Feel yourself becoming that very mother energy. Pray for all beings that they may know their freedom and any other prayers that may come to mind. Close with deep gratitude and walk freely in the world as your own natural presence.

Journal your own sacred heart energy.

Mother of the Spirits

Listen to my instruction and be wise; do not
disregard it. Blessed are those who listen to
me, watching daily at my doors, waiting at my
doorway. For those who find me find life…
Proverbs 8:33–35 NKJV

Our mother's cosmic womb is where all life comes from and from where all life continues to draw its nourishment and energy. There is nothing that is outside or excluded, there is nothing too dark or too light, too fundamental or too liberal, too ignorant or too lost. All beings, all spirits, are nourished by the perpetual river of the mother's energy and love that flows through all dimensions and realms. Nobody is denied.

An earthly mother is aware of the energies that motivate her children, even if the child is saying something other or is not aware themselves of what is motivating them. Our cosmic mother goes beyond our simple psychology and watches over her children as different spiritual forces play their role in influencing and guiding souls. In reaching into our spiritual maturity, we also are asked to become aware of these forces, and, even more so, to choose those whom we wish to join and work with, as there are many different energies abounding, all with varying motives or gradations of service to the One.

Just as on this earth, there are those beings who are more concerned with their own welfare and exerting their own power, so there is the same in the other dimensions or astral planes. We may prefer to think that the other realms are only populated with divine angelic beings, but unfortunately, on certain planes, this is not true, and so we must learn discernment as we open ourselves to receive assistance from beings beyond. Just as there are tricksters on this earth who will present themselves as all goodness, yet something other is motivating them, so too it is in the spiritual realms. They are in competition with the One, if you will, trying to get our attention and energy and seeking to divert us to their throne.

The way we can draw angels of the true light to us is through our thoughts and prayers. If we uplift our minds and hearts, seeking to know these angels, invoking and inviting and keeping our hearts clear of negativity, then they will desire to be around us. We may begin to feel their presence and experience helpful thoughts and whisperings in our soul or circumstances in life being arranged with greater ease. We may find it is easier to sit longer at our prayer and meditation and find that we lovingly do so.

Just as there is an infinite array of people on this earth, so too it is with the angelic beings. Unfortunately our world has portrayed them as very fluffy, soft beings, but this is not always true. There are certainly those who do bring the energy of tenderness and comfort, but there are also those who bring the power of the One through to us in many varied ways, though of course the power is appropriately veiled so we can feel it without falling down unconscious. Any encounter we read about with the archangels in the sacred texts begins with "do not be afraid." This fear is a natural human reaction to a great surge of power and energy coming to greet us. There is a natural drawing back, if you will. However, there are also those angels who will rest lightly around us, restricting their power so as not to frighten us, all as our soul is willing and able to experience.

In seeking to know the angels of the true light, we must first restrain any negativity and then be willing to spend time cultivating a relationship with them. This can be done by consciously coming into meditation and openly inviting them and sitting in their presence. There may be no particular exchange of words, but we are looking to develop an awareness of their energy. If we can develop sensitivity toward these beings, then we can also more readily spot those beings of the false light that may masquerade before us, seeking to gain our worship. This usually comes in the way of our inner feeling. The angels of the true light will draw us closer to the One with the corresponding feelings of love and compassion for all beings. Angels of the false light will make us feel uneasy, as if something is not quite right. There will be no love for the One or others, and there may even be words of praise toward you, seeking to puff you up and make you feel important. Do not be alarmed, however; use this opportunity as your cosmic mother would by praying for and uplifting this spirit, asking that they may come back to the true light and to serving the One, remembering that we all come from the same cosmic womb.

I invite you to take up the prayer and invocation for Archangel Mumiah, known as the energy and angel of the womb of the mother. Mumiah is known to help and assist with all things to do with the sacred feminine and for the revelations of the mother. She also assists healers and in all areas of healing.

Prayer to Mumiah

> I welcome and invite you, Mumiah
> Womb of God
> Womb of the mother
> May you come and enfold me
> > in your wisdom
> > in your sacred feminine ways
> May I come to know my own
> Feminine wisdom
> And may all health and harmony
> Be restored to my being and all beings.
> I thank you.

Chant

> *Ma-Ya Ma-Ya Mum-iah* (moom-ee-ah)

Meditation

After taking up the above prayer and chant, open to the presence of Mumiah. Allow her to enfold you in her womblike way. If you have any health-related concerns for yourself or another, then place your question to her. If you wish to know more about the mother and feminine wisdom, then also ask this of her. Then take time to simply be in the quiet with her, and ask if there is a blessing she would like to give you. Remember, the answers and blessings may come immediately or they may be revealed through your life circumstances. Whatever the case may be, bask in Mumiah's presence, and, when you feel complete, give thanks. Come and be with her as often as you can to develop a relationship with her. It is good to have a few very intimate spiritual friends rather than many acquaintances.

Journal your experience with Mumiah.

The Way Is Born

To serve the Queen of Heaven is already
to reign there, and to live under her
commands is more than to govern.

St. John Vianney

Mother Miriam's metaphysical and physical womb created a matrix for the light of Yeshua to come into the world. Her and Joseph's spiritual knowledge was of such an advanced level that their souls were capable of consciously drawing in a soul of great magnitude such as Yeshua. They also created a home environment where the light of Yeshua would be nourished and he would grow through and in mystical wisdom teachings. They may have been simple folk in this world, but their soul capacities were of another gradation and world altogether.

In her physical incarnation and in creating this matrix of light Mother Miriam opened the way for Yeshua and his followers to bring forward a radically new consciousness and wisdom (Yeshua's disciples were known as Followers of the Way). In her ascension Mother Miriam became that matrix, ascending into and becoming the archetypal fullness of the cosmic mother. Every possible combination of energetic existence and life form lives within this mother matrix and brings forth the form of consciousness for all creation.

Mother Miriam, knowing this true, expansive nature as her own soul, entered into and became the mother of all creation. And it is through a human soul—and, in this case, Mother Miriam's soul realizing this—that allowed for the fulfillment of the transcendental/cosmic nature of mother, or Shekinah. What we do not understand in our world is that the ultimate fulfillment and ongoing expansion of the Living Presence depends upon us realizing our nature. It is not a one-sided action of humans becoming who they are and everything else beyond remaining stagnant. No—consciousness and being are always expanding in all of life, heavenly and earthly. Certainly there is that sacred, eternal place within the Living Presence and within us all that does not change, but so many other layers of being and consciousness are evolving at the same time.

When we speak of ascension, what is it that we really mean? It is usually defined as rising to a more powerful place. It can also be described as the impermanent becoming the eternal. In the case of Mother Miriam it was her impermanent body that transformed into her body of light, or her eternal light body. In an Eastern Orthodox document entitled *The Account of St. John the Theologian of the Falling Asleep of the Holy Mother of God*, dating back to the fourth century, it tells of the account of Mother Miriam's assumption, or ascension. It begins with Archangel Gabriel coming as messenger to Mother Miriam, speaking that her life on earth was complete. Being caught up in the clouds of the Spirit, some of the apostles were transported to be with her in spirit. Yeshua also appeared, telling her not to fear. Then her face shone brighter than the light, and, rising, she blessed those around her. The account goes on to say her body, filled with this same light and pouring forth the sweetest fragrance, was then taken to a sepulcher. For three days the voices of invisible angels were heard singing and praising the Living Presence, and all the while her body remained incorruptible until it fully ascended.

With the fullness of this ascension came the crowning of the mother as queen of heaven, the supernal Shekinah, in all of her glory. Now her earthly mission was truly complete and yet, at the same time, just beginning again as becoming mother to all. It matters not in which form we think of this ascended mother, but more that we acknowledge her magnitude and our earthly mission, understanding that this mission extends far beyond this earth and adds to the continuation of the blessing and growth of consciousness in all beings, in all worlds and universes.

This transformation of the earthly body to the eternal light body by Mother Miriam was a great blessing for us all as a means of showing the possibility for humanity, and not just a special grace or mission reserved for her and Yeshua alone. Through the centuries there have also been other beings who have demonstrated our grand and eternal light nature through the transformation of the physical being: Teresa of Avila, Clare of Assisi, and Paramahansa Yogananda are just are few examples of bodies that did not immediately decompose. What does this transformation really say to us—and, even more, what does it ask of us? It is, of course, a guiding light in our dense world of physicality, reminding us of divine possibility for the human being. It is also an invitation to make ourselves ever more available to the archangels and the light of the Living Presence, to let the light infuse us both on a soul and a physical level. It is a preparation for the transfiguration and resurrection body when that day may come for us.

We may be quick to dismiss that such a thing is possible for us or relegate it to a long-ago, legendary past, but at least we can begin where we are, open our heart, and invite our eternal light body to be present. It is much closer than we know. The queendom of the Living Presence, the queendom of the Shekinah, is near.

Prayer to the Queen of Heaven

Mother, Queen of Heaven
In all of your glory I come to you
Help me to know what is possible for me
Help me to believe in my own light
May it resurrect within my body
Within my soul and mind
We speak of wholeness, Mother
And yet we believe it only goes so far
We stop ourselves
    and why?
    Why is it that we don't believe?
What is it that stops us from knowing
    our true light?
Come, Mother, in all of your divine array

And wash me clean of doubt
Free my heart from disbelief
Free me from myself
May I know my light as you know yours.

Chant

Ha Isha Ha Elyona Amma Israel (ha eesha ha el-ee-oh-na ah-ma
is-ray-el)
Woman of light, mother of all humanity

Meditation

Coming into your mother-ground, invite the Queen of Heaven to
be present. Invite your body of light to be present. See or sense this
mother extending light from her heart to yours. See her extending
light from her mind to yours. See her extending light from her body
to yours. Take in this light as long as you are able; then, giving thanks,
allow her to merge with you. Let yourself ground this energy in the
fullness of your body and being, and walk gently back into the world.

Journal all that you feel.

Author's Note: Mesopotamian legends have repeated references to a
supreme deity/goddess as "Queen of Heaven," and Sumerian prayers
address "the Mighty Lady, the Creatress," and "the Mother who gave
birth to heaven and earth."

The Blue Flame

I am calling to you, all people;
my words are addressed to all humanity.
Proverbs 8:4 NKJV

The color blue has long been associated with Mother Miriam, with her personified image showing a blue mantle with a white inner robe. When this image comes to mind, it can also draw forth from our souls the notion of a misperceived perfection, as Mother Miriam has been wrongly revered as the silent perfection of false humility that all women should be. This erroneous understanding of perfection and humility has been the source of bondage for many.

The mother does represent silence, but not in the way it has been taught to us. Rather, this silence is an inner silence, a receptive spaciousness to our greater soul and the greater Spirit. The color blue in the psychology of color has been described as concentric, or looking inward. In Luke 2:19 we read that she treasured all things spoken to her by the Spirit and pondered them in her heart, very much indicating an inner looking and listening, along with her receptivity to conversing with archangels. The color of psychology also describes blue as heteronomous, allowing others to perform an action and taking a more passive role. Here we come to understand the true meaning of passive as not allowing someone to step all over you but allowing those who are here to act to take their rightful place, hence Mother Miriam's ability to allow Yeshua to rise into his fullness while she fully supported him from the womb all the way to the tomb. This is true humility, knowing your place of strength and allowing another to come into theirs.

In the Tree of Life the color blue relates to the branch of loving-kindness and mercy, and the color white relates to the head of the tree, which speaks of the eternal, the infinite, the primordial light. When we consider that Mother Miriam's inner robe is always white, it tells us something about her absolute, purified, and transparent nature and being. The blue outer robe of loving-kindness and mercy reflects this eternal light and nature in loving action.

Historically, the color pigment of blue was rare and therefore used only by royalty or the very wealthy. It was also the last color to be named; before its naming, it was simply referred to as the color of the sky or the color of the sea. From this, some religious historians have deduced that the color blue was only fitting for one who came to be known as the Queen of Heaven, honoring her spiritual royalty and also her status as mother of this earth realm through the colors of the sky and sea.

This blue-and-white image of the mother represents our own inner transparent, eternal nature and our own loving-kindness. The blue-and-white flame is also a purifying energy that is readily available to us. Purification is different from fixing something that is perceived as wrong or deficient. It is a type of alchemy that transforms the gross into the subtle and draws out the very nature and essence of our being into its most radiant form. Who does not wish to be their most radiant? Do we ever contemplate our radiance and what this may be? It is strange how we hang on so direly to what keeps us small, perhaps because we do not understand the ease with which it may be transformed.

Our Mother of the Blue Flame, however, can bring forward a blissful, transformational encounter, easily transmuting the old metal into a new form. We need only be willing. And we can come joyfully or fearfully or in peace; whatever is present can always be transmuted to deeper levels in her presence. This transformational prayer is not something to undertake only when we are troubled. Do you notice how much more intent and focused we are in our prayer when we are struggling with something? When things are flowing and joyful we tend to back off our prayer time and the intense focus, and yet, if we also come at these joyful times, it gives opportunity for that joy to be purified and elevated to even more sublime gradations. It can then be shared with others as well, by praying for them in this state. The prayer of joy and ecstasy is a great gift to our soul and all souls; don't miss it because you are off playing in the world. Pray first, then play!

The following is my rendition of the Magnificat (Luke 1:46–55), the prophetic words Mother Miriam spoke to the crone Elizabeth, the mother of St. John the Baptist, as they shared the glories of their blessed pregnancies:

> My soul magnifies the goodness of the human soul and the
>   goodness of all creation.
> My spirit rejoices in my true image as being a daughter of the
>   mother.
> May true humility rest upon me; may I know that I cannot
>   know everything, nor am I expected to.
> I am a blessing of the mother here on earth. I am a blessing to
>   the people and the land.
> The mother of creation has done wondrous things for me and
>   the raising of my soul.
> The mother's love is faithful to me.
> May all arrogance lay down on the bed of self-worth and love.
> May I believe in the promise of the world to come, and may I
>   know that as a sacred daughter I am helping to create that
>   world and all worlds into eternity.

One can only surmise the level of purification these two women encountered during their many lifetimes to ready their bodies and souls for the mission that lay ahead of them. Blessed indeed! Are you ready for your soul mission? It seems to me that we have a number of mini-missions, if you will, with many steps that take us from one mission to the next, each building upon the other, each purifying and readying us for a greater level and gradation of being. In time these mini-missions coalesce and draw us into the place we were born for. Along the way may we know joy in our purification, and may our soul magnify the Beloved in all we do.

Prayer for Purification

Mother Miriam, teach us what it means to purify in love
To know the joy of the Spirit as we willingly transform
May we look deep within and let our Beloved grow
Magnifying her in the world through grace and the
  purity of selflessness
Not putting ourselves down
But allowing ourselves to be raised up
  by the spirit of loving-kindness
  by the spirit of love
Who loves every inch of my human self
  and all of humanity
May I know the eternal truth of this
May I know the eternity of my soul.

Chant

Ha Isha Ha Elyona Amma Israel (ha eesha ha el-ee-oh-na ah-ma
  is-ray-el)
Woman of Light, mother of all humanity

Meditation

Breathing into your mother-ground and feeling a peacefulness
of soul, draw yourself into your heart and breathe, feeling a natural
expansion of your heart with every breath. See or sense a blue flame
in your heart and let it gently burn. You may see the flame as being
edged with white. Invite the presence of the mother to be with you,
and simply be with the flame and your breath. Specific things may be
revealed; just let them be transformed in the flame, whatever they may
be, or nothing may come at all. Whatever your experience, simply feel
the joy of willingly releasing, of willingly transforming.

Journal your gentle purification.

The Interior Solar Plexus Star

*Often using our power is merely a matter of
understanding that we do indeed have the power
to begin with. That understanding becomes
solidified through use and experimentation,
and results ultimately in gaining confidence.*
Anodea Judith, *Wheels of Life*

As we saw, the Mother of Light is both immanent and transcendent, having one foot on earth and another in the heavens, much like Tara in the Buddhist tradition. When we come to know our divine mother we will know she is always intimately involved with her creation and creatures. There is great power in this ability to be involved in both realms, not favoring one over the other but understanding the need for an ongoing interrelationship in order for the ultimate fullness of creation to come into being. The interior solar plexus star gives us this power to engage fully in all realms, but if we enter into fear, then we shut down our natural power.

The most important quality regarding the solar plexus is the redefining of power, moving from the ego lording it over others, or having power over others, to using our power for the good of all. The question becomes, who are we serving with this power? Only when we are feeling powerless do we wish to serve ourselves because we are afraid we will not be taken care of—that we will not be noticed, that we will be left out, and all the many other inadequate feelings that can arise. And if we fall into this false serving and try to lord it over another, which means ultimately trying to control another, we become extremely angry when they do not cooperate. By using the power of choice and using our will to serve the good of all, the energy of the interior solar plexus star can begin to flow freely and unobstructed. Sometimes it manifests as a gentle strength; at other times it can be a powerful force, or perhaps you may experience it as a steady, vital flow, energizing and inspiring. Whatever form it takes, this energy provides a vitality of life, freeing you from any inertia or feelings of depression.

Our bodies are a good place to start if we are feeling any kind of lack of energy or inability to be inspired. Start stretching, let out any sounds or groans, jump up and down, open your arms and chest wide. Do some aerobic exercise. The solar plexus sits just below the sternum, so in opening this area we begin to shift the energy and invite a physical flow. Similarly, if we are experiencing any digestive problems or feeling pain in the area of the solar plexus, this can be an indication that we are still carrying fear of our power or feeling our power center being attacked somehow. By engaging our choice and will and asking for appropriate healing, the emotional and spiritual roots of this will be revealed and ultimately dissolved.

The reality is, many people on earth simply do not want to be here, especially those of the spiritual persuasion. A few years ago I had a medical situation that revealed a rare form of aneurysm. In the first few days leading up to the aneurysm diagnosis it was initially thought I had a mass on the pancreas. I thought that my time had come to leave this earth, and I was very surprised to find what a huge relief this was for me, thinking, *I am to get out of here finally! Interesting.* Of course this was followed by other emotions, but it showed an underlying desire not to be here. With such energy at play it is impossible to truly embody or be here at all, and the power quickly drains, with the solar plexus closing down. When this happens we can wander through life not really inhabiting our lives at all, which has numerous repercussions, such as feeling anger, powerlessness, and an inability to connect with others on deeper soul levels. We then search for all the ways we can blame others for our predicament, falling into victimhood and even further into lack of our own personal power and confidence. On top of this, shame can also appear and drive us even deeper into that dark, loveless pit.

This is where our will can become our greatest friend and ally (instead of taking up its somewhat regular opposite position). We can use the fiery energy of the solar plexus to put an end to these fruitless cycles by drawing in the power of our true will from the upper crown star into our solar plexus (as described in the following meditation). We can then ask that we have the willpower to begin engaging in ways that are conducive for this true will to come into being. This will help build and allow us to embody our inner power, giving us the confidence that we have the capacity to do so and having the courage to come out of hiding and actualize this in the world. As Anodea Judith states in the above quote, first we need to know that we have the internal power, and then we need to experiment and put it into action. In this way we will build our confidence and come to know our capabilities. By experimenting we will also come to know where our gifts do not lie and confidently move away from them, not in shame or with self-criticism but simply with an understanding of where we are not meant to be. This also opens up the way for connection and admiration of others' power, for they will excel in those areas we do not. The mother of many faces reveals herself through us all.

"The quality of strength lined with tenderness is an unbeatable combination"—these words from Maya Angelou speak resoundingly of Mother Miriam and all she undertook upon this earth. Mother Miriam showed us the true strength and power of humility, of not only allowing, but also aiding another to excel. She demonstrated the power of choice as she chose again and again to serve the good of all, and she came into the fullness of her power as the Queen of Heaven, still serving each one of us today, ever ready to assist us in knowing the fullness of our own power. Hail Miriam, full of grace! May we learn from you. May we remember to ask you for your help.

Meditation

Focusing on your interior star of the solar plexus, envision or feel a radiant golden sun-star. Breathe into this a number of times, and then open to the energy of the crown star located at the top of your head, letting the energy of true will gently come into your solar plexus star. Let the brilliance shine out, reaching from the sternum down to the navel and upper abdomen. In this moment choose to use this power for the good of all and offer your life and vitality, your gifts and light, for both you and others to excel. It is important that you include both yourself and others; there is room for everyone at the inn. Happy birthing into your power.

Journal your power experience.

Further Practice

Return to your journal entries of the Our Mother of Light chapter and absorb them, bringing all into your body. Pray for any further soul clarifications. Anytime you feel your interior star of the solar plexus is out of balance, return to the Our Mother of Light chapter and know your liberation is at hand.

And now, Our Mother of the Dark lovingly awaits.

5

Our Mother of the Dark

> Mary said, "Until you know the darkness of
> Sophia, you will not acquire her Light."
> *Tau Malachi, The Secret Gospel of*
> *St. Mary Magdalene, saying 55*

The deeper our journey takes us within, the deeper and greater subtlety of shadows we encounter. These shadows have been protecting our soul until we are ready to look into them and see the radiance and light they are watching over. Our Mother of the Dark, or *Sophia Nigrans,* which can be translated as Dark Wisdom or Black Mother, is a great force within us, and she is a great liberator of being.

Meeting Na'amah

And as to Na'amah...she is alive to this day, and
her dwelling is among the waves of the Great Sea.
Raphael Patai, *The Hebrew Goddess*

We return to our story of Lilith. After witnessing Eve and Adam getting together, Lilith flew back to her self-imposed wilderness where her anger churned into rage. Her rage begat deep rage, and this grew prolifically. The Creator of All was deeply disturbed at this fully empowered being reducing herself to such a fierce and painful place of existence. Three angels were sent to appease her, asking that she stop this raging, but she would have nothing of it. She then drew within herself and emanated another being: the Queen of the Night; in Hebrew she is called Na'amah. This queen has the power to birth or subdue the darker forces at will. These forces, of course, are all those negative energies that keep us from our own inner power and natural realization of being.

The Queen of the Night, Na'amah, had a very specific job to do for creation: to enter into the darkness or ignorance of creation and help liberate beings from their own bondage and ignorance. On the way to her destiny she had to experience all the negativity in order to set it free, even right down to denying the pleas of the Creator for her return. She has done us a great service in opening the doorway of cosmic ignorance to reveal the truth that lies within, and she can help us return, even when we think we can't or simply don't want to. It is interesting to note that the name *Na'amah* has come to be associated with the meanings "pleasing to God" and "beautiful and intelligent woman," as formerly she was known as the "charmer" or "seductress." Na'amah's service to humanity—of cosmically lighting up its deep ignorance—is also joined by her raising the beauty and intelligence of the feminine to become embodied. Her dwelling place, the Great Sea, is the Shekinah; that is, Na'amah is an active principle of the divine feminine presence.

But let us first look into what she was born of—that is, the rage of Lilith—and how it applies to us.

Feminine rage, if not uncovered, can be a deadly friend to live with, and it often makes its presence known in the most terrible and harmful of ways. The overt expression of this is, of course, easily spotted, and we all need to take responsibility for how it takes form in our world. The more subtle form, though, can take the shape of punishment, either projected onto others or onto our own self. And it can be so integral to our way of being that we do not even realize we are engaging in such painful behavior.

You have done nothing wrong. We cannot hear these words enough. There seems to be a constant source of reasons for self-criticism and thinking we have done something wrong. This is an age-old feminine malady going right back to Eve, continuing through the alleged witch time, and following us still today, even if only in our hearts, frozen in another time. There is a natural progression that occurs from this thinking that we have done something wrong; we enter into self-blame and self-punishment, not allowing ourselves to feel love or the joy of life, not allowing ourselves to know freedom of self or to succeed or feel the joy of success. We keep ourselves bound and small, and ultimately we lie down in lack of self-worth and self-hatred, or at least self-dislike. What an insidious and fast train those dark forces and energies—and we—ride, keeping us in a place of absolute lies. It is time for Na'amah to peer into and pierce through these long-held illusions.

There is no such thing as punishment existing in the Creator. Yet, if we find ourselves punishing either others or ourselves, then on some level we do believe that punishment exists beyond us. We are archetypal creatures and we do what we believe is true, even if, and especially when, these beliefs are so deeply unconscious. These beliefs, of course, often stem from layers of our soul still carrying past religious teachings causing illusory bondage. *Enough!* May you choose to like yourself just as you are, may you choose the best for yourself and your life, and may you know the freedom from rage and punishment, both of the past and the present.

Prayer to Queen of the Night

Na'amah, Queen of the Night

Uncover any rage that still lives within me

>That which lies secretly plotting my undoing

>That which cripples me in this life

May it return to an energy pleasing to the One

Pleasing to my own soul

Piercing the darkness of ignorance

Of wrong-doing and shame

May I know there is nothing to be punished

May I know there is no punishment at all

May the Queen of Night within me

Reign in her true beauty and intelligence

Amen.

Chant

Nay-ah Nay-ah-ma, Kali Imma (ka-lee ee-ma)

Na'amah means the fertility of the mystical feminine death,

>being reborn into unity; Kali Imma is Dark Mother

Meditation

Breathing deeply into your mother-ground, invite the Dark Mother in the form of Na'amah, Queen of the Night, into your space, into your being. You may envision her as a beautiful feminine figure shining with a dark radiance and full of strength, power, and knowledge. Allow her dark radiance and beauty to shine upon and within you, blessing you and drawing forth what needs to come forward. Let all wrong-doing, shame, rage, and self-punishment be transformed in this radiant beauty. Let the ignorance return to wisdom for you and all beings. Give thanks, and pray that womanhood may return to its sacred power.

Journal your transformation.

Sexual Rage

My heart burnt within me
with indignation and grief.
Elizabeth Gaskell

There is nowhere more potent in our lives where rage comes roaring through than our sexual rage—that is, when it is allowed to do so. Our greatest feminine power lies in our sexual nature, which is well known by the negative forces and energies that seek to disempower the feminine energy in young girls, boys, adolescents, women, and men. There are many who walk the long road back to trust due to this very disempowerment.

Whether or not we have personally encountered the very physicality of this terrible abuse, the associated feelings and need for protection can be understood and shared in one form or another. There has been a violation of one's most intimate and sacred space; there has been betrayal, often by loved ones; there is shame and ultimately outrage. My own journey through this has been long and painful as I released and continue to release the trauma from my heart and body. Ultimately it is a journey of liberation as I compassionately watch over this trauma body as if she is a younger sister in need. The layers of self-imposed protection slowly dissolve, new choices are made, and safety and trust return. Do we all not experience these things to varying degrees in our journey?

A great liberator in this process has been recognizing that I journey with this not only for myself, but for all those who have been violated. It is the deepest healing, and therefore the deepest power, that arises for humanity. Sometimes this rage begins as an irrational anger or as an overreaction to something happening in our lives. It is as if we are swept up in a raging storm that has been brewing within us for years, and that is because it probably has. If we take the time to be with it and ask what is the real root, then it will surface and find its voice and liberation in a beneficial way that does not linger in blame. Through prayer we can ask for the necessary healing, and with faith we can know it will be given to us.

Another way I enter into this healing is through joining my heart with others. The atrocities we hear about daily—through news of our sisters and brothers being abducted and sexually exploited or brutally raped in the light of day—quite frankly breaks my heart wide open. Their pain is my pain, and this is where I can be of true service: through prayer. When we widen our prayer to include others who are also in places of pain and dire need, our own pain seems to naturally dissolve and heal of its own accord. In this way, their liberation becomes our liberation, and ours becomes theirs. Most important, however, is that we begin with ourselves and then open to others. We must not leave ourselves out—this includes the pain and the joy! Have faith in yourself, as the mother has faith in you, and remember you are co-creating with her, so it is not just up to you. Ask for assistance in the moment, and all will be revealed.

Na'amah understands well the sexual rage; was she not born of Lilith's rage over her own sexual power being diminished? I am sure we have all experienced sexual repression to some degree in our lives or our lifetimes, and even if it is not relevant now for us, let us remember those who are still imprisoned either internally or externally. May we all be free to know the truth of our sexual energy and its power and sacred expression.

Prayer for the Healing of Our Sexual Nature

Na'amah, I call upon you
Please help free me from the fear
    and shame of my sexual nature and power
Let the truth of your radiance
Shine deeply into the night of my soul
Awaken me from this night-mare that I have been riding
Let betrayal be free
Let violation be free

Let pure protection reign
Not binding or keeping out
But gently watching over this soul
    and all souls
I thank you, Na'amah.

Chant

Kali Imma (ka-lee ee-ma), *Ah-Yah-ma Ah-yah-ma Ah-yah-ma*
Brings the powerful healing presence of the Dark Mother

Meditation

Breathing deeply into your mother-ground, settle into your being of peace. Invite Na'amah to soften sexual edges, to cut through fear and falsity. Breathe in her dark radiance and allow it to transform all into the light. Extend this radiance to all beings, especially those bound by the sexual forces of domination and violence. Let the sexual being heal both us and the soul of the world.

You may also want to place your focus on someone you know who may be suffering in this way or perhaps a person or place that has caught your attention in the news. We have many sisters and brothers in literal physical bondage; may our prayers be given freely for their liberation. Wherever your heart is breaking open for another or for a particular situation, there is the power of your prayer waiting to be prayed.

Journal your prayers.

Self-Sovereignty and True Will

*And you have driven far from me the emanations
of Self-Willed that beleaguered me.*
J. J. Hurtak (translator), Pistis Sophia

Na'amah teaches us to how to know our true will and subsequently our sovereignty of self or inner authority, which ultimately means we know and can confidently say *yes, this is what I bring for the world and its healing and evolution*. Sometimes this can be a whole life-journey just coming into this knowledge, especially as we navigate our way in and through our self-will. And of course we are also healing and evolving all of the time and therefore must allow for our being to be constantly refined and for the truth to come into new forms. Enter Na'amah.

We saw how Lilith refused the request of the angels and the Creator of All asking her to stop the birthing of her rage. This self-willed refusal spiraled her into even greater isolation and pain, through which Na'amah was born. Somehow it was necessary for the energy of self-will to be exposed and liberated through this Queen of the Night. Na'amah withdrew into the deepest night in order that the light could envelop self-will and draw it back into union with true will.

We all know the danger of handing our will over to another, whether it is to someone outside of us or to our personality/self. We also know the futility of seeking our authority from another or from the personality. This business of will and self-sovereignty or inner authority resides within, and it is a very intimate conversation between the soul and the mother. I would rather make a mistake that comes directly from my own self than do something supposedly correct at the bidding of another person. With the former I will learn and grow and know self-sovereignty. With the latter I will always remain in need or even addicted to another person's affirmation of my being.

Now, of course, discernment is most important when it comes to our will. Whose will is at work, and on whose authority am I acting? There has been much written and taught about claiming our inner voice and inner authority. In my own experience, when I am claiming my voice, claiming my authority and place in the world, it is my personality trying to bolster itself in accordance with worldly expectations, even if clothed in a spiritual garment or container. Our true inner authority comes quietly into place, with no outer statements or show; it simply becomes an action of being, which we have come to know and embody in our lives. Authority is given when we are already living it, not the other way around of claiming and then living.

I have seen this all too often with myself and other women. There is an intuitive sense that we have this wisdom and an inner knowing, yet because of our lack of self-worth and trust in self, we have yet to fully embody and start living it with confidence. We try to proclaim and speak our wisdom but, as yet, our lives are not in accord. The inner strength has not been developed to back up the intuition, and therefore much frustration ensues as we scratch at our depths but remain on the surface. The way we proclaim our authority is not by shouting it off the rooftops but merely allowing the vibrant spirit within to come alive in accordance with who we are and what we are here to give. Too often we are seeking authority for something other than what we are here to do, and when it doesn't go so well, we end up even more frustrated and with even greater feelings of unworthiness.

To come into the true dwelling of authority we need to look at our will and see the major role it plays. Our will does not reside anywhere on the outside. It is in the deepest chamber of our being, and, in turn, it is connected to our true desire. As we move through life we move in and out of desires—some true, some false, and, correspondingly, some connected with our true will and some with our personality-will. How do we know which one is which and when? *By the fruits you shall know them.* As we reach into the truth of our desires and trust them, so shall our true will work in accord with them. Inner knowing and peace confirm our intuitions, and with more and more experiences of such inner trust and confirmation, our inner authority gains a natural confidence that simply is. Teresa of Avila came to be especially masterful at discernment and the inner workings of the soul, and she wrestled greatly with her own self-will and that of others, but ultimately, after many years of inner vigilance, she became victorious.

Certainly, Na'amah must have been watching over and prodding the many renegade mystics over the centuries who have followed their inner authority, leaving behind all outer authority and reaching into the deep and mysterious inner worlds, then drawing them back into the outer world. All traditions experience a dying of the old and a rebirth into totally new ways. This is essential for the ongoing development of the soul and our cosmos. When things stay the same for too long, they are simply no longer valid and must be rebirthed for the current generation. If they do not move, then they become bound in dogma, even if they were the liberal ones to start with! And so the role of the mystic and the self-sovereign one are synonymous. It is today that such ones are needed more than ever, as not only are our religious paradigms collapsing but also our spiritual ones. We are in a grand spiritual evolution, or perhaps revolution.

It is good to know when to listen to someone you trust on the outside, and equally good to know that no matter what is said, it is ultimately your own inner authority that you must follow. And even if you make a mistake, it doesn't matter; forgive yourself, learn, and move on. Seek Na'amah's assistance whichever way it plays out. She will help cut through, wherever and however the energy needs to move and transform. May we all know our true will, self-sovereignty, and inner authority, and bring this as a gift to the world.

Prayer for True Will

Na'amah, I seek your assistance here and now
The truth of my desire cries out
Help me to hear and listen to her
Show me where true will lives
Where does she sleep at night?

Is she hungry?

Does she want to come and play in the light?

I am waiting here for her and for my desire

I have a feeling they are waiting for me

I have a feeling they have been waiting a very long time

Tell them I am coming, Na'amah

Tell them I am coming

Tell them I am here

I am here.

Chant

Nay-ah Nay-ah Nay-ah-ma

The fertile and mystical feminine death being reborn into
the unified will

Meditation

Come with the intention of knowing your true will. Invoke the presence of Na'amah and envision her as a strong, black, beautiful woman, with an inner white brilliance streaming from her heart and mind. Align yourself with her breath and begin to breathe with her. Align yourself with her heart and mind. Let all false desires and self-will fall away. Let her inner white brilliance ignite your own, and let your true will shine forth. It may not have any shape or form but simply be a feeling. Sit with this and do not force it into anything; this is how self-will works. When you feel complete, give thanks, and breathe into and ground your strength of being.

Journal your impressions.

Repeat this meditation in the next few days, and when you feel there is openness and a receding of self-will, you may ask what you are here to give. Allow the answer to reveal itself in its own way and time. It may come immediately; it may reveal itself through synchronistic events in life. It is important to not force anything but trust in the timing of the revealing.

Real and False Pride

Let me no longer be lacking, O Adonai, for I have had
faith in your Light from the beginning. O Adonai,
Light of Powers, let me no longer lack my Light.
J. J. Hurtak (translator), Pistis Sophia

Of course, Lilith's refusal to listen to the Creator of All and the emissary angels also has the energy of an outer pride and arrogance, which Na'amah was literally birthed into. As we know, there is never just one side of a story. Here is the other side.

What would have happened if Lilith had listened to the angels and stopped her raging? Na'amah would not have been born, self-will would not have been liberated from its own ignorance, and where would that leave us? Or perhaps Na'amah would have been birthed into her rightful glory and the power of feminine beauty and intelligence. Here is where our free will and the uncertain nature of how our human destiny is to be played out is such a mystery. True will is free will; equally, self-will is free will. And so the mother follows us at every decision and on every path we walk, waiting in pure loving patience for us to decide how we are to live and who we are to be, and then she responds according to our choices. There is spiritual maturity when we can consciously step into this realization and be prepared for the consequences, whatever they may be.

Who really knows what the outcome would have been if Lilith had listened and acted on the angels' pleas. Maybe she was not meant to listen to them and something deep within was driving her to help the liberation of humanity from its self-will. Or maybe if she had listened, humanity would've taken a different course? The only thing we do know is now we are the ones setting the course.

Pride has two faces. It can be a spiritual pride in our sovereign selves or it can be a false pride in a self that feels lack. The latter also wears the mask of arrogance, trying to make up for any feeling of lack it detects. Let us know when we are falling into the false pride. You will feel it in your body. You will become like a strutting rooster pushing out your chest and tilting your head and chin, with all your defenses lining up to cover your heart. Interactions will be about trying to prove and claim who you are, and denying and judging the other before you. Be honest and go beneath these gestures and words that are seeking to prove a power that is not real; ask for purification and you will open the way for true spiritual pride to start growing within you.

The true pride will be as if you are quietly tending to your garden, and when someone approaches you will turn in complete openness and compassion, and you will rise to meet and greet them right where they are. Words and gestures will come effortlessly, whether tender or firm, all as needed, and your spirit will be uplifted in an empowerment that does not tower over or lord it over another but rather opens the way for truth to be known. True pride also naturally evolves when one is engaged confidently in one's place in the world, and yet confidence is not necessarily something that is felt; it is simply being engaged in a rightful way where everything feels in its place, in alignment. I have noticed the only time I am actually aware of confidence is when I am lacking it or if I begin the rooster strutting, which then very quickly turns to arrogance.

We are by nature a very arrogant society, looking down upon others who are different, truly humble, and happy with simplicity of living. We have over-valued the mind that seeks only its own so-called godly power, and we fall prey to false spirits that seek to seduce us into the illusion of a false power. We each have our own particular false god that we idolize because it serves to make us feel powerful when we have felt powerless for so long. Equally, many have fallen prey to disempowerment of soul. The journey now becomes how to resurrect into the true spiritual pride without being caught and becoming a slave to the false pride of arrogance. Sometimes it is so subtle that we need outer help in seeing it—or are we too arrogant and proud to receive such help?

Na'amah showed me both faces of this pride, and she danced over and burnt away the false one, and danced, celebrated, and lit the fire of the other. Thank you, Na'amah. And so it continues. I pray that the true spiritual pride be known by all women and the feminine energy, and by all men and the masculine energy, and that our arrogance be burned into ashes, rising as the phoenix into the true pride of Na'amah, the dark and beautiful one.

Prayer for Spiritual Pride

Na'amah, I welcome your searing white flame
In my heart of hearts
    burning away all lack and self-pride
Let me not strut and defend and claim
    the falseness of power
    that tries to take residence in my soul
But let me open to the truth
Subtle and gross
So that you may dance upon
My being and we can celebrate
The true face of pride
That lives in you, and me, and our wondrous
    wild beauty.

Chant

Na'amah (nay-ah-ma), Na'amah, Na'amah, Queen of the
    Night; Na'amah, Na'amah, Na'amah, dance in delight

Meditation

Calling upon Na'amah, ask that she may show you any areas where false pride is lurking beyond your view. Envision a clear white flame in your heart and, breathing deeply, let it burn what it chooses to burn. Feel the delight in this purification and, if inclined, physically dance your liberation, celebrating the opening for your spirit pride to be known.

Journal the truth of your pride of being.

The Feminine Intelligence

I am the gnosis of my seeking, and the
finding of those who seek after me...
and it is within me that women exist.
Anne McGuire, *Thunder, Perfect Mind*

For a very long time I have pondered and wondered what the feminine intelligence is and how it is uniquely expressed. I intuitively felt that it would take a different form to that of the masculine. Yes, the source of this intelligence is the same, but the expression of it must have a different face. As I looked around I saw two faces being expressed by women: one was an exact replica of the masculine mental intelligence, and the other was an emotionally heart-based feminine love, but one I could not comfortably associate the word intelligence with. I felt there was something other to be known, some form of intelligence that reached deeper into the soul, an intelligence in and behind the heart, if you will, that was much broader than either the masculine or feminine faces were showing.

The heart is the interior star, or chakra, that joins the lower interior stars with the upper stars. The heart is the gateway—the portal, if you like—to enter into wisdom far greater than our normal human wisdom. But this gateway/heart is not one fused with sentimentality or spiritual naiveté. It is a gateway that only the spiritually perceptive can enter. In Proverbs 8:12–14 we read, "I, Wisdom, share house with Discretion, I am mistress of the art of thought...To me belong good advice and prudence, I am perception: power is mine!"

Interestingly, on the Tree of Life, the branch associated with wisdom is called both Sophia and Father. When we climb the tree, just as when we climb into our upper interior stars, we enter a place that is neither feminine nor masculine, but both are unified into something wholly other. For this unification there must be complete peace between our inner Adam and inner Eve, our inner Adam and our inner Lilith/ Na'amah, and our inner Eve and inner Lilith/Na'amah. Where there is strife, there can be no unification. And where there is no unification, there can be no greater intelligence.

A meditation experience can best demonstrate this. I saw myself as a young woman standing by a stream. A young man approached and as he stood beside me, we both gazed into the stream, witnessing my reflection constantly changing from maiden to mother to crone. He did not flinch or back away but lovingly appreciated the faces that appeared in all of their forms: dark and light, young and old, beautiful and ugly.

The young man and I then stood facing one another and, gazing at each other, I found myself merging with him, and I became him. A horse appeared, and now as the young man I climbed upon this horse and began riding swiftly. I then found myself becoming the horse, feeling every muscle as it worked hard and yet so beautifully coordinated and unified in its running. The strength of the horse was coursing through my being; it was exhilarating. I then became aware of a bow and arrow that was being taken up by the rider, and I now became that arrow filled with intense concentration and focus, seeking only my target, flying through time and space with a swift intensity, devoting every ounce of my energy to my task. And then I, as the arrow, collided with my target, and there came such a creative explosion in that moment—world upon world upon galaxy was born at this moment of impact or what I could also call our union. It was such a spectacular occurrence that no words can capture the feeling of ecstasy that ensued.

Through this meditation experience we can see that my masculine knew and loved my feminine through witnessing and appreciating all of her dark and light faces, and my feminine knew and loved my masculine through experiencing his strength, his focus, his one-pointed devotion. Was the feminine the target the masculine was aiming for? Yes, I believe so. Our point of collision (in cosmic terms) or union (in earthly terms) is what we are all seeking—the return of the inner feminine and the union with her inner masculine partner and energy. We have been struggling for so long to do this on the outside in our relationships, but we often neglect the inner realms and the depth of encounter that it requires of us.

In terms of the intelligence, as expressed through this meditation, we are being asked to bring forward all of our feminine faces and all of our masculine strength of focus and devoted concentration, bringing into union all of our intuitive and mental abilities. When we are able to do this, we give birth to a whole new creation, a whole new intelligence that we can no longer call feminine or masculine. We have stopped our development by narrowly saying *this is the feminine way* or *this is the masculine way*, calling each other names, and all the while berating our own selves in the process. Yet, in truth, the feminine does open to all, and the masculine does desire the feminine in her fullness. We love each other immensely.

Na'amah is the wisdom keeper of our inner world and the world to come. Her perception as Queen of the Night looks right through the darkness to see the true light of the energy of the interaction, of what lies in and behind the heart, and she helps birth through an intelligence in the brilliance of her light, which each of us will experience and express in our own way.

Prayer for True Intelligence

> Na'amah, help me back into the fullness that I am
> No more seeking in the dry desert land
> Trying to know union on my own
> You are fertile ground, Na'amah
> A ground so fertile that all of life
> > teems from your soul
> A ground where your magic and ritual
> > make love with your strength and focus
> > weaving together a love triad
> > that bursts forth in cosmic ecstasy

Bring me home, Na'amah
Bring me home to that fertile ground
Home to the true intelligence that we are
The intelligence on fire with love.

Chant

Nay-ah Nay-ah Nay-ah-ma
The fertile ground of being and intelligence

Meditation

Come to this meditation with the intent of uncovering your deepest feminine and masculine beliefs and desires. Ask for the brilliance and intelligence of Na'amah to be your guide. Breathe deeply into your feminine being and ask whether she loves the masculine one. Breathe even deeper, and ask again. And again. Be with what arises, and ask for appropriate action and guidance.

Now breathe deeply into your masculine being and ask whether he desires the fullness of your feminine being. Breathe even deeper, and ask again. And again. As above, be with what arises and ask for guidance.

Then go within and envision Na'amah as the divinely intelligent dark one with a white flame at her brow. See yourself with the same white flame within your brow. Commune with her divine mind and intelligence, letting it ignite your own.

Journal what Na'amah reveals.

Revisit this meditation periodically and see how your layers of appreciation for the feminine and masculine energies may grow and any layers of negativity may dissolve. Also revisit anytime you wish to ignite your divine mind and intelligence.

Remember to ask Na'amah to assist you. She is a powerful force of dissolution and opening.

Resurrected Elegance

She is a garden enclosed, my sister, my promised
bride; a garden enclosed, a sealed fountain…
Fountain of the garden, well of living water,
streams flowing down from Lebanon!
Song of Songs 4:12–15

One definition of elegance is refined grace. Grace can be understood as a flowing energy of light and wisdom from the creative intelligence, or the mother-creator of all that is. And *refined* can mean "to be free from dross, to purify," hence refined grace and our natural elegance evolve when we can allow this light-wisdom energy to flow unobstructed into our being through the constant purification of our lower nature. When we are able to do this, the innate beauty and harmony—the elegance—of our soul is naturally revealed. The flowing grace never stops; we are the ones who disrupt its flow when we do not surrender gracefully to the purification.

The holy crown, or root of the Tree of Life, is known as a river or fountain of light from which this consistent flowing grace comes. It streams down through all the branches, each branch revealing a quality and energy of the Holy One. A sealed fountain, as spoken of in the above Song of Songs quote, indicates one who is in a constant flow of grace. Nothing from the outside can disrupt or disturb this flow. The masterful person can allow the dross to arise, the purification to happen, and the grace to flow, all within a matter of moments. And so the fountain remains sealed and flowing. When we chew over our dross and therefore extend our purification, we subsequently cause a breach or leak in the sealed fountain, and it may feel like grace is no longer flowing. Actually, it is; we simply have lost awareness of it as we are tending to our chewing. And the longer we take, the further away we step from the fountain or river of light, though in a twinkling of an eye, in a change of awareness, there it is again. The choice is ours.

The sealed fountain, a garden enclosed, also speaks to one who is not using the energies for any personal gain but is sealing their energy and keeping their soul garden clean and clear to work for the good of all. By doing this, an added understanding of the subtlety of the forces and of energy used negatively is easily recognized, and with the blessings and power of Na'amah, this one will rectify, as soon as they are able, either these energies within themselves or in dealing with others. As is so prevalent on this earth, we tend to take natural states of being, such as elegance and beauty, and disrobe them of their spiritual power and significance, using them falsely for our own self-aggrandizement and gratification.

If we remember, Na'amah's name also has the association with charmer and seductress. Here we move into the negative feminine darkness, known and lived out by both men and women. We all know the proverbial good-looking male charmer who flirts and charms their way at a party or gathering, seeking and giving attention, and drawing energy toward themselves to try and fill a very real sense of lack in their being. And I am sorry to say that I have all too often witnessed the seductress at work in the female form and body. It is as if an energetic net is cast over the one they seek to know/control, cleverly drawing them into their own auric field and literally feeding off the energy of the one who becomes enraptured by the beauty and elegance before them. In fact, both people are being fed, for the male also is energetically feeding off this negative feminine power, having his ego bolstered, among other things! And often what ensues is the male then being manipulated into doing any manner of things to serve and ostensibly help the feminine one in need.

This is the spirit of seduction at work. Sadly, even with supposedly very awake beings, I have witnessed this at play and have had it described to me as merely being sparked by the other. Yes, this can be so if it is a natural unfolding and meeting, and it is even more enjoyable when it is in the Spirit, but when there are feelings of lack or manipulation and a motive in and behind it, then we are dealing with another kind of energy at hand. This spirit of seduction can be very persuasive, and it makes us feel good and gives us a temporary and false aliveness, but essentially it is casting a false power over another to do our will. How often do we try to do this in our life? How often do we try and bend another's will to do our own? Oh! Where and when does the flow of refined grace turn to a manipulating willfulness in our lives? Or, put another way, how often are we trying to manipulate life, or God?

May we return to our purified elegance, our purified beauty, calling upon the true name of Na'amah in all of her grace and power.

Prayer for Spiritual Elegance and Grace

Na'amah, I see you in your beauty
I feel a harmony and grace
    flowing through your soul
A natural elegance
    that no one has witnessed before
A natural elegance
    that speaks my name
    and calls my own beauty forth
My own flowing grace
    that no one can interrupt
    or stop or interpret or deny
May I not try to manipulate this grace
Or bend it to my will
May I not seek power over another
Or fall prey to the spirit of seduction in all
    of its forms
May I return to my natural purified elegance
Flowing free in the winds of time
The desert winds now blowing
    with love and beauty and harmony
The desert rose unfolding
    with the grace of elegance.

Chant

Ka-ah-la-ya Imma (ee-ma)

This is the same name as Kali Imma, Dark Mother,

but with Kali elongated

Meditation

Seeking your own and Na'amah's liberation from any form of seduction, invoke the energy and image of the Dark Mother. You may envision a Black Madonna that you resonate with or let an image come to you. Then ask that any of your hidden manipulations be revealed. Set them free in the vibration of Kali Imma, the Dark Mother's name, and offer it to her. No need for shame or guilt, just a gentle honesty and offering. Let the Dark Mother purify it.

Then see or feel grace flowing unobstructed through your whole being. Let the desert winds, the wings of the Shekinah, gently touch you with true elegance and grace.

Journal your true elegance.

Justice of Darkness

I am black but lovely, daughters of Jerusalem...
Take no notice of my dark coloring...My
mother's sons turned their anger on me,
they made me look after the vineyards. My
own vineyard I had not looked after!
Song of Songs 1:5–6

Justice is a means of seeking a redress of balance. It is the action of right wisdom, or the true meaning of what was formerly known as righteousness. Justice also takes on the role of guardianship: wisely watching over, skillfully speaking out, and acting according to inner knowing.

Na'amah cannot speak or act if she is still relegated to the realm of the desert wasteland, clothed in the shame of darkness. She cannot watch over or provide guardianship from a place of imbalance or if she is still bound by our fear. You see, Na'amah lives beyond the edges of the society of our soul, her darkness and her power feared not only by others but also, and maybe even especially, by women. And yet she, within us, can bring forward a voice of power that will make even the angels stop and listen. Mostly, we shy away from this voice and go back to our safe hiding place that we have been carving out for lifetimes.

The feminine energy has been exposed to an ongoing pillory in our world—a public scorn, punishment, and humiliation. And we women have been right up there throwing our own rotten eggs, mostly at ourselves. But what happens when we stop throwing, start listening, and begin to wisely watch over our souls? First, our vision must be clear. We must witness all with neutrality: the light, the dark, the luminous, the painful. This neutrality can lead us to our inner vision, where a direct experience with the Living Presence can reveal and communicate the situation at hand. Of course, there are varying degrees of lucidity in these communications, but by visiting our mother-ground of being daily, it then becomes easier to access and experience a clear vision. Sometimes we are a little hazy and other times there is a compassionate clarity. The latter is from where our skillful speaking arises.

Of course, we have all experienced the not-so-skillful speaking as words burst forth out of too much silence and hiding. But with time and patience we can remain out in the open and learn the art of speaking in the moment with a gentle power or, if necessary, a firm power when it is warranted. We naturally progress to right action when informed by our clear and compassionate vision and our inner knowing that we must trust, listen to, and act on. If we are mistaken, then let us apologize and know we are learning. If our inner knowing is fruitful, let us give thanks to our soul and to the wise feminine within. Let there not be gloating or diminishing another but a gathering of everyone in the midst of our ongoing evolution.

Na'amah is also known as the Queen of the Night, as she has the visionary capacity to penetrate the darkness of any situation. She has the brilliance of light to draw forth the wisdom contained therein, revealing the power to speak and act in the way of righteousness, or right wisdom. She is the queen of our heart who knows no difference between day and night, light and dark, but lives with them reconciled within her. This is the truth of Na'amah; this is the truth of us. We need not fight the darkness anymore. We need not fear it or run from it for we are also this darkness, and within it lies the sacred jewel of our diamond being, or soul.

Justice is returning the dark beauty of the soul of the world to her rightful place within our souls and within our world, knowing her alchemy to be the transformative elixir that can help our human evolution. This dark beauty of the soul of the world includes all people of all colors, all countries, all genders, and all religions. The garment of justice that needs to be re-dressed first and foremost is the re-dressing of our own soul. Some questions to ponder: What garment are we wearing? Is ours worn down into complete disrepair or is it merely outgrown? What injustice are we being asked to bring into balance in our lives, and what garment will allow us to do that? These questions will naturally lead us to the injustices we are called to on both the personal and the worldly level.

I pray for the balancing of the feminine and masculine and the earthly and spiritual energies; for the healing of all injustices past, present, and future; and for the inner soul of Na'amah to be brought back into the world, where the Dark Mother's voice will be heard, her actions heeded, and her wisdom acknowledged. May it be so!

Prayer for Justice and Guardianship

Na'amah, I seek the truth of your guardianship
Where your night vision reveals the sacred light
>> in every thought
>> word, and action
>> that pours forth from my soul
Let me not run from your darkness
Let me not run from my darkness
But stand in its power of revealing
>> its balance of knowing
>> its sight of pure wisdom
Let me place your garment
>> of power upon my soul
Freeing us both from the shame
>> of the dark beauty that the
>> soul of the world brings.

Chant

Ka-ah-la-ya Imma
The healing and compassionate presence of the Dark Mother

Meditation

Invoking the presence of Kali Imma, sense or feel her dark compassion. Let her appear to you in any form or feeling of the Dark Mother/ Black Madonna. See her smiling upon you. Know she brings the compassion of truth that can transform any injustice inflicted upon her children.

Let a feeling come forth of an injustice, and feel both the personal and universal significance of this. Take this to the Dark Mother and offer it to her, asking for her compassionate transformation. Let this transformational energy and power suffuse your soul, mind, and body. Taking up this new garment, walk in the world as you are called. This may take the form of a worldly action for a particular cause or it may take you deeper into prayer for the soul of the world and the return of her fullness.

Journal what is being asked of you.

The Interior Heart Star

*Set your heart, therefore, on what I have to say,
listen with a will [with desire] and you will be
instructed. Wisdom is brilliant, she never fades.
By those who love her, she is readily seen, by
those who seek her, she is readily found.*
Book of Wisdom, 6:11–12

As previously spoken, our interior heart star is the connector between our upper and lower interior stars. It is where our personal and cosmic hearts meet, and where wisdom, if we desire and allow it, can flow in her shining brilliance, cutting through the ignorance of our small heart and world.

We can learn deep compassion communing with the Dark Mother, as we know all beings and forces, including those of a darker nature within ourselves and others, are all birthed from the mother. Self-acceptance, self-love, and nonjudgment reveal the doorway into greater wisdom, where we can also commune with angels and archangels of light, and all beings from other realms. For this, we do need to have a healthy level of self-worth free of self-criticism, otherwise we will doubt and dismiss our communications. If we begin to build relationships with any beings, earthly or heavenly, we will in time experience our unification with them—that is, we will understand and know they are in us and we are in them. It is a truly magnificent experience, one that humbles and empowers all at once. If we are able to experience this unification, we are moved from the conceptual catchwords of "we are all one" to actually feeling and knowing it to be true. Spiritual concepts are easy to say, but by opening to our greater cosmic heart, we can then move into the *gnosis*, the knowledge, of the truth. There is great power and peace in this.

We are all called to keep moving into greater unification—to know ourselves as Magdalene and Yeshua did, as the embodied Living Presence. It is not a sin to know that you are like your creator. When doubt of this possible unification assails, it is good to take up an affirmation that I was given: *I can, I am, I will embody my realized feminine being.* If we are consistently surrendering our ego desires and ego will to our true desires and true will, then this affirmation has more of a chance to be experienced, and we will not fall into false ego inflation or ego deflation. We will also come to know our place in the cosmic and earthly realms. This is a great gift when we can take our place with angels and humans alike, moving with ease and grace in and through them all. This is what living with an open heart truly means, taking us far beyond our personal relationships to include cosmic ones also.

While meditating upon this chapter to be written, I was very aware of a robin outside on the chestnut tree. In *Animal Speak*, Ted Andrews tells of the legend of the robin and how, by pulling a thorn from the bloodied crown on Yeshua's head while he was on the cross, the robin obtained its red breast. This legend speaks deeply about our compassion for others, our unity of feeling with others, and how we all have a connection and responsibility for one another's journey. Here it must be stated, however, that this responsibility does not mean we take on the pain or healing or even that we hold others. Too many women do this and burn themselves in the process. Rather, we actively engage in our own compassion and help another in a way that is empowering to them. We often say *I will hold you in prayer*, but this implies that we are carrying it. Rather, let us say *I will pray to the mother for you*, and then let the mother hold and bring to pass what is needed, which may look radically different than what our human heart may tell us is necessary.

Another aspect of the robin is that it is associated with spring, new growth, and fertility, all speaking to the greenness of life, the color associated with the heart. Is our life green and fertile? Is our soul experiencing new growth, opening to all of the facets and faces of love? Do we know our place in this world and other worlds or are we keeping ourselves small and bound, with our hearts covered and restricted? Do we allow ourselves to feel love in our life or do we perceive there is a lack of love? Love is not lacking. Perhaps we should all write that over and over until it begins to seep in at the edges of our consciousness and slowly pries open our small hearts. Or, even better, by venturing into our cosmic heart, we will know this to be a reality where we can invite the small heart to come and know this too, and keep reminding and reminding when she forgets. Love is not lacking. Love is here, now. On earth. In the heavens. In our shining, brilliant hearts of wisdom. She is alive. As Anodea Judith writes in *Wheels of Life,* "Love is not a matter of getting connected; it is a matter of seeing that we already are connected within an intricate web of relationships that extends throughout life." May we all see and know this connection; may we all know the meeting place of the cosmic and human heart and find our place in this great and wonderful cosmos.

Meditation

Coming into your heart area, take time to breathe in and behind the heart, opening to your greater cosmic heart. See a green shining star growing larger and larger, filling the whole of your chest and shining with a radiant brilliance. Use the breath as a means of opening any feelings of internal constriction. Enter into and enjoy the expansion, and open to the connected web of life on all planes. Know love is present.

When you feel the meditation is complete, consciously feel the connection between the lower and upper interior stars through the heart, moving from the heart to solar plexus to navel to root and back up to the heart to throat to brow and to crown. Come back to the heart, breathe, and give thanks.

Journal how your heart feels.

Further Practice

Return to your journal entries of this Our Mother of the Dark chapter and see what most strikes you or what is still calling you. Go and be there. Pray and chant and meditate on what comes to you. Anytime you feel your interior heart star is constricted, return to this Our

Mother of the Dark chapter and ask to know your connection, your compassion, and your place.

Now, the Cosmic Crone of Light invites us to come and meet and know her.

6

The Cosmic Crone of Light

Strongly she reaches from one end of
the world to the other and she governs
the whole world for its good.
Book of Wisdom 8:1

The crone takes us into territory that is completely other than this world and its ways. She lives with the vision of the greater cosmos and how this world can and must serve the divine plan. She has no patience or vision for anything other. If we truly desire a more intimate knowledge of this great cosmic grandmother and are in alignment with the divine plan, she will aid us by bringing true knowledge and an awakened life. If we are not in alignment, then she will skillfully expose the falsity and draw us toward what is real.

The crone in her life-giving aspect is known as the Ancient One of Knowledge. In her death-bringing or destructive aspect she is known as the Hag of Chaos or Hag of the Void. It is her life-giving face that we will enter into here, though it must also be said that to the crone herself the life-giving and death-bringing faces look exactly alike. It is only we who see or experience them differently. At times they become so entwined, however, that even we cannot differentiate them.

161

Meeting Iggaret

*If you are eager for wide experience, she
knows the past, she forecasts the future…
she has foreknowledge of signs and wonders,
and of the unfolding of the ages and times.*
Book of Wisdom 8:8

Lilith's story continues through the birthing of Iggaret. The angels of God were sent to pacify Lilith, but when they witnessed her unrelenting and prolific birthing nature through Na'amah, they took a fateful step and boldly threatened to destroy Lilith. This drew forth Lilith's deepest rage and also her deepest strength of all, and through this Iggaret, the hag as crone, was born with two faces: one as the Ancient One of Knowledge and the other as the Hag of Chaos.

Lilith, as this crone, proclaimed who she was to the angels, saying, *I am the very soul of creation and the very soul of humanity. You would seek to divide us? Impossible; you do not know what you speak. You cannot destroy me, for if you do, you will destroy all of creation and all of humanity.* She appeared to them as the great cosmic womb-ocean, filled with every potential form of creation. She then showed herself as the great cosmic destruction, with every life form returning to where it had come from, dissolved back into the womb of eternity. Iggaret was showing herself as life and death itself, and as the very force of creation and destruction. We could also call her Kali, the Morrigan, and many other names from all traditions.

The angels bowed low and admitted they had misspoken, and added that they were incapable of destroying such an emanation of creation itself. Lilith withdrew Iggaret back into herself, but the unleashing had happened, as it needed to. Our creation as we know it was now on its destined course of birthing and its ultimate return and liberation—or, put another way, for its dissolution or destruction making its way into true life. As the Ancient One of Knowledge, Iggaret has full vision and knowledge of this creative dissolution of liberation.

Iggaret lives outside of space and time as we know it, with her cosmic vision extending far beyond our small earthly realm. Our lives, in her view, are merely a blink in the cosmic eye; she is much more interested in the human evolution and life-wave as a whole rather than the small details of our individual lives. She does not operate in the ways of the world but rather will confound us with her ways, which are devoid of reason and empty of our perceived notions of human fairness, spiritual expectation, and any form of explanation. In fact, she can and will stealthily move in and quickly destroy any or all of these if they remain obstacles to our evolution.

A most vivid example was when I was traveling in Southern France and I was given a vision of a community to be birthed, complete with a detailed description of property, buildings, and people. Within less than an hour I was driving down a mountain road, and as I came around a bend there was a tree branch overshadowing the road, and upon it was a golden eagle. I stopped to take in the awesomeness of this grand bird. Her eyes penetrated deep within me, almost to the point where a little nervousness set in. And then she took flight and began to fly along the roadway; I intuitively began following. We went around curve after curve down the mountain, and I was marveling at this occurrence as I drove. Then as we reached the valley floor she flew off into the trees on the left and I instinctively turned into a long drive on the right. Following the driveway, I was led to a property exactly as my vision had detailed. Further investigation revealed all of the visionary details were in place, and even more astoundingly, the property was for sale. All was in order.

With appropriate people and with the finances in hand I returned some months later, prepared for a new chapter of my life to unfold. But the return journey did not elicit the expected result. The property no longer held the energy of the initial attraction. I could not even point to one thing as a deterrent. To live there simply did not feel the right thing to do. But I was led here; how could this be so? I prayed and prayed, but there was nothing. No word, no feeling, no image, no guidance of any sort, not even a no. There was nothing, not even after many days of incessant asking. It was as if the vision that had transpired on my previous trip was wiped clean, with no explanation and no reason, logical or otherwise. How could something so divinely inspired suddenly evaporate? And so we all went back home. Why did this happen? Welcome to surrendering to the crone. My lesson was to trust in what I did not or could not understand—the unknowable face of divinity—and to simply let go and move onward. Too often we create our own answers to our childlike "why" questions just to give us a sense of security, but in this instance I could not even offer myself that. It was the mystery that sought and won me.

Iggaret will also play with us mischievously. She is a grand trickster, and some of my experiences include her making physical things appear and disappear, trees blooming one moment and barren the next, pets dying and then resurrecting, all creating gaps in the mind consciousness where she can introduce us to the greater realities that lie in and behind this relative reality that we all inhabit. Iggaret's mind does not know duality. There is nothing in opposition, for her mind-womb is the cosmic pregnant-emptiness of creation, surging with an unparalleled life force. If we do not fear this life force or try to grasp onto it, then it can move through us at will. If we try and resist her, though, we may find ourselves in an unpleasant place of panic as we grapple with the sensation of losing control.

We must remember, however, that she is our grandmother of a deep and wide wisdom who only desires our freedom, and she will do anything for that liberation to be known. When we know this, and when we can open to her unorthodox ways, we may find we meet her in the form of the trickster, through her mischievous sense of humor, or through any form she deems necessary to teach us what is to be learned.

As we remember her words, that she is the very soul of creation and the very soul of humanity, then we must recognize that we also are all that she is, including the great cosmic mind-womb of spacious no-thingness, in which is contained the great and ancient knowledge and the every-thingness, or the chaos. We are being called to be co-creators with her to help free humanity from its slumber, and to free creation from anything that binds. And, even more, we have a responsibility to do so. Our lives and wisdom and truth are needed, for it is we who are now the messengers and co-liberators for one another. Are we willing to let go into our cosmic grandness, losing ourselves in the state of empty spaciousness in order to find ourselves? Yes, it can be scary, but it's also a great freedom as we shed binding beliefs and the duality of this realm to peer into the greater realities of existence.

The crone is known in many traditions and myths, and she very often appears in disguises that society disdains. She can be fierce and will give anything for your freedom, even taking your life as you know it to give you the true life. This may be in the way of divorce, losing your job, a serious illness, or moving you on from spiritual beliefs and communities. Even if we feel we are losing everything, she is seeing it as taking off a garment that is too small and giving us an eternal garment of a much greater wisdom.

Prayer to the Cosmic Crone

Ancient One of Knowledge
One who lives beyond
You who are my soul
    and the soul of all creation
May I know the place where you live
The place that will free me from
    any and all beliefs that still bind me
The place where the ways of the true life
Are honored and known

The place where I may know the
   spaciousness of my soul
May I be like you, great crone
Not dimming my light for anybody
Not apologizing for who I am
May I know the humor of light
And the light of humor
Right through to my bones.

Chant

Ah Ba Ya Rechabiyah (rey-ha-bee-ah)

This chant is to connect with Archangel Rechabiyah, who is known to bring expansiveness to our experiences, to broaden our being into a grand and open place.

Meditation

Open to know this cosmic crone who is the very soul of creation. Let her appear as the Ancient One of Knowledge or any form she chooses to reveal herself. Breathe into your soul with slow rhythmic breaths, and then on the out-breath go into no-breath and rest in the gap of this no-breath, the gap of the cosmic crone. When needed, take an in-breath, breathe out, and again rest in the gap. Know this gap to be beyond space and time, beyond concepts and words. It is the entry into other states of consciousness. Keep repeating this pattern of breathing until it feels natural to stop. Gently move into your life, aware that the gap, or greater awareness, is always there.

Journal your meeting with Rechabiyah and this cosmic crone.

Crone of Vision

Blessed are you among women, and blessed is the
fruit of your womb! But why is this granted to me,
that the mother of Adonai should come to me?
Revised translation of the Gospel of Luke 1:42–44 NKJV

Crone Elizabeth, mother of John the Baptist, spoke these words in the above quote when Mother Miriam visited her. Miriam, then a young woman, or daughter, sought out the company and affirming knowledge of the crone after Archangel Gabriel gave the news of her imminent pregnancy. Upon Miriam's arrival, Elizabeth was clearly given the sight or vision of the soul Miriam was to be birthing. And what followed was the great and beautiful spirit-filled exchange between this daughter and crone, prophesying their visions of what was and what was to come. Miriam's words were described through the rendition of the Magnificat in chapter 4.

Elizabeth herself was no stranger to the miracles of the Holy One, her own pregnant womb bearing testament, as she was well beyond childbearing age. Miriam and Elizabeth stayed together for three months, with Miriam seeking the protection and knowledge of the crone in those crucial months of pregnancy, both physically and spiritually. During this time they engaged in prayers of protection for one another and their unborn. They were given the prophetic gnosis of what was to come through their respective pregnancies and birthing for the world, and they were frequently visited by the angels and archangels bringing blessings for their lives and the lives they were carrying. They became as spiritual midwives for one another and for the soul of the world, looking far beyond the ways of this earth and gazing into the land of the living, the universes, and realms of the eternal.

With the aneurysm previously mentioned, I was offered an experimental surgery with a 50/50 chance of survival. It was an extraordinary time that included a variety of emotional states and deep spiritual experiences, and ultimately I came to what I call the three levels of vision. The first level is the very human one, where Yeshua's words *take this cup from me* describe the reality of a future pain that is known, but with every fabric of your being not wanting to go in and through it at all. The second level is the ability to see both the pain and anguish and the beauty and wonder of this life and all that is asked of us as we live and grow in this world. The third level is something completely other—it is hard to convey in words. The best I can say is, it is like a vision of the Golden Land, where there is no longer separation between light and dark or sorrow and joy; all is in its natural, pure state and order just as it is. This is the vision of the crone, the Ancient One of Knowledge, or the vision of God.

What perhaps is most important regarding these levels of vision is that we are meant to move in and out of them all, not simply staying in any one of them. This is what being an authentic human being means. It is also what a skilled spiritual practitioner does, ably moving from one level of vision to another, all as needed in daily living. Naturally, we have our vision-keepers, much as Elizabeth and Miriam were, but they too also experienced the other levels of reality. We are not here to escape anything but to live it all fully, with the knowledge and faith that all will be delivered in accordance with the greater plan of existence.

My own aneurysm experience certainly revealed this fullness of living when I was given, at the third level of vision, great spiritual delights and visions that unfolded with time, including the gift of mystical heart prayer for myself and others. I was also taken into my emotional body and asked to feel the deep-seated pain that I had not been willing to feel before. The purification and release from this was widely and wildly liberating, thus bringing together the pain and beauty of this world through the second level of vision. And there were times where I simply wept with the anxiousness of it all, wanting out in any way possible (the first level of vision). And yet in time these feelings also transformed into very beautiful and tender moments, drawing me closer to my own vulnerable humanity, which asked of me to truly receive the love of my human companions. So precious! And so the levels move in and out of each other constantly. Recalling this reminds me of the words that Elizabeth also spoke to Miriam, telling her she was blessed because she believed in the fulfillment of the things told to her by the Beloved One. Through my experiences I also believed and knew in ways I had not known before. I opened to the greater plan or destiny of my life.

How the greater plan plays out in our lives, however, is up to us. It will play out, but know that we are co-creating in every moment, facilitating or obstructing according to our own will and vision. Humanity is on a course that we each have a responsibility to help direct. May we take up company with this Cosmic Crone of Vision, asking for her guidance and her wisdom that extends far beyond our normal range of sight. May we choose to develop our own greater vision, while at the same time being aware of all levels of reality that we are asked to live in.

Prayer to the Crone of Vision

Cosmic One of the Great Vision
May you elevate my consciousness
And sight this day
May I be restored to all levels of reality
Honoring each as they require of me
May I not seek to escape, nor become
Bound by my smaller vision only.
One of Great Wisdom
May I abide with you awhile
Give me your eyes to see
Your mind to know
Your faith to believe.
Take me, Crone of Love,
Into your hallowed womb
And birth me anew.

Chant

Ruach Elohim (roo-ac el-oh-heem)

The spirit of Elohim. (It was this spirit of Elohim who came upon the waters of creation and brought all of creation into existence. Focus on the brow opening to the greater vision of the cosmic crone.)

Meditation

Coming into the calm of your mother-ground of being, ask Miriam as daughter and Elizabeth as crone to be present with you. Bring forward a time of great difficulty that you have experienced, are now experiencing, or know you are being faced with in the imminent future. Feel into the very humanness of this: feel the pain, the anxiousness, the desire to have this cup taken from you.

Then rise to the next level of vision, and see and feel the situation's freedom and fear, beauty and horror, all equally sitting side by side.

Asking to know the next level of vision, expand into the Golden Land, where there is no longer any of the above feelings but a pure vision of all goodness, all rightness in what has happened, what is happening, or what will happen. Know the mother's great mercy.

Journal what is most poignant to you from your experiences.

The Cosmic Cauldron

*The work of woman is transformation: making
something out of nothing, giving form to formless
energy...She is both container and contained...
She transforms matter and is herself transformed.*
Nor Hall, The Moon and the Virgin

The cauldron is a well-known symbol of the womb of rebirth. It contains the very properties and energy of life itself: a primal matrix where the immortal and mortal meet in states of flux, in liminal places of life and death. The cauldron is a container where the dark waters of chaos are churning in a formless potential, waiting for the weaving of their energies into a desired form. We are at once the container and what is contained therein, and we are being called to become the weavers of these formless energies, assisting the crone, the guardian of the cauldron, in her transformational duties.

The cauldron is not simply a symbol of old, or relegated to pagan or Celtic traditions; it too has many forms in and of itself. Nicholas Mann in *The Silver Branch Cards* writes:

> The Cauldron is the agent of transformation. What is placed within it will be transformed or have the power to transform whoever partakes of it. The hungry will be fed. The artist will become inspired. The dead will come to life. Wine will be transubstantiated.

In the Gospel of John 19:34 we read that when Yeshua parted from his body, a soldier pierced his side, from which blood and water flowed. In the Sophian tradition there is a story told of how Magdalene took a cup and filled it with this flowing mixture of red and white fluid. When she did this, she was chanting divine names and prayed for the healing of the world, and thus she made and consecrated the Holy Grail. It was said that this cup, this grail, could effect great miracles, including healings of body, soul, and spirit. Some even thought it could deliver the knowledge of immortality; in truth, what this means is gaining the knowledge of eternal life and the transfiguration or resurrection of the physical being. Nicholas Mann continues:

> The quest for the vessel capable of effecting this change is an enduring theme in Western religion, literature, cinema and psychology. The mystery of change that takes place within the cauldron—whether a cup, a womb, a tomb, a reactor or alchemical alembic—creates the bridge between the worlds. It is the vessel through which the procreative and original impetus of the universe prevails.

When we think "grail" we immediately think of some medieval ornate goblet, but in reality it was probably an earthenware bowl. Such bowls were the common drinking vessel at the time of Magdalene and Yeshua. And of course being made of the earth, it naturally relates to the great mother, the womb or cauldron of life, and equally to the form of the crone, the womb or cauldron of death, for these are both one and the same cauldron. Even though the patriarchal religious law was the main order at that time, it had not been that long since the Canaanite Goddess had been in every home and probably secretly still was. So when we think of the grail as the vessel through which the procreative and original impetus of the universe prevails, as written by Mann, we are drawn deeply into the primordial matrix of all life. In some Gnostic traditions it is said that Mary Magdalene herself is this grail, this primordial matrix. Having received the fullness of her divinity and humanity, and knowing this procreative impulse of the universe within her, she could draw forth and weave the energies of the life-giving cauldron/grail in and through her life. The words Mann writes of the sacred grail vessel and the beliefs of the Gnostic traditions speak of one and the same thing to me.

How are we called to weave these crone energies into our own lives? How can the chaos of the inner swirling waters bring forth new life? In what way does the procreative impulse beckon us to participate in this great life, death, and rebirth transformational cycle, giving form to formless energy? How can we as women transform our minds and bodies through alchemical means of prayer, movement, and ritual that have a solid energetic basis for bringing true transformation? Being a neo-traditionalist, I personally have found the strength and depth of the mystical Judaic-Christian and Gnostic traditions as providing the necessary foundation for a Living Spirit of transformation, and in openness I allow this tradition to grow and emerge in new ways and forms as needed within me. Without a living foundation we are often only entertaining spiritual concepts and ideals or rituals of old that are no longer alive with the Living Spirit. In our desire for renewal, we can also shun the very life-giving foundation itself. May we each find our living tradition of the crone that brings forward true transformation.

Prayer to the Ancient One of Knowledge

Ancient One of Knowledge
You know these secrets of transformation
    Of bringing forward something from nothing
    Of giving form to the formless
You have no fear of the swirling waters
Begetting life and death and life again
Show me this way in my own life
Teach me how I may reach deeply into my
    own primordial matrix of being
And honor the impulse of creation that
    surges through me at every moment
Do not let me fear in bringing this forward
But teach me to weave it in and through
With healing prayers for the world
And all of creation.

Chant

Ruach Elohim (roo-ac el-oh-heem)

Focus in the very center of your head, deep inside, and imagine a brilliant white light as you chant.

Meditation

Take yourself deeply into your mother-ground of being. Feel into the dark spaciousness of your own womb/grail/cauldron. Let yourself become this. You may even envision yourself as a grail cup or cauldron, and let the Great Mother of Transformation pour into you; let her fill you to overflowing. Let every cell in your body be transformed; let your mind and soul be transformed. Allow the Ancient One of Knowledge fill you with herself in any way she wishes. Then let these transformational blessings flow out to your family, your community, and the world. Let your vision open to see where these blessings are needed, and let them flow there.

Give thanks and seal your womb/grail/cauldron with this gratitude. Journal your womb/grail/cauldron mysteries.

Raven Crone

What is blacker than the raven? Only death.

Old Celtic saying

My first meeting with the crone came in the form of the Morrigan from the Celtic tradition. She is known to lure people to either their mystical or physical death, and their renewed life, through appearing in any manner of guises, from maiden to hag, and even in the form of the raven. Cuchulain, the great Celtic warrior, came to his demise as he refused to make love with her in the form of a hag—that is, Cuchulain refused to know and become intimate with the Morrigan, rebuking her advice and following his own instead. In fact, he encountered the Morrigan (who appeared to him in various forms) on four different occasions, but in choosing to follow his own counsel he met an untimely physical death. If only he had the humility to bow down and commune with the Morrigan in the way she desired, not only would he have lived, but he would have also reigned in the fullness of his power.

Fortunately, my initial meeting took on another quality. I was in Ireland at the Well of Tara, also known as the Well of the Dark Eye or the Well of the White Cow. I had brought with me offerings of flowers and was spending time in quiet prayer and communion with the land, the waters, the mother herself. The well is below a small mound, and reaching down into the waters I felt a flowing consciousness overtake me—what I can only describe as the fluent waters running through my mind and soul. It was powerful. It felt as if all of life and death was flowing through me, a continual birthing and dying, and with this uninterrupted flow I felt a deep sense of my own free and creative mortal and immortal nature. They were all flowing harmoniously together.

When this experience came to a natural stillness, I arose from the place of the waters and, with eyes closed, I remained standing in front of the mound, praying in gratitude. When I opened my eyes, immediately before me, pierced into the ground, was a raven's feather. It was not lying flat but standing straight and tall with the quill firmly planted in the ground, radiating energy of utter strength and pride, and it seemed to emit a warlike cry. I looked nervously around, aware that these were the energies commonly associated with the Morrigan in the form of the raven. It was as if she had left me her calling card in case I did not recognize her in the experience of the waters. I was aware that her dark eye was watching over me, ready to feast upon any white cow of false belief I may have been carrying within me.

I walked reverently back to my car, saying *so she does exist*, still looking around somewhat fervently and in trepidation. After all, the Morrigan, as the raven, was renowned for picking over her targeted corpses in the mythical stories. She did not let anyone go falsely back into the world.

Through this experience these myths came alive for me. They were no longer stories that were removed from my time and personality and long-ago heritage. They were real living energies that pointed to something far greater in our midst and in our souls. What were previously adventurous, psychologically revealing stories were now becoming energetic realities. It is the crone in all of her wisdom who tricks us into experiencing them and her firsthand if we are willing to follow.

Prayer to the Crone Raven

Crone of the Raven
Trickster of dark wisdom
Fly into my soul
And release the flowing waters
That have become stagnant.
Purify these waters with your wings of strength
Let my feminine pride return in its fullness
Let me not be afraid of emitting
My war-cry into the world
As together we watch over souls and creation
As together we are the soul of creation.
May I fly with your wings to other realms

Other realities
Bringing back wisdom to share
With our earth children.

Chant

Listening to the grand variety of raven calls is the chant here. Let the vibration of their call enter you and speak to you.

Meditation

If possible, do this meditation outdoors where ravens are. And if you have one, hold onto a raven feather while entering into this.

Ask for the spirit of the raven to be with you. See and/or imagine every aspect of the raven—feathers, color, beak, eyes, and so on. See the raven flying, jumping, feeding, cawing, talking. Saturate yourself in raven energy, and then open yourself to the crone in this form. Ask her to reveal to you whatever message she has to convey. It may come straightaway or much later. Remember, no expectations with the crone!

Journal your raven findings.

Author's Note: As I was lying on the beach contemplating the crone, a raven swept down from the cliffs and landed very close to me. She had this ever-flow of water streaming from her beak and was looking right at me. She kept hopping closer and closer with this water still streaming. It was a little unnerving and mysterious, as this was certainly a new sight, but I knew she was giving me a message. As I pondered this, my experience in Ireland and the flowing waters of the well came to mind, and so here it is, at her command.

As I am of Celtic heritage, I delight in finding where the Celtic stories of old inform and blend with my Christian heritage. I pray that both traditions be renewed and reborn in the crone's wisdom for our contemporary soul needs.

Mysteries of the Moon

The moon was perceived to be a gathering
place of the dead, the storehouse of the seed
of life, and accordingly a feminine being.
Demetra George, *Mysteries of the Dark Moon*

With our planet ever moving in great cosmic cycles and ages of different energies rising and falling, our moon came to symbolize these ages through its own cycles in the form of creation, preservation, and destruction of life. The human woman herself also came to be aligned with these cycles, with the new moon as the maiden and bride, the full moon as the mother, and the dark moon as the wise grandmother.

We must not become too linear when we look at these cycles, as just as there is transitional overlap with the great cosmic cycles, so there is with the moon and our own cycles. In fact, our power lies in our ability to access the energies of each cycle as our soul calls us to do so, regardless of our chronological age. Here we will look at the phases of the dark moon.

The dark moon is the age of gathering in; it is the time where we withdraw our energies from the world and live deeply within the primordial womb. It is where we access a different light and wisdom that is only known to those who are willing to sit in the dark of their soul… and simply be. As we know, the crone exists outside of time and space, and so when we gather to join with her in this cycle, we sit on her non-time, not our concept of time. It is in her primordial womb where she will destroy what needs to be destroyed in our lives, and she will also plant the seed of new life that needs to grow. We see this in the cycle of the moon herself, with the three days of no apparent moon representing the destruction, and the first sliver of the new moon as the new seed of life. Hence the crone and maiden (or daughter) have a very distinct relationship.

When we look at our physical death process we also see this same cycle occurring. After we take our last physical breath, we enter into an inner dissolution and come into what is called the black path, which is akin to entering the very primordial womb, or space from which creation came into existence. The soul is known to abide here for three to four days before the continued journey into the afterlife states, where we experience different states of consciousness, or encounter the *bardos,* all according to our level of awareness reached here on earth. Seeds of our life experiences create the way for our new, emerging life, and ultimately we are reborn in a cycle much like the moon.

It is important to remember that at no time in our life or death journey are we ever abandoned. If we find ourselves in the dark of night with no light, no answers, nothing at all, this lets us know we are in the dark phase of the moon, or, in the language of the mystics, the dark night of the soul. As the mature mystic knows, the Holy Presence does not disappear, we just cannot feel or perceive it; but if we stay the course we will rediscover once more that Presence in the great no-thingness. And so it is with the crone. If we can learn to abide in peace, in the no-thingness of this life, then we are training ourselves also to be able to abide peacefully in the black path of death. Watch what happens in this life when you are in the dark phase; you may become restless, listless, impatient, bored, angry, demanding, worried, self-doubting, and the list goes on. If we can learn to abide peacefully in life, then we also will be able to abide peacefully in death and thus be open to experiencing the great divine vastness that opens the way to our clear light of consciousness and being.

Unfortunately, the darkness of night came to be feared a very long time ago in our human history, with inner demons being projected outwardly. The moon, being unpredictable in her sky journey, came also to be associated with these fears of the inner and outer night. And the female human body, aligning with these moon cycles, unfortunately was also driven into the collective recesses of human fear. We need to ask what ancient collective fears still lurk in our own souls. Our bodies are directly related to our full spiritual embodiment, which is the ultimate liberating transfiguration or resurrection experience. We cannot enter into our freedom of being if we are still engaging in the self-critical war with our bodies. Any form of criticism against our physicality—whether it is through a belief in an imperfect form or its gender affiliation and associated feelings of lack—is paving the way for spiritual obstruction. What is obstructing your own embodiment? The crone will show you if you are willing.

Another good question is, are we also willing to walk the black path in this life and know perfect peace? When Yeshua appeared to his disciples after his death and said "peace be with you" twice to them (John 20:19–21), he was gifting them the peace in this life and peace in the afterlife. Remember also that Yeshua arose from the empty tomb, or the empty womb, three days after his death. He knew the primordial womb and its cycles, fully regenerating life in the newly garmented or resurrected body in the then-cosmic solar cycle. Now we are being called to know this resurrected body in the current cosmic cycle of the lunar moon and energies. The dark phase of the feminine is slowly ending; the seed for rebirth has been planted in the new moon womb of feminine leaders, as we are now witnessing. The fullness of the feminine moon rising will reveal the future full embodiment. It is interesting to watch and see how these phases are manifesting, with old and new cycles colliding and rubbing against each other, and transitions cosmically overlapping. May we all know peace through these times.

Prayer to the Crone of the Dark Moon
> Cosmic One of the Dark Moon
> May I know your spacious darkness
> As my own soul and being
> May I not be threatened or afraid of
> > what lurks beneath the surface of
> > the bright moon of my life
> May I know peace with it all.

May I abide in the spacious no-thingness of life
    and also of death
Seeking my own resurrected body
Within the empty womb.

Chant

Ha-Aysha Ha Elohim (ha-aysha ha el-oh-heem)
The primal fire of creation

Meditation

Begin with gentle and natural rhythmic breathing, then shift to
the breath of no-breath or what I sometimes call the death breath,
where you exhale and then simply sit in that space with no breath at
all. This is the same as breathing into the gap. Feel the expansiveness
of this no-breath place; feel the spaciousness all around you and in
you. When needed, take in another breath, and keep repeating this
sequence gently and naturally. Then feel this space as the primordial
womb, as the body of the moon in her darkness. Let yourself know
complete peace here. Let anything and everything arise and be looked
upon with love; no need to do anything more. Let Grandmother of the
Dark Moon bless you, and know peace as you continue on your cycle
of life and death.

Journal your dark moon blessings.

Owl Wisdom

The owl is a symbol of the feminine,
the moon, and the night. It has
been called a cat with wings.
Ted Andrews, *Animal Speak*

The myth of Lilith continues with it speaking of Lilith's association with certain he-demons and she-demons called *incubi* and *succubi*, respectively. These spirits are said to be sexual in nature and come to those lonely men and women in the dark of night, lying with them and giving birth to further demons of their kind. The *succubi* were understood to be responsible for men's sexual dreams in the night and their subsequent nocturnal emissions.

One can only really smile at these words written by men of God who were obviously incapable of owning their sexual needs by night and any repressions that they forced upon themselves by day. Once again Lilith was demonized, as was the moon, for both aroused such passions. And let us not forget the owl, also associated with Lilith and the moon and understood to be another harbinger of these nocturnal dreams and the terrible sex-power demons that rendered one helpless in the night. In one sweeping gesture of unspeakable fear, feminine sexuality was relegated to the world of dark magic and sorcery, as were women themselves, and perhaps this was the most fatal demonization of all, for it is in our sexual and desire power, our kundalini, that our true resurrection power lies. And so my smile turns into the crone's screeching power of the owl as she helps to divest us of these projected lies.

Today we hear the demonization of Lilith through such statements as *she asked for it* and *boys really can't control themselves—it's not their fault* and the continued objectification of women in between the sheets and on the streets. And so, too, women have joined in this very destructive game in their own way of trying to find their sexual expression and are calling it sexual liberation. And yet what they are playing out is a soulful destruction of a great and sacred mystery. We see this particularly when there is lack of discernment by women when entering into sexual partnerships, or entering for reasons of loneliness, affirmation, or adoration. The purity of sexual desire becomes distorted, and therefore so does the sexual and soul power.

Enter the screech owl, who is often associated with Lilith in crone form. She will swoop in undetected because of the silence of her flight, picking her prey effortlessly and devouring it whole, all within a moment in time. The prey has no time or means for recourse from this one who is known for her excellence in hunting. She is courageous and ferocious, emitting her screech when her young are threatened. And she is also at times a collective hunter—that is, she will cooperate with others to gain prey, each displaying their own ferocious individuality yet joining together for the success of all.

Owl medicine teaches us to look into the darkest depths and to see and hear what others cannot. It teaches us courageousness in the face of what appears to be a force that has tried or is trying to destroy us and ferociousness in standing for the truth of our being and all beings. Screech owl teaches us that we are not alone—that in joining with others we can and will liberate whatever needs to be freed in the dominion of our souls and our bodies.

Crone Owl is masterful in seeking and devouring her target even when there is no moonlight, and so when we befriend her we can be assured that all that lies in the darkest of dark nights of our soul, waiting to be liberated, will be revealed. Rather than a fearful thing, let us celebrate the masterful ways of such a huntress, knowing that through these abilities our soul will know a greater freedom and expansion of light than we have ever known. It is interesting to note that the eyes of an owl are yellow in color, symbolic for bringing the light of the healing sun and illumination into our dark night.

Sex and power are so aligned in the female body that it can be a long and arduous journey retrieving and liberating the millennia of associated projections, yet again and again I am reminded that this is one of the reasons why I am here. Willingly and sometimes not so willingly, lovingly and sometimes not so lovingly, I screech in the night for my young—my own personal young and the ancient and contemporary young, my personal woman and collective women, my personal feminine and the cosmic feminine.

In my own personal night-search and the subsequent revealing, I have experienced old energy patterns or archetypal energies being released. This can bring feelings of great relief, deep fatigue, and the need for dream integration, which is then followed by renewed energy. It can also bring a type of trembling to the soul and body as it reenters the world, a newborn that is still fragile in its reawakening. It is important at these times that we follow the directive of the body and whatever it may require of us. This will aid the integration of the new reality being birthed and give it the necessary strength for walking in the world, unrelenting in its wisdom and standing firmly in the power coming forth from its slumber.

Let us come forward and stroke this inner owl, this cat with wings, and invite her into our dreams of the night, learning to fly silently into the regions of our soul that we have not visited before. Know that it is here that our deepest treasure lies.

Prayer to Owl Wisdom

Crone Owl
Take me into your dark wisdom
    of the night
Teach me to fly with your silence
    and grace
Your precision and sight
Teach me to hear the still
    small voice
Teach me how to let it grow
Until it fills my soul

With the thunderous sound
    of truth
And the brilliance of the
    new moon seed.
Teach me true redemption
The redemption of illuminated bodies
And hearts and minds
Knowing nothing is irretrievable
Nothing need suffer in the dark silence
Let there be light, O Crone of the Night
Let there be light.

Chant

Let there be the owl's flight of silence whispering in your soul or the owl's call in the night; immerse yourself as you are directed.

Meditation

Take yourself outside, into an area of nature if possible. Choose the dark phase of the moon (new moon) or the full moon. If you have an owl feather, take this with you, with the intention of communing with Grandmother Owl.

Breathing into your body, open your soul to the mother-ground of being. Allow your soul to be lifted into the night sky. Feel yourself becoming as the night owl, flying silently in the night, eyes sharp and open, ears alert and focused. Let this owl fly you into the deepest darkness; watch as her hunting unfolds and see what she chooses as her prey. Let whatever unfolds speak to you symbolically; if necessary, ask for further elucidation as to what occurs.

Give thanks to Grandmother Owl and all the collective energy of Owl. Allow yourself to receive their blessing and ask that you may walk with this renewed energy in the light of day.

Journal your owl wisdom.

Crone as Shapeshifter

[S]he was given a pair of the great eagle's wings
to fly away from the dragon into the desert, to
the place where she would be looked after.
Revelation 12:14

Creativity and fluidity are two energies that are at the very source of our feminine being. When allowed to be present in our lives they can bring great mutability to our being and experience. This mutability is essentially shapeshifting and is completely natural to all of humanity, but—as with many of our abilities—we have become divorced from them, relegating them to the world of fancy and fairytale, unfortunately often with a negative and fearful connotation.

Ted Andrews, in *Animal Speak*, writes:

> Shapeshifting is not just transforming into a beast, as is often described in ancient myths and tales…Shapeshifting is a matter of controlling and shifting our own energies to fit the needs of the moment—being able to draw upon those qualities and energies necessary…If you can adapt to change, pleasant or otherwise, you are a shapeshifter. If you can turn a foul mood into a pleasant one, then you are a shapeshifter. If you can adjust your behaviors to relate to a wide variety of people and life conditions, then you are a shapeshifter.

Many years ago, while visiting a friend's property in the northernmost part of New Zealand, it became quickly apparent that this was unspoiled land where the elemental beings were freely roaming and choosing to reveal themselves. I saw tree spirits, fairy beings suckling their young, gnomes, and all manner of beings going about their daily business. And then my attention was taken to another being; I cannot say or describe what she/he/it was, for it kept changing and mutating before it solidly formed into any one thing or being. Sometimes it appeared as a form of much beauty and then in the next moment was mercurially moving into a grotesque figure, and then into something other that does not even have a human name. It was a truly mesmerizing and astonishing experience to witness the energy changing in this being, which encompassed many forms without becoming solidly any one of them.

What is the difference between this being and us? The knowledge of its fluid nature, the skill to allow the energy to move unimpeded, the lack of grasping onto any one form. In spiritual language we may say this is allowing the Spirit to move through us. Shapeshifting, however, calls us to consciously engage and invoke the different energies of the Spirit as needed in our life. It also asks us to become comfortable with the expansiveness of our empty, fluid, and creative nature, from which all such forms arise and where they dissolve back into. And we must stretch ourselves into this expansiveness, coming to realize our cosmic nature as well as our human nature. We may enter into a very shamanic form, such as the passage in Revelation quoted above, speaking of the woman being given eagle's wings. The eagle can fly us far above the earth, giving us the vision of the Ancient One of Days, where we know we are living upon this earth but are not participating in or partaking of its distorted ways. And we may similarly engage with other animals' energies, each bringing a particular ability and quality, as we have also seen with raven and owl.

We may also enter into shapeshifting through embodying the energy of certain divine personas, such as the divine mother. Think of all her various forms in this world; talk about the masterful act of shapeshifting! Our divine mother does not limit herself, and so we must not limit ourselves either but learn to join with her energy whenever and wherever it is needed in a particular moment. For instance, in working with my sister's soul when she passed, I found she so desperately needed to feel the love of our own earthly mother's energy but was unable to open and accept this due to her pain and anger toward our mother. So, praying that she would receive this mother energy, I witnessed my own being become this very form and energy, with my sister then able to take in the mother love in this way. In time my sister was able to accept the love and healing, then move beyond her pain, continuing on in her afterlife journey.

As Ted Andrews wrote in the previous quote, shapeshifting becomes as simple as changing our mood or behaviors as desired. By becoming masterful in simple ways, then we can also expand into greater horizons. Let us begin by catching those negative thoughts and instantly shapeshifting them into positive ones; this in turn will shapeshift how our lives manifest around us. Then we can begin to experiment and expand with the greater energies as described above.

Prayer to the Crone of Shapeshifting

Grandmother Crone

In your vastness

In the empty space of your belly

May I know myself as you

May I not be afraid of the dark space you inhabit

May I not fear getting lost and losing my way

But rather let me be embraced by your darkness

In the wild cosmic starry night.

Let me fly with your eagle wings

Let me breathe with the breath of fire

Let me give birth to another star in our galaxy and beyond

Let me know I can do all this and more.

I am your granddaughter

Teach me your ways

And bless me while I take a ride

Across the night sky.

Chant

Ha-Aysha Ha Elohim (ha-aysha ha el-oh-heem)

The fire of creation burns away any notion of the solidity
of self

Meditation

Come with the intent of experiencing your mercurial and shape-shifting nature. Enter into your mother-ground of being, breathing rhythmically and naturally, and gently allow yourself to fall into the great spaciousness of your being. Feel the outer edges of your body soften and slowly dissolve. Feel the fluidity of your nature, with the possibility of arising and dissolving into different forms.

You may wish to choose a particular animal and envision yourself as becoming its form and energy.

You may wish to choose a particular form of the mother and envision yourself as that form and energy.

Or you may wish to simply open to the crone and follow where she wishes to take you. Whatever arises for you, go with that, even if it is surprising to you. Allow your natural fluidity to take you where it will. And if dancing and movement help, as they often do, then prepare yourself for this sacred shapeshifting dance.

Stay with the image/form/energy as long as you can, and when it feels complete, see your own body/form arising. Spend adequate time grounding into your own form until you feel you are fully inhabiting your body. Give thanks for what was revealed.

Journal your impressions and feelings of shapeshifting.

The Interior Throat Star

But Norea turned with power and, in a loud voice,
she cried out up to the holy one, the god of all,
"Rescue me from the rulers of unrighteousness
and save me from their clutches—at once!"
The great angel came down from the heavens
and said to her, "Why are you crying up to
god? Why do you act so boldly toward the holy
spirit?" Norea said, "Who are you?" The rulers
of unrighteousness had withdrawn from her.

Bentley Layton, The Reality of the Rulers

The passage above is from a lesser-known and more esoteric text of the Nag Hammadi Library, written in Greek sometime in the third century and probably originating in Egypt. It is a variation or retelling of the Genesis myth. As one knowing her godlike image and retaining her divine consciousness, Norea is Eve's virgin daughter. The rulers of unrighteousness (those turned away from God) sought to lead her astray, defile her, and make her their servant on this earth. She clearly defies them and through her loud voice and boldness of spirit she saves herself by her prayer of command that she be rescued "at once." She then, with equal boldness, questions the origins of the great angel. By this time the rulers clearly recognize this is not a soul to be easily dominated, so they depart.

These rulers of unrighteousness had also assailed Eve in this myth, but as they pursued her and caught hold of her, she turned herself into a tree, leaving only her shadowy reflection resembling herself. It was this reflection that they defiled, and "they defiled the seal of her voice." Giving birth to Norea, Eve spoke, "[God] has produced for me a virgin as an assistance for many generations of human beings." That is, Norea—who, in knowing herself and not having her voice defiled—resists those who would seek to dominate and silence her, and is subsequently able to help humanity return to its spiritual root and knowledge.

As has been previously mentioned, the crone and the daughter are intricately related. I have heard many elderly women say that once they reach their elder years, they finally feel the freedom to say what needs to be said, no longer afraid of what others will think of them nor feeling compelled by what society asks of them. They are firmly confident in their own being, speaking out against and defying anyone who seeks to rule over them. Like Iggaret, there is also the capacity for a greater knowledge to be known and spoken now that they are not bound by the ways of this world. Are we able to speak out against the current of unrighteousness in our society, in our homes, at our work, or has our voice become defiled? And are we still collaborating with that defilement? Yes; women and the feminine aspect of men have been silenced for far too long through both religious and cultural means, but we do not need to continue being coerced by such unrighteousness. Are we willing to stand up with a loud voice and speak what needs to be spoken or are we false peacemakers driven into the silence of fear?

Eve's story in this myth tells us something very valuable: that the only thing that was defiled was the shadowy reflection resembling herself, not her true being. How interesting that her true being becomes the tree, bringing to mind Lilith's tree dwelling on the Euphrates and also the Hebrew goddess Asherah, who is known as the Tree of Life, the giver of all life and divine attributes. In fact, in the myth when Eve is being pursued by the rulers of unrighteousness, she actually laughs at their foolishness and blindness, for they do not see what she becomes and what she willingly gives over to them. Eve has a greater understanding that no harm can come to her being in the form of this tree, as it is the truth of her being, and this can never be defiled. This tells us that no matter what has happened to us upon this earth, it can never defile our inner Tree of Life, our inner radiant being, our spiritual root. We are not flawed in any way. This is another statement of truth that we need to hear over and over again. *You are not flawed in any way.* Let this sink deeply into your being. This is what both Eve and Norea demonstrate and want us to know.

The old Judaic-Christian falsity that we are flawed needs to be eradicated from the consciousness of humanity. In the Hebrew tradition there were many laws adhered to regarding *korbanot,* which are sacrifices or offerings to God. The root word for *korban* means to draw close, and there were a variety of offerings seeking to reinstate this closeness to God. The books of Leviticus and Numbers tell us of a common element in these offerings, and that is the need for an unblemished animal. No imperfection of any kind was acceptable to be given to God. As with all laws, religious or otherwise, there is a tendency by humanity to transfer, absorb, or misinterpret, with dire consequences on a personal level. Translate this unblemished law and project it onto humanity, and suddenly we become unworthy of God's love or of drawing close to God. Add the Christian belief of Christ dying for our sins, and what hope do we have when it is improperly taken into our psyches and believed in a wrongful manner? We come up as being blemished, sinful, and flawed. What a very heavy cross to bear! We need to lay this cross down and draw close to the knowledge of the crone, who in her visionary capacity holds our flawlessness in her mind/womb/consciousness and in her speaking affirms the goodness of all beings.

Our voice, our interior throat star, is where our creative power finds its expression. There is great power in speaking our prayer out loud, as when we speak something verbally we set it in motion and bring it into life, into existence. There is a vibration that begins to tremble in the soul and something Other takes over. When we are truly open the Spirit can then pray through us, and we will pray things we never imagined or even knew to speak. Magdalene co-created the grail with such prayer. The crone Elizabeth and the daughter Miriam entered into great prophecy and words of the Spirit by speaking out loud together. Vibration is key to our voice and our interior throat star. When we speak or chant divine names or mantras, it is the vibrational quality that is important. Do we feel the vibration through the whole of our body? Do we feel the quality of that divine name or chant transforming us? If we wish to reach into this interior star, this is where we must travel. It is not about sounding good or feeling light of heart through singing; it takes us much deeper than that. It leads us to our spiritual root, who we are, and who we are becoming. As Anne McGuire translates in *Thunder, Perfect Mind,*

> I am the voice of many sounds and the utterance of many forms...
> I am the utterance of my name.

Meditation

You can do this sitting or you may enjoy standing and moving your body as you sound. I find that movement can help loosen the sound.

Bring your focus to your throat center. Envision a beautiful cerulean or sky blue star shining brightly. Breathe into this color and begin to gently sound *Ah*, feeling the vibration. Let the sound be elongated for as long as your breath allows. Repeat many times, not being concerned with the sound but with the vibration. Then sound *Ma* and repeat as above. Then sound *Ee* and repeat; then *Ma* and repeat. Take your time with each, and then join them all together: *Ah-Ma-Ee-Ma.*

You can also take up *El.* Repeat as above. Then *Oh* and repeat. Then *Heem.* Elongate each sound and then join them together: *El-Oh-Heem.*

When you feel complete, let yourself continue to feel the vibration even after you have stopped sounding. Give thanks and go speak your soul into being with loving-kindness and vision.

The vowel sounds in all of the wisdom traditions of Judaism, Buddhism, Sufism, and Hinduism are known to reach into and open the way into the spiritual realms. They also have a very practical use of opening the throat star.

Go out into the world and see how your speech may have changed. Are you stronger and speaking with greater clarity in your communications?

Journal your experiences.

Further Practice

Return to your journal entries of this wondrous Cosmic Crone of Light. Acknowledge how you may have grown and expanded. What now seems in the realm of possibility? Anytime you feel your interior throat star is constricted or you are falling into fearful silence, return to this Cosmic Crone of Light chapter and ask to know the vibration of your spiritual root and your voice in this world. Ask that you may speak your name and being into existence.

You are now invited to visit the Crone of Dissolution and the Dark.

7

The Crone of
Dissolution and the Dark

In all chaos there is a cosmos,
in all disorder a secret order.
Carl Jung

The Crone of Dissolution is also known as the Hag of Chaos, the Hag
of the Void, or the End of Days. She is the one who brings dissolution
to our world, and in order to do this she will reveal what needs to
be dissolved, often with ensuing chaos. But within this chaos and the
accompanying destruction, there is a great and cosmic order at play,
and an ultimate life-giving outcome.

Crone of Death

The death of what's dead
is the birth of what's living.
Arlo Guthrie

I have always had a fear of the Hag of Chaos, which was born from the myths and legends of her mystically destroying others. When I looked deeper into this I discovered an inherent fear of the death of my physical being, and perhaps even more so of the death of my small-mind consciousness or life as I know it.

It is an odd phenomenon that many say they are not afraid of dying, yet they will cling to their daily life and beliefs with such gusto and with fear raising its head at even the most simple of changes. Perhaps it is time to inquire again, as death is what we may call the mother of all change, and every other fear of change stems from that ultimate fear. When we can really know that death is merely a change and releasing of garments, a revealing of the inner garment, then we can begin to relax and open to not only the adventure of the death process, but also to this life we are living and whatever change appears to us while still in this body. It is also important that we do not look upon our physical death as an escape from this life, for wherever we go, there we are, even in death. Things do not get miraculously resolved with that last gasp of breath. The forgiveness and resolutions are still waiting to happen, and the heart and consciousness are still waiting to expand. Know there is no escape from yourself on this side or the other side, so it's best to not delay but tend to all things now.

We may also find ourselves afraid of larger energetic movements in our life, as this energy can sweep us off our controlling feet and literally place us in a new consciousness-locale. The crone is certainly a large energy, and she does not apologize or dim her light for anybody—something we all could learn from!

Once while I was attending a gathering, there was a ritual being entered into in a purely spontaneous way. Though I relish the spontaneous, there was something in the way the ritual was being undertaken that was unsettling to me. I tend to work within a container and then let the spontaneity happen within that context. Here, I was not experiencing any container, and I was feeling the pure chaos of the movement and the moment. For some this may have been enlivening, experiencing the creative energy giving birth in this way. For me it was uncomfortable, but I stayed with it. Toward the end of the ritual I saw shards of that chaotic energy dispersing throughout the circle, and one of those shards pierced my heart.

Upon walking home I was in a strange state, and I knew something was happening but I did not know what. And then my vision opened, and I saw the reality of our life here and how we are projecting everything—that nothing is as it seems. All our thoughts of others and ourselves are bound in multitudes of false perception, and we then project those all around us and hear and perceive everything through the same erroneous filter. Now, this could have been a wonderfully liberating moment of awakening, but unfortunately fear came by for a visit, and small-mind consciousness did not want to admit this reality witnessed; after all, what would happen to all its constructs and projections? It would lose its life and die—or so it thought. Little did it know it was being born into a new and wonderful life, but alas, not yet.

The fear continued to grow and grow. It felt like fear was being overlaid with more fear and then all fear, and then I heard it: Iggaret's unmistakable laughter. It was a haunting laugh, even a taunting laugh. I saw her out beyond space and time in the form of the Hag, emitting or transmitting a continual piercing laugh. This laughter penetrated my mind, and in that moment a great surge of energy came through me, and I spoke out loud, "It is only fear." Immediately all the fear was gone, leaving me with a grand spaciousness of soul/mind/consciousness that I fell into and rested deeply within. There was nothing to be done here, nothing to be thought, simply being in the spaciousness with the essence of repose claiming me. What a liberating place to be!

Now, I write this experience in order to show that if we stay with the Hag of Chaos, whose antics open the way for us, we will be liberated. Also, sometimes we may not go all the way with her, and we may only experience great discomfort or panic in her presence, for indeed she can sometimes be shocking to the soul. It is one of those large movements that affect the soul in one way or another. Whatever your experience, either in the past or perhaps in the future, know that Iggaret has your back and your soul. She is your Grandmother of Wisdom.

Prayer to the Crone of Death

Grandmother of Death
May we speak?
I come to you to lay down
All my fears
My fear of leaving this body
Of leaving this small mind
And all its worries way behind.
I know they are only temporary
But do I really know this?
Can I mourn their death now?
Daily?
Even moment to moment?
Maybe then death and I can be friends.
Maybe then you and I can be friends
And I will not fear your piercing energy
And laughter in the night
But welcome you into my bed
Where you will slay all that needs to be slayed
And resuscitate all that needs to breathe again.
Give me the holy breath, crone of my soul
And let me laugh like you in the morning
As I rise a new woman into unadulterated love.

Chant

Ruach Elohim (roo-ac el-oh-heem)
The breath of life and death

Meditation

See yourself lying as a corpse, your body dead and lifeless. Look at it closely and love it, and thank it for all that it has offered you and for all the places it has taken you in this life. Now see your small mind and all of its worries and concerns—see it also dead and lifeless, finally at rest and in peace. Thank it too for all that it has done for you and how it so valiantly tried to take care of you. Then, when you are ready, let them both be blown away like dust in the wind.

Feel into your consciousness/soul/being and thank it for continuing on; open yourself to the changes and adventures now to be encountered.

When this is complete, come into your body, take your small-mind by the hand, and draw both mind and body into their rightful place as you go about living in the world.

Journal your death feeling.

The Sleeping Dragon

*Beware the sleeping dragon. For when
she awakes the earth will shake.*
Winston Churchill

While taking a morning walk on one of my visits to Scotland, I saw the land before me with a very different perception. No longer was she the gentle rolling green hills I had been seeing every morning, but before me I saw the living, breathing form of a dragon sleeping. It was not my fantasy-imagination or too many King Arthur stories; I was feeling her in my very body—I felt her breath and I felt her power. I knew she was sleeping a dreamless sleep, and I also knew she was destined to wake, bringing forth her power in and for humanity.

Our ancestors have long acknowledged the symbolic nature of the landscape as revealing specific energies, more recently referred to as ley lines. It is something we would do well to reacquaint ourselves with, for in this way we can co-create more efficiently with the land spirits to bring forth and utilize the natural energies contained therein.

The dragon has long been associated with the primeval serpent or snake, and many sixteenth-century alchemical texts speak of the two aspects of this dragon-serpent as representing both the female and male energies through its association with the moon and the sun or the colors of white and red. In these alchemical texts, red is associated with the masculine and the blood and sun as life-essence, and white with the feminine and the moon, the body and physicality. When we venture into kundalini or serpent power teachings, however, we encounter a slight switching of these energies, with red representing the feminine and the fiery aspect of the soul or the life-giving blood, and white representing the masculine, cooling, and transcendental nature, or the life-giving semen.

Where these alchemical texts align with serpent-power understanding, however, is in their acknowledgment that both the feminine and masculine energies need to join in order for the serpentlike kundalini energy to be brought into a place where it can be properly used as an evolutionary force. As the alchemical text the *Theoria Philosophiae Hermeticae* states with reference to the dragon, "I carry in me the force of men and women." And in the *Aurora Consurgens*, "Woman dissolves man, and he makes her solid."

This makes for an interesting contemplation. How can our feminine nature dissolve or perhaps soften our masculine force? And how can our masculine nature aid our feminine force in becoming more solid? When we are too fiery, can we bring in the cooling aspect of our more transcendental nature? And when we are too cool and detached, or floating in our ethereal or mental nature, how can the fiery aspect redefine and draw down to earth and physicalize the situation at hand?

The dragon as serpent has also been depicted as the ouroboros, most commonly depicted as a serpent in a circle eating its own tail, representing the life and death cycle or the eternal nature of being. The ouroboros was also depicted as two self-consuming dragons of light and darkness, and even as a *tria prima*, which consisted of the transformation of body, soul, and spirit. As a seventeeth-century alchemical manuscript relates,

> All things are brought together and all things are dissolved again…
> for nature, turned toward itself, transforms itself.

In Kabbalistic teachings the feminine is associated with the dark face of God and the masculine with the light face. The dark feminine face is known to have the ability to penetrate and understand the mystery in the darkness. John O'Donohue elicits a perfect understanding of this as he writes, "Light cannot see inside things. That is what the dark is for." The dragons of light and darkness represent the masculine and feminine energies waiting to emerge and transform into their purified state. The masculine aspect of the kundalini serpent energy can be understood to be in the crown of our being or our inner Tree of Life waiting to be formed by the light. The feminine aspect is coiled in the darkness at the base of our spine, the root, or the dragon nesting in the dark at the base of Lilith's tree, as spoken of in the Sumerian myth in the Daughter of the Dark chapter. The dragon, the serpent, the crone, and the daughter are all inextricably linked in the darkness, waiting for their time of awakening.

What did Winston Churchill know about this sleeping dragon? Some have posited that it was a purely political reference to China arising in its power. Others have surmised that he was referencing the book of Revelation and the powers of destruction arising there. Still others say he stole the quote from an ancient source. No matter what he did or did not know, within the esoteric text of *Pistis Sophia* there is a passage that speaks of Yeshua putting on the garment of the fullness of his power and light, and when he did so, not only did the earth shake and quake, but also the heavens too. So great was this power that it shook the very foundations and terrified all within these realms. Many cried out for him to return to his dimmed form. When the sleeping woman awakens, she too will shake the very foundations of this earth, and when she learns to ride the dragon of her power and light, all realms will also shake and shudder, for at that time they will know a new existence has come into being. May it be so, and may you not return to your dimmed form!

Prayer to My Sleeping Woman

> May my sleeping woman awake
> Willing to the dissolution
> And to the solidity as it is needed
> Help me, dear crone, to masterfully
> Learn the art of riding the dragon of
> Power and light
> May I not fear its power but know
> The earth and the heavens and all contained therein
> Support me in my journey
> Waiting for the moment of awakening…
> For then they awaken too.

Chant

> *Ruach Elohim* (roo-ac el-oh-heem)
> Spirit of the creative force

Meditation

Take yourself out into an area of nature that holds a special energy for you. Come with the intention of entering into and seeing anew the actual symbolic formation of the landscape and what energies lie within. You may wish to bring a small offering of herbs or flowers or whatever you are called to.

Take your time simply sitting and breathing with the land. Open to it and commune with your breath and body however you are moved to do so. Look and see with your eyes in and behind your eyes, with the vision of the crone. Open to receive the blessings and support from the land. In turn, bless the land. May you both awaken to new revelations and visions.

Advanced Meditation

Taken and adapted from an experience at Montségur, France, which is one of the Cathar castle remains.

Envision the ouroboros as a golden, circular serpent with its tail in its mouth. See its energy moving in a circular fashion from your interior root star, coming up and around the right side of the body to the brow, and then back down and around the left side of the body. Keep breathing and feeling the movement of this serpent-circle energy.

Then, seeing the form of the caduceus (the medicinal symbol of snakes entwined on a central pillar), allow your ouroboros to become one snake with two heads. Envisioning a pillar of light in the middle of your body, see the snake weaving up this pillar—entwined together as one body but with two heads joining at your brow. Let these heads join as one. Breathe up and down the central pillar of light, allowing this pillar to reach through your crown and upwards, and all the way down into your feet and the ground.

When complete, give thanks and send out blessings to humanity and this earth and any prayers that come to mind.

Journal your visions.

The Dragon Awakes

And I shall tell them of the coming end of
this realm and teach them of the beginning
of the eternal realm to come.

John D. Turner (translator), Three Forms of First Thought

The dragon has long graced our mythic world with its magnificent and often terrifying presence. You will notice in stories and movies (our modern-day myths) it is always the dragon that is the last of the beasts that need to be fought and overcome. Who is this one that we get to ride and command if it does not kill us first?

Dragons have been given a positive connotation through being described as guardians of treasure, often symbolically representing a hidden wisdom. This secret wisdom is known to give great power—a power that can destroy if not used in the proper way. The negative force ascribed to the dragon is one of pure destruction, of fighting against the force of good so that it may have the ultimate power and control. In different geographical locations and at varying historical periods these same attributes have also been assigned to the crocodile, the hippopotamus, and the primeval serpent, with all of them coming to represent the dragon and all bringing forward the fear of death and destruction.

Behemoth, the hippopotamus creature of land, is described as first among the works of God (Job 40:19), and Leviathan, the crocodile creature of the seas, as one who has no equal on earth, being created without fear (Job 41:25). Both represent the dragon energy in the ancient Near East. No one could survive their destructive life-taking force, yet at the same time they were considered God's greatest of creatures, as being the first-created and equal to none. We can equate these creatures with the great dissolution power of the crone.

The dragon in the book of Revelation has also been represented as Samael, or Satan, the one who fought in the heavens and was cast down upon the earth, raging against the woman and child, or humanity itself. He joins forces with the beast from the sea and the beast from the land, seeking to deceive humanity into a false worship. Here we have the ultimate myth of good versus evil—or the penultimate question: who does the grail serve?

Samael is also called the primeval serpent, and there is a story that speaks of him becoming Lilith's husband in the desert-land when she was raging and birthing demons. Remembering that Lilith can also represent the serpent, we come back to the union of the masculine and the feminine. If we are bound to the destructive masculine and the destructive feminine, we will surely call up the beasts of land and sea from within us. If we are in command of these inner beasts, however, we are then able to ride them and use their ultimate power for the good of humanity. Rather than raging at humanity and destroying our own happiness and those around us, we will be serving the goodness of all. This is the personal level, but there is also a greater cosmic level, and that is where the dragon as crone arises.

There is the abyss where we can say the dragon—meaning the guardian or keeper of secret wisdom—resides. The abyss is not some large, dark nothingness; rather, it is everything and anything that keeps us in separation. It is also the force of destruction or dissolution in constant flux. One who can face the vision of a larger world or cosmic dissolution and understand the necessity for such a movement is on the way to knowing the secret wisdom and learning how to ride the dragon. Dissolution or destruction is not seen as negative or evil but an ultimate fact for every world system. So, when it is spoken that Leviathan is God's greatest creature, then we can begin to understand, when in divine alignment, that such a being or energy as this one will bring about a great transformational change. Having no fear, as Leviathan embodies, is essential to riding and using our own greater transformational power.

The crone dragon has been much maligned as we perceive her as only bringing war and destruction, but through this she ultimately brings peace and new life. Nothing more grand can be found than her secret wisdom.

Prayer for the Revealing of the Truth of Dissolution

Open my mind, dear Crone of the Dragon
That I may know the truth of your destructive nature
That I may feel its liberating power for all of humanity
Let me not turn my face away
But be willing to the vision of the night
In my own soul and that of the world.
May I cease fearing and trembling
And stand firmly in my grand being
Knowing war and peace to be one
One within me, one within all
Revealing your secret wisdom of
True life.

Chant

Elohim Tzavaot (el-oh-heem tza-vee-ot), *Ya Mi Ha Michael* (mick-ee-el)

Invoking the presence of Archangel Michael helps to burn away all aversions, fears, and old forms of consciousness; he also gives protection.

Meditation

Begin by feeling any aversion you have to the thought of destruction, and then let yourself keep falling into that, deeper and deeper. Open to the light of the crone within the midst of this destruction. Let yourself be elevated to the cosmic dimension of this dissolution, and begin to see the new life being born from within this seemingly dark chaos. Let the new life keep opening and growing until there is no destruction left. Rejoice in the new consciousness that arises from such a powerful movement of love.

Journal the dissolution and the birth of true life.

206

Crone of Destruction

This ignorance of the father brought
about terror and fear.

Robert M. Grant (translator), The Gospel of Truth

Distortions and the shadow nature live in every created being, and in our world there is nothing more frightening or more destructive than this being lived out through the Hag's inverted nature. It is where the basic moral consciousness no longer exists and where the heart has become so hardened by hatred that the only possibility seen to exist is through destroying what is perceived as the enemy. One is taken over, if you will, by a volatile force that hears no reason and sees this enemy as only on the outside of oneself.

Have we not all experienced some time in our life when our fury, our rage, is so great that a deep hatred arises toward the one allegedly causing our pain, and we want them to disappear from our sight and lives, or metaphorically kill them off? Of course, for most of us this passes, and with our evolution of consciousness we have learned to take on a much greater sense of self-accountability. But what of those who have not evolved in such a way and have fallen prey to this force, which perpetuates such deep darkness of soul? I once had an experience with the Hag, Iggaret, in her darkest of all darkness, where I literally saw her face before me and she was speaking of her absolute hatred toward the masculine and the need for their destruction. Fortunately, I was in no way inclined to her words and simply told her, "No, we are not going to do that." She quickly disappeared.

But what of those souls who also experience such voices and visions and *do* listen? These are the poor souls who have become so bound in their own hatred that now they plot the destruction of others, particularly the enemy outside of oneself, who they understand as causing their greatest pain. And so what manifests are orchestrated mass shootings, emotionally volatile murders, and organized political destruction. We must be careful in reading this and not fall into saying it is Iggaret or the Hag who is responsible, that it is the violent, unbridled feminine energy that causes all this death. Yes, she does bring death, but it is up to us to choose how this energy is lived out; it is not she, per se. Again, we cannot blame something or someone on the outside, whether it is a visible or invisible force and energy.

Iggaret appearing to me and speaking the words of destruction did give me pause for contemplation. I sought to see the ways that I was entering into a more subtle destruction, whether through words or emotionally restrictive actions, so her visit became enlightening to me. It also felt like both invitation and warning. I could follow the dark thread and execute it outside of myself in some subtle form or I could use that energy to destroy the thought itself. With my simple statement of *no* this was accomplished, accompanied by a feeling of great lightness and elevation. Something remarkably dark just got liberated in that moment. I also prayed for this liberation to be extended into the world where it was most needed.

Sometimes we may also encounter the darkness or hatred being directed at us from someone outside; what are we to do then? Our greatest protection is always to draw near to the Holy One, calling upon the divine names and those archangels given the vocation of protecting the human one, such as Archangel Michael and Archangel Kamael. (Please see previous chapter for a Michael chant and the end of this chapter for a Kamael chant.) We may also be directed to simply remove ourselves from the presence of the one bringing the darkness or negativity, internally saying *no, I will not engage here.*

What also can be most effective is to look upon the soul with whom you are encountering the darkness and seek to find the absolute goodness that lives within. This requires shifting our human looking to our divine gazing, as it is not about finding the good human traits but rather the essence of that one's being—the ultimate goodness that lives in all, no matter how much pain or hatred resides within. We can do this with all beings, whether in human or spirit form, and so any fear we may initially feel can quickly turn to strength. We can then also echo the words of *Thunder, Perfect Mind*: "I am strength and fear."

Sometimes when we are encountering a lot of negativity in our lives, it could be a wayward spirit stirring our own internal negativity pot, so to know this basic form of protection is very useful. (Please see appendix II for more protection practices.) I have also had spirits of different forms and descriptions hanging around seeking this very liberation for themselves, and so the more attuned we become, the more helpful we are to all of our cosmic brothers and sisters.

The Crone of Destruction was sent forth from the power, and she is found by those who seek her through their desire to dissolve deeply held negativity and equally by those who find her through their hatred. The choice is ours, and always ours, through our free will and desire. May all beings return to their absolute and natural goodness through the dissolution of their distorted and shadow nature.

Prayer for Humanity's Return

We pray for the return of those
bound in hatred
bound in others' and their own destruction
We pray for the return of Iggaret
That she be known in her dance as the slayer of
negativity, not as the one who perpetuates
We pray for the goodness of choice
and will and desire to return
For the raising of consciousness
from its dire place of willful destroying
May we, the race of humanity
Remember our sovereignty
And act as royal souls
Serving the absolute goodness of all.

Chant

This can be taken up for yourself or others you know who are in need. Envision a ring of fire around you, invoke the presence and protection of Archangel Kamael, and chant somewhat forcefully *Elohim Givor* (el-oh-heem give-or), *Ah Ya Ko Ma Kamael* (ka-mee-el).

Meditation

You may do these below meditations separately or following one another, all as it feels natural to you in the moment.

Part One

Coming into your mother-ground of being, allow yourself to feel the energy of Iggaret in her liberating form, knowing her as your ally. You may envision her as the Hag, dancing and laughing wildly. Allow any hatred, old pain, or where you may be subtly or not so subtly seeking to destroy another or a part of yourself (often emotionally) to arise. Offer whatever arises to Iggaret's transforming nature. Follow where you are taken and let there be an alchemical transmutation of these energies. Know you can serve many through this experience, bringing the liberated power from heaven to earth. Pray that all those bound in this same way as yourself be freed.

Part Two

If doing separately, begin as above, opening to your mother-ground of being and feeling and envisioning Iggaret. Bring any fear to her and let her dance over it. Ask to be shown the jewel that lies within that fear. Allow her to transform it into strength. Sit in that strength and feel it first in your mind, then in your heart, and then in your belly, letting it fill your whole body and being. Give thanks for the crone's liberating nature.

Journal your liberation.

Hag as Nightwatcher

*My people listen to my teaching, pay attention to
what I say. I will speak to you in poetry, unfold
the mysteries of the past…that a generation
still to come might know it, children yet to be
born. They should be sure to tell their own
children, and should put their trust in God.*

Psalm 78:1,6–7

Lilith's story has one more element: in the form of Iggaret, she vowed
to make war upon the children of Adam and Eve. Miscarriages, deaths
of babies, and any kind of malformation in a child came to be understood as the workings of Lilith through Iggaret the Hag. And any
children who went missing? These too were stolen by this Hag, who
stalked them through the night.

There is a rendition of this Hag story that tells of this vow of war
against Adam and Eve's children as being spoken only about those
children who were considered weakened in soul, and who were not by
nature concerned with the greater will of God. She spoke that it was
not God that she had a problem with, nor the children who walked in
right ways, but rather the poisoned and domineering ways of Adam
and the weakened and sick state of Eve. Iggaret was a preserver of true
and authentic life, if you will, of the feminine and masculine energies
being lived as intended by God. How she has been distorted!

The distorted Lilith, in the form of the Hag, rises in our world today
through the slaying of our innocent children. Work and sex slavery;
physical, emotional, and sexual abuse; literal murder; genital mutila-
tion; denial of food and shelter; and the ultimate denial of love and
who children intrinsically are. There are so many ways to slay a child;
let us count the ways. The Hag, however, is also rising to bring the
truth of her mission, where all of the above and more are being sought
out and revealed, and we are ever so slowly finding ways to rectify such
dominating hatred toward all of God's children.

How is it that we have slain or still are slaying our own child? Again, let us count the ways, not in a way of morbidity or narcissistic reflection and victimhood but rather in a liberating exploration. Once more we witness the deep interrelationship between daughter and crone as we move into this area of youth. The daughter, in having her slain child revealed, will seek ways to heal herself with a predominant focus on her own unfolding life. The crone, on the other hand, will take these soul memories and use them for the greater good of all. Like Iggaret, who seeks the purified and strengthened form of Eve and Adam, we can help uplift the daughters and mothers who are weakened and sick, we can compassionately bring new paradigms to sons and fathers, seeking to draw them back to the sacred and unified life as intended for the feminine and masculine energies.

We can renew our intention again and again not to become slayers of humanity—particularly not of our own humanity. Let us be kind to ourselves and one another, and learn to uplift rather than push down. Let us remember what it is to trust even in the darkest of nights. In this way we will ride with Iggaret through the darkness, becoming night watchers and not night slayers, seeking the resurrecting light in the deepest night of our soul of the world and all of her children.

Prayer of Protection

Grandmother Crone
May I join with you in uplifting the lives
    and ways of our children
So they may remember the true God
Not the false god of wounded and ignorant parents
For those who have had their trust shattered
May they learn what true love is
May they know protection where it has been absent
May all domination and submission be laid to rest

May willingness to trust be born
And may purity of heart reign.
Amen and amen.

Chant

Ah Ya Ko Ma Kamael (ka-mee-el)

Ask that Archangel Kamael go to a child most in need of protection in this very moment. May his ring of fire surround and protect this little one. The Shekinah in her wisdom knows exactly where this is needed and will guide your prayer and Kamael accordingly.

Meditation

Bring forward a memory of your childhood—one that may have been painful but now gives you deep compassion and caring for others who are experiencing this and who are in need of healing. Holding the memory in your heart, see it filled with light and a resurrected love; feel it become a transformed strength, a gift for humanity. Then see all this energy go out to the world, and ask the Shekinah to guide it to where it is most needed, asking that it bring healing to souls, returning their trust and faith in both humanity and the great mother.

Journal the great gift you bring for humanity.

Crone of Unknowing

Mary said, "If you know what the world is, you
will no longer desire it, for you will see what is
beyond the world. When you see what is beyond
the world, in that day it will be in the world."

*Tau Malachi, The Secret Gospel of
Mary Magdalene, saying 79*

Our world is built upon self-interest and becoming somebody of importance in society's eyes. We feel we must become somebody who is noticed, listened to, and admired if we are to have any worth in this world. And this can equally apply to the spiritual world, for it surely has its own unique societies. Most everyone begins their spiritual journey with extreme self-interest at heart—to become the special enlightened one, the one who is closer to the sacred, or to enter into a form of self-righteous service—but with spiritual maturity we hope and pray for the constant purification to reveal a truly humble heart.

True humility lies in being willing to know nothing. As we read earlier on, Yeshua gave Magdalene the heart advice of seeking to become nobody. He also spoke of the need to seek to know nothing. This can be both frightening and liberating. We need to have the courage to go in and beyond our initial human reaction of knowing nothing. Could there be anything worse in our world? Knowing nothing automatically speaks of failure, worthlessness, uselessness, irrelevance, of being overlooked and not seen or heard, and it can bring about a depressive state of being, wandering in a sea of extreme lack of worth or, at its worst, an ocean of despair. When we venture into this territory our initial response is to get out of it as quickly as possible, trying to fill ourselves with all sorts of knowledge that will guarantee we are noticed. We will try to bolster ourselves up with all sorts of self-proclamations about who we are or what we know, falling into the deception of self-important arrogance. Panic may even set in, saying *I don't know what to do*, and we may feel a dense blackness of nothing. This is such a very difficult place for the human one to abide in.

214

If we go further, however—if we *really* feel into knowing nothing—we can be spiritually jettisoned into new territory. We can find ourselves being taken into the absolute vast spaciousness of the Crone of Unknowing, where we now enter into the mystery and wisdom of being, which is knowing the sacredness of no-thing. We expand beyond the confines of the worldly ways to something far greater, where the rules of this world no longer apply and where satisfaction and contentment are found in completely different ways. When we are given this experience we see our world with new eyes. We see the continual cycles of insecurity set into motion by the very structure of the world. And as the quote at the beginning of this chapter says, "If you know what this world is, you will no longer desire it..." We need more than a vision of a new way; we need to experience something other. In this way we then feel it in our soul and therefore are able to bring it back into our bodies and the world. Again, as the quote says, "When you see what is beyond the world, in that day it will be in the world." Here we can say that to see is to experience, and through this experience we can return and integrate it into our lives. Does this not describe the whole spiritual journey itself?

The crone, as we know, lives beyond the confines of this world and its ways, so if we truly wish to bring another world into being, then we must be prepared to travel beyond this worldly structure of self-interest and not only be willing to die to the old ways but literally and energetically experience and enter into the new. It is like we are removing an old garment and placing on a new one, one that will give much greater freedom and happiness. We just need to be willing to travel through some dark restricted territory first. But when we realize that this territory is a false construct, then it becomes easier to let it go and enter into much greater wisdom and light.

Prayer for Not Knowing
Crone of Unknowing
Crone of Another Wisdom

Take me in flight to your land
Show me your ways
Give me eyes to see what is real
May I no longer believe what the world tells me
May I place my trust in you
And bring back to this body, this mind, this world
The truth of existence
May I be willing to travel and to die
Knowing true life will be given
True happiness and contentment of being.
May it be so for all souls.

Chant

Ruach Elohim (roo-ac el-oh-heem)
The creative breath and sacred mystery

Ritual Meditation

Prepare a place where you may enter into a fire ritual, either a fire-pit outside or a fireplace or fireproof container indoors.

On a piece of paper write all of your natural gifts—all areas in your life where you excel or exhibit wisdom. Then acknowledge that the mother gives all of these talents. Ask for their greater purification, and ask that they may be released back to her through the crone in order that even greater wisdom may be given.

Take up the above chant, and then, when ready, burn the paper. See the smoke as rising back to its heavenly origins. Be willing to fall into the unknown. Feel the ecstasy of this.

And then, in the silence, open yourself to the cave of the crone and receive the greater wisdom waiting to be given. You may become aware of this in the moment or later that night or it may take time to come to you—all as the crone wills. May you be open to the wisdom continuing to unfold as you walk in the world.

Journal this greater wisdom given.

Grandmother of Primordial Wisdom

I am union and dissolution. I abide and
dissolve. I am perfect mind and rest.
George MacRae, Thunder, Perfect Mind

When we are willing to enter into personal dissolution, moving from the smaller self to the boundaryless nature in spirit, we are able to experience an expansion far beyond our imaginings. It is a place that brings great freedom and true peace of mind. Suddenly all becomes quiet, emptied, and yet fully connected. The mental being comes to rest, the polarities unite, and if we are able to keep abiding here, then another form of wisdom—one much greater than we have encountered before—reveals herself. This is the great Grandmother of Primordial Wisdom.

One morning when I awoke there was nothing, just an emptiness of mind and being. It was as if every belief, every concept, every teaching, every bit of knowledge and wisdom I had gained was no longer there— all had suddenly vanished. Instead, there was a great spaciousness, so empty and yet seemingly full and teeming with an unbidden life. Underneath I felt an eternal bubbling well of joyfulness, for no other reason than its own sake of joy. And yet I cannot say I was thinking any of these things, for there was no thought; rather, it was soulful impressions or sensations, all contained in a great big no-thingness.

I began to make friends with this no-thingness, humming as I washed the dishes and looked out upon the blue sky, taking myself out into nature and dancing with her magical beauty. All was still and quiet in my mind, and so very, very peaceful. And then, ever so slowly, thoughts began, but they were not the usual thoughts of mind; they were now of a greater nature. Some spoke of a promise for humanity, some were so wide and expansive that they could not land upon this earth, and others could only be described as deep soul communion. They were not of this world or its ways, and yet here they were setting up home in my soul. I welcomed them and remained with them as long as I could. A part of my soul had been deeply touched and revealed. It is a privilege to be visited in this way. I also became aware that it becomes our responsibility to create the soul conditions for this natural spaciousness and wisdom to visit and abide with us. This great grandmother desires us more than we know. The question is, do we desire her?

As with all experiences, there are countless variations as to how we may respond to such encounters, and at other times I was not quite so willing to the dissolution of my smaller self. This provoked a tension within my soul as it sought to expand. My smaller self became fearful of the expansion and wanted to desperately hold onto its well-defined boundaries and who it knew itself to be. As the expansion continued there arose that perennial question of *who am I?* The smaller self was furtively glancing around trying to find and define itself. This can either progress into varied levels of panic or simply close down the experience, reverting to the familiar, solid, and small relative reality of being. When there is no tension or holding onto oneself, this question does not even arise, and there is simply a marveling and awe and wonder at the universal nature. From the awe and wonder comes the opening to the greater wisdom of being. Again, another cutting of our experience at this awe and wonder stage may happen; however, that is just the beginning—the entry point, if you like—for this wonderfully wise and cosmic grandmother Sophia to reveal herself.

What may also restrict the fullness of such an experience is rushing too quickly back to our reality, trying to fill it back up with what we think we know or with distractions or cupcakes or whatever else we use to fill the frightened gaps in our soul. Sometimes the largeness of our experience is unfamiliar and so we clamor for our familiar life, where we feel falsely safe.

Remember, the mystic soul delights in the mystery, in the unknowing, not in its own small wisdoms. May we not wait for great random experiences but willingly cultivate our mother-ground of being, from where we will fall easily into the dissolution of our self and into our own great no-thingness. It is here that we come to know the union of our perfect mind and rest; this is the spiritual knowledge and experience that we all truly desire. May you cultivate your ground well.

Prayer to Sophia Wisdom

Great Grandmother of Primordial Wisdom

You live in places far beyond our normal reach

Beyond our thoughts and mind

And even beyond our small wisdom mind

I come to open to you

To your spacious womb-consciousness

Where the joy-filled delight of wisdom and
     being live

May I sit with you awhile
        and become as familiar with you
        as I am with my own small self?

May I lay this smaller one aside for now
        knowing I can and will return to her?

But for now may I come and immerse
        my being in yours?

Freeing myself from these limited boundaries

Enjoying the freedom of the grand spaciousness

And opening to the greater wisdom, if and when

She wishes to reveal herself.

Affirmation

I am Wisdom herself.

Meditation

Come into your natural breath, gathering yourself into the greater love. Bless your smaller self, assuring her that she is loved and cared for and that she will remain with you even when she lets go. Returning to your breath, focus in the middle of your brow (or third eye) and slowly let the boundaries of your body expand. Keep reaching out further and further until you feel no boundary at all around you, and feel yourself let go into the womb of the grandmother, the womb of spaciousness. Let your consciousness simply abide here. If the smaller self rises in fear, simply reassure it that all is well and keep breathing. Remain here as long as you are able and give yourself room and spaciousness, not filling your being up in any way.

When you feel complete, give thanks to the grandmother, draw your energy and self back into the boundaries of your body, and come visit her often.

Journal your experience of expansion.

The Interior Brow Star

*In your last life you were called to be a seer, but
you withheld yourself from your holy soul…May
you be true to yourself and follow the Spirit.*

Tau Malachi, St. Mary Magdalene:
The Gnostic Tradition of the Holy Bride

To access this interior star we must learn how to come into the quiet and depth of mind and be able to sit in the peace of this with no disturbance of regular thought. It is a place of darkness, of no-thing, of no-body, of no action. It is the place of repose. Only when we are able to do this does an inner vision open, one where there is direct perception of another reality.

Many years ago I visited the Aboriginal lands in central Australia. I had a driver drop me off out in the desert land far from the nearest town, agreeing to be picked up in five days' time at the same drop- off point. I then walked for some miles even deeper into the desert. There was nothing and nobody for many miles. I made camp and was simply there, alone—or so I thought. With no distractions, nothing to do, and nothing to occupy myself with, there came to visit oh-so-many thoughts. It was extraordinary to watch the mind at work. One minute I was thinking how wonderful it was to be out there in the desert alone and I never wanted to leave, the next moment I was internally crying and thinking how much I hated being there and I just wanted to go home. Then I was thinking how happy I was, and then how sad, then how courageous, then how fearful, then so calm, then so agitated, then so peaceful, then so angry. It was like watching a furious game of table tennis as thoughts bounced from side to side, back and forth, back and forth, in their duality, until they sped up so fast that they simply stopped. It was as if I was plunged into a deep, dark, empty cavern… and what a relief, what peace.

From this dark place of no-thought, real spiritual experiences then began to occur. I entered into other realities, other dimensional spaces, and I was able to visit realms far beyond our own. One was of a beautiful race of people of all colors with their faces raised toward what seemed to be a creator or, perhaps more accurately, the energy or force of creation itself, and they were singing the most wondrous, harmonious song of praise while gently swaying in their bodies, which appeared much less dense than ours. What was most noticeable was the clear feeling of unity and peace amongst the people and their unification with the energy of creation they were singing to. Their song seemed to be a transmission to the energy of creation itself, which was being reciprocated in kind. It was a harmonious balance of being and life force. It brought forth my own harmonious balance, which stayed with me long after my visit and strengthened my inner visionary capacity in a whole new way.

This visionary capacity then finds its place of manifestation through unification. For instance, being taken to the other realms, I found myself in unification with elder or enlightened beings. Though we had no form to speak of, we were all present as one consciousness, one mind, and we were creating a force field of conscious intent and inquiry as to how best to offer assistance to humanity. No description can adequately describe the experience or feeling associated with this, except it was like participating in one big mind or, as they call this in Aramaic, *mochin d'gadlut*. Another similar experience was finding myself in unity with many light beings, and we were creating a unified vibratory field through chant, which was directed toward greater realms and the light of creation. The commonality with all of these experiences was the ability to fully let go of my earthly form with absolutely no thought of self or for self and using the visionary capacity for a greater good. Returning to the earth and this form, I can say that the forgetfulness or dissolution of self is the key to any greater consciousness and is true freedom. The Buddhists speak about this in terms of emptiness and bliss, and Yeshua takes these spiritual truths and demonstrates the emptiness of death and the blissful embodiment through the Resurrection, a true manifestation of unification.

In *The Gospel of Mary Magdalene* we read that Magdalene had a vision of Yeshua after his death, and she enters into direct conversation with him. She asks the question, in a moment of vision, "Is it through the soul (*psyche*) that we see, or through the spirit (*pneuma*)?" He replies that it is through neither; it is the *nous* between the two that sees the vision. He says that where this *nous* is, there lies our treasure. What is this *nous*? This Greek word can be described as the higher mind or spirit mind, and it receives and transmits the fire and light of the Creator to the other elements of the human being. This *nous* is the meeting place, if you like, of where the divine and human mind join in a single dwelling or, in Leloup's words, "it is an inclusive third state where the two imaginally become one." This is not fantasy or the imagination as we would normally understand it; it is where mystic vision is given, where wisdom is born, and where deep feeling arising from the experience is felt in the soul and body, and thus becomes a full transmutation of the being and spirit. This is gnosis. Teresa of Avila also speaks of this felt quality, describing it as a certainty placed there by the Beloved, and even if the soul does not experience it again, the certainty itself never leaves. If, however, we do not feel it in the other elements of our human selves, it remains an experience of mental consciousness only. What Yeshua and Magdalene are discussing is something more, and this ability gives Magdalene the knowing and power to dispel the fears of the disciples and to encourage them to enter the world and become fully human, as Yeshua had been teaching them how to do.

To become fully human first requires the visionary capacity to know what this means—that is, to see the dwelling place of the Living Spirit in human form. This is what Magdalene was able to witness with the resurrected Yeshua, and thus she was able to become this in her own being. Her mind, emotions, and body were obviously in a state of deep grace and repose to be able to have this visionary capacity and to be fully conscious and able to enter into communication with the vision.

How can we more fully enter into our communications with the Spirit? How we can dissolve our chattering mind long enough to reach into our visionary *nous*? And how, like the crone, can we move from personal to universal or cosmic vision?

By practicing whatever brings us into the quietness of our being and by being willing to go further and deeper and longer. Also, to have equanimity toward what you will be shown or what you may experience. It may not always be according to your small mind's understanding. Go beyond with the crone into the dissolution of her dark night, enter into your visionary mind, and know her grace will guide you. In time you may find remarkable things occurring, such as time stretching out into both the past and the future, where you are able to gather valuable spiritual information. You may find you have greater seer capabilities than you thought, which allow you to now help humanity on its journey. Let the visionary mind grow beyond the astral planes of channeling, and keep going and keep going. You just might find your own Sophia or Christ-mind, or what can also be known as Buddhahood. And when moments of vision do come, be like Magdalene and engage with them. Ask for greater clarity and understanding. Ask how they may be beneficial for all. In this way, the energy of creation can give more, and in turn you can give more back. It can and will become a harmonious song of praise and unity.

Meditation

Lie down on the floor and use any music that may help your mind to relax and let go. Ask to fall into the quietness of mind and being. Then, focusing on your interior brow star, see a violet color gently spreading across your mind and forehead. Immerse yourself in this color and find a place of rest here. Ask the Shekinah if there is anything she wants to communicate with your spirit mind, and be in a mode of receptivity without expectation. Allow whatever happens to happen, and keep coming back and resting in this place, knowing your vision will open in accordance with your soul needs and gifts.

Journal what your spirit mind received or what you felt.

Further Meditation

Revisit all of your journal entries for the Crone of Dissolution and the Dark. Rest in them. See if any fears remain, and open to their transformation. When you experience too much chatter in the mind or feel your interior brow star is cloudy and unclear, return to this Crone of Dissolution and the Dark chapter and ask to know the dark quiet of your mind; ask for your visionary capacity to unfold.

As you are ready, move into the Virgin of the Clear Light.

8

Virgin of the Clear Light

> Now the young woman was very beautiful
> to behold, a virgin… And she went down to
> the well, filled her pitcher and came up.
> *Genesis 24:16 NKJV*

The Virgin (or Mother) of the Clear Light is the pure radiant awareness of our nature. It is the spacious ground of our being that has always been, is now, and always shall be in its perfected state. This Virgin is also known as our awakened being or pure mind; she knows the eternal well of the living waters and needs no other to show her the way, for she is the very well and the very waters; she is the Way.

Virgin of Wholeness

I am the forever whole.
Our Lady of Guadalupe

A woman of great light who is now known as Our Lady of Guadalupe appeared to the shaman Juan Diego in 1531 at the Hill of Tepeyac in Mexico. "I am the forever whole" is one of the names that Our Lady of Guadalupe relays to Juan Diego, and she speaks of her true nature as a virginal wholeness of being that has not and never will be compromised, divided, or separated in any way. The story of Guadalupe reveals how we may come to know this "forever whole" within our own being. The following is a traditional telling of Guadalupe with a revealed addition.

When Juan Diego was going out one morning to commune with the Great Spirit, he heard a celestial singing, like angels, and then he heard someone calling his name. As he ran toward this voice he came upon a celestial woman in all of her radiance. She asked where he was going. He replied, "Patroness, noblewoman, my daughter, my mother, my grandmother, I am on my way to your home, your dwelling, seeking the spiritual essence the sacred priests teach us." And she said to him, "Know, my youngest child, I am the forever whole and perfect maiden Saint Mary, Holy Mother of God, Holy Mother of the Giver of Life, Holy Mother of the Creator of the Human One, Holy Mother of the One Who Is Distant and Near, Holy Mother of the Creator of Heaven and Earth, Primordial Wisdom, the Great Grandmother of All." Wow!

Juan Diego firstly acknowledges that this celestial woman was the giver of all life through calling her patroness. He then offers his respect by speaking of her royal or noble being, and yet equally claims her personally as his daughter, mother, and grandmother—all of the feminine energies as one energy and being. Recognizing her as the very spiritual essence that his indigenous and shaman priests had spoken of, he acknowledges her home and her dwelling—that is, her being—as the very place that he was seeking to commune with. This Juan

Diego, though a simple man (as he speaks of himself), is obviously well advanced in his spiritual attainment, which he demonstrates first by being able to encounter and remain conscious during such a visitation. And second, he is able to draw together great spiritual respect with deep and familiar intimacy through his conversations with this celestial woman and by recognizing and naming the cosmic energies she embodied. What a great example Juan Diego is for us all; through persevering with and cultivating our spiritual life, we also can open ourselves to see, name, and speak the wholeness of this Virgin.

As Juan Diego was capable of this speaking and recognition of the perfected Virgin or Maiden, it allowed this noblewoman to reveal herself in ways of great depth. Beginning with naming her eternal wholeness, she reveals this "forever whole" as the perfected Maiden, the daughter who has blossomed forth into her wholeness of being and then opens herself to become the Mother of All Life. She speaks that she is the Mother of the Son and Mother of the Creator, the one who brings forth the human being and heaven and earth. She declares that she is the Mother of the Distant One, that is, Father Sky Spirit, and the Near One, Mother Earth Spirit. She then reveals herself as grandmother in the form of primordial wisdom, the Great Grandmother of All. What a beautiful rendering of our true nature as forever whole, while at the same time revealing the manifold energies of human and divine, spirit and earth, feminine and masculine, all as one indivisible whole. When, like Juan Diego, we can open to the Virgin, she can also reveal her—and our—true nature to us.

It is interesting to note that Our Lady of Guadalupe is known as the Brown Virgin, thus uniting the dark and light aspects of the Great Mother. There is a blessed weaving together of indigenous, pagan, mystical Jewish and Christian symbolism, and all traditions through the name and being of primordial wisdom. She is indeed Mother of All. And we are all her children, born to be and become what we can acknowledge and experience as our own noble and forever whole selves. In fact, we already are that, and we are just a glance away from seeing this—from acknowledging and knowing this to be a reality within our own being. Let us take a spiritual clue from Juan Diego and, like him, seek to commune with this dwelling place, the home of our spiritual essence and being, the Grandmother of Primordial Wisdom and the Perfected Virgin of the Clear Light that never dims or divides.

Prayer to Our Lady of Guadalupe
> Virgin of the True Perfection
> You who are forever whole
> May I come to know this within my own being
> To know my perfected daughter
> My Mother of All Life
> My Grandmother of Primordial Wisdom
> As one indivisible whole.
> You are the ultimate weaver of energies
> Of cosmic and human life
> Weave me into the very fabric of who I am
> And who I am becoming.
> Climbing upon the hill of my spirit
> I seek to commune with you and my life essence
> May you welcome me to my home
> As I dwell in you.

In this chapter we will take up the chant *Eheieh*, meaning "I am and I am becoming." We will then follow the chant with an affirmation.

Chant
> *Eheieh* (ah-hi-yah)
> I am and I am becoming

Affirmation
> I am forever whole.

Meditation: Connecting with Our Lady of Guadalupe

Find an image of Guadalupe and either place it before you or hold this image in your mind. See her smiling upon you and opening her mind and heart to you, willing to give you all. Surrender all thought to her and ask to know your forever wholeness. Fall gently into her presence, breathing with her and communing with her in any way she guides. Simply be open to receive and dwell within her. When complete, give thanks and take these blessings into the world.

Journal your connection with Our Lady of Guadalupe.

Witnessing the Pure Light

You have beheld the Truth of the Soul of Light in you.
Remember yourselves, and you shall be as I am.
Tau Malachi, *St. Mary Magdalene: The*
Gnostic Tradition of the Holy Bride

There is a story told in the Sophian tradition where one of the close companions of Mary Magdalene asks her about the true nature of the transfiguration and asks that Magdalene reveal herself in all of her forms. It was known that Magdalene was not only present at Yeshua's transfiguration but also experienced this great blessing and ultimate revealing of truth within herself at the same time. The companion asking for this was seeking to know the fullness of her own sacred womanhood and knew that this was alive in Magdalene.

Magdalene agreed to show her and the others present, so she came into her pure light-being and revealed the Daughter of Light, the Mother of Light, and the Grandmother of Ancient Days, followed by the radiant darkness of Lilith, Na'amah, and Iggaret. And then in and behind all of these faces, and yet beyond at the same time, she revealed the clear or virginal light of her nature. All were left in awe and wonder at such a radiant display, and the disciple who had asked for this to be revealed spoke that "In you the light and darkness are joined, and there is perfect being, perfect intelligence, and perfect delight. Truly, you are the daughter of the great mother!" Magdalene replied, "What I am, so also are you." Here, Magdalene clearly shows the depth and fullness of the feminine soul, with the light and dark faces of the daughter, mother, and primordial grandmother united in the clear light nature—the many as the one. As we have seen throughout this book, each aspect brings specific energies and qualities that are always seeking the fullness of our being and expression, and which actually come from and are indivisible within our own virginal being.

There are three gradations through which we will experience the movement of Spirit in our lives. The first is through vision, the second through hearing, and the third through knowing. Of all of these, knowing is the most valued and is understood to be the most accurate or authentic. With visionary experiences we may easily misinterpret their meaning or have no idea of their meaning at all. With hearing we can often put words in our own ears, especially those words we want to hear that will make us feel good about ourselves. With knowing, it implies that we had no prior thought in the mind about such a thing, thus distinguishing between our mind-knowledge and our spirit-knowledge. Too often we may mix these up and keep ourselves on the surface knowing only. What this spirit-knowing gives us is an increased wisdom and opening to greater realities that we could not know from any other source. Gnosis is another name for this knowing that comes through our own inner experience.

What Magdalene demonstrated through the above display is that it is possible for each of us to know the fullness of our sacred womanhood. In fact, it is where we are all called to live, so let us not fall into the falseness of some long-ago wisdom that it was only alive in the time of Magdalene and Yeshua. In *The Secret Gospel of St. Mary Magdalene*, saying 26, a woman says to Magdalene, "You are the holiness of womanhood we have been waiting to see." Magdalene replies, "What have you been doing while you were waiting? If you see this in me, then it is in you. All the while it has been with you! What were you waiting for?"

So, of course, the question still applies: what are we waiting for? The fullness of our sacred womanhood is alive here and now—first, if we believe it to be so, and second, if we are willing to spend time and open to our own internal encounters and experiences. And as a wise teacher once said, if not now, when?

Prayer for Sacred Womanhood

> Magdalene, daughter of the Great Mother
> You opened your soul, your mind, and your body
> Giving yourself fully to your own true nature

To the sacred womanhood that lives within us all.
I come this day seeking my own sacred image of
    this womanhood
My own sacred fullness
And that which lies in and behind
    my own pure light nature.
May even for a moment I glance at her
And she at me, losing and finding myself
In the indivisible light of my being.

Chant

Eheieh (ah-hi-yah)
I am and I am becoming

Affirmation

I am the essence of sacred womanhood.

Meditation

Come into awareness of your breath, following your own natural rhythm. With every breath allow yourself to feel an expansion of soul and heart. Envision Magdalene before you; connect your heart energy with her heart energy and breathe in this exchange between you. Ask that you may be shown or experience in some way your own image of sacred womanhood. Release all expectation and just be with whatever evolves.

Journal your feeling and experience of sacred womanhood.

Desiring the Clear Light

*All will be clothed in light when they enter
into the mystery of the sacred embrace.*
Jean-Yves Leloup, *The Gospel of Philip*

We return once more to the absolute necessity of desire. Without desire, the creative life force does not become activated, evolution limps along or even regresses, and our soul power atrophies, just as our muscles do through lack of use. We forgo our innate wisdom and our ability to be clothed in light. We forget the sacred embrace and no longer know how to send forth the power. And this is not just a personal loss but also a universal one. As J. J. Hurtak says in his commentary in *Pistis Sophia,*

> In fact, the expansion of the universe comes when consciousness awareness changes and, ultimately, is able to give birth through the spiritual creative (female) energy, bringing about the completion of the gnosis of the mystery. Without that creative energy elevated and restored there can be no continuation of evolution as it was originally given.

It is essential that we understand the creative nature of the Radiant Light Being. It is not some far-off, blissful, inactive state that has nothing to do with life; it is life itself—the true life force from which all emanates. She, this Virgin Light, lives in us, and it is up to us whether we choose and desire to live in her. If we do, we begin to make our way toward a conscious unification where there is a beginning and a completion eternally occurring and where the power of powers can live and go forth in and through us. It is desire that keeps this eternal nature and the life force in momentum, and without it there are no creative and evolutionary impulses that propel us into our greater humanity.

Again and again the feminine nature and soul need to get comfortable with the word and energy of power, finding her own way with it and understanding power as a natural part of her strength—something she simply is. She also needs to know that the clear light nature of her being is attainable—that it also simply is if she desires it. We should never underestimate the power of desire. Think of a time when your heart was truly on fire with desire; was there anything that could've stopped you if you followed it? In her book *Daughter of Fire,* Irina Tweedie writes, "You must want the Truth as badly as a drowning man wants air." We can rephrase this to say you must want your clear light nature as badly as your small self wants love. Perhaps now we can begin to feel the fire, and if we cultivate it and let it continue to burn, we may find it burning away the smaller self to reveal the clear light in and behind. We may then also be able to enter into the grander truth of the words of the master poet Hafiz:

> Fire has a love for itself
> It wants to keep burning.
> It is like a woman
> Who is at last making love
> To the person she most desires.

Ah, now here is the true and deep communion of love. Can we keep burning with desire for our own true nature in such a way? Can we continue desiring with a love that wants to keep burning? What fans the flames or the spark within us? Irina Tweedie also writes that "the roads to God are as many as human beings." It is up to each one of us to find our road or pathway of desire. A clue is hidden in what makes you feel alive—what lightens your spirit and opens you to the delights of your inner Beloved One. My own feminine soul revels in its manifold nature. Sometimes I sit in the deep well of silence before my altar, at other times I am playing in rivers and lakes and communing with the trees and birds. I dance, I chant, I pray. I enter into moon cycle rituals and rites of passage in my life. Mostly, I follow the desire in the moment, and in this way the sparks keep glowing and growing, the flames burn, and even when it feels as if the fire-pit of my heart has been rained upon, I come to my prayer and meditation with the knowledge that there is an inner brilliance still shining and radiating, even if the sky of my soul looks darker than the blackest night.

As we stir the desire and come to know our power, we are then asked to take command and use it for the good of all. Teresa of Avila described this time as reaching into spiritual maturity, which she experienced ten years before her death. She said that the Beloved had now put her in charge of her own soul; that she could no longer do her own will but only what aligned with the divine will. It is important to remember that the divine will is within us, contained within our deepest desire. Like Teresa, may this desire lead us to our place of maturity, and may we know that all those who seek will find the inner knowledge and wisdom of their soul, opening the way to the true radiance of their inner light.

Prayer for True Desire

Fire of True Desire, I call to you
And invite you back to my heart
Back to the origins of my soul
And my Being of Light
May we fan each other into delight
Into the radiance of truth
May I learn once more to commune with
And command the power of my soul
Using it for the good of all
In this world and all worlds
May I believe and know this to be possible
May I know it is already so.

Chant

Eheieh (ah-hi-yah)
I am and I am becoming

Affirmation

I am true desire; I am clear, radiant light.

Meditation

Drawing yourself into the state of quiet, fall gently into your breath and then envision or feel a flame within your belly. Let it bring to life a deep desire from within you. Then, as you are ready, see the same flame within your heart and let it burn away any false love and draw forth your deepest love and compassion. Then move to your brow and let a brilliant white flame burn in the center of your head, opening to your pure and radiant mind. And now see the same flame at your crown, pouring forth the pure, radiant light.

Feel your belly, heart, mind, and crown come into alignment and sense your true nature in and behind them all. Abide as long as you are able and give thanks to your Clear Light Being and the light of creation.

Journal the purity of your desire.

The Perfection of Being Alone

For I am the first and the last...
I am the bride and the bridegroom...
I am the incomprehensible silence.
Anne McGuire, Thunder, Perfect Mind

Human aloneness can be one of the greatest obstacles on our spiritual journey. It can draw us into false love, relationships based on need, or into a lower vibration of living, as we try to squeeze out some semblance of belonging. Many of us still carry the impression of our child-aloneness in the form of isolation and have not fully matured into an adult-aloneness, or the welcomed depth of solitude. When we are able to move from the darkness of aloneness to the light of aloneness, we can shift and experience the all-oneness of our being and begin to enjoy natural human and otherworldly connections in an elevated way.

As we engage with the way of perfection of being alone, it requires a great level of spiritual maturity, which is necessary for us all, whether we are partnered or single. Only in this way can we fully encounter one another and ourselves in the Virgin Light, in the truth of being. *I am the first and the last.* These words attributed to Sophia, the feminine presence in *Thunder, Perfect Mind*, are the exact replica of *I am the alpha and the omega, the first and the last, the beginning and the end*, as spoken by Yeshua through John in the book of Revelation 22:13. This mystery and way of being is not relegated to any one person or any one gender but is an archetypal image belonging to humanity as a whole. It is an understanding that we all have within us that spark of life that was there in the beginning, before creation, and will be there at the end. In the Gospel of Thomas, verse 18, some of Yeshua's disciples ask him how their end will be. He replies by saying, "Have you discovered, then, the beginning, that you should look for the end? For where the beginning is, there will the end be." Our aloneness is a key to experiencing this beginning.

I am the bride and the bridegroom. Remembering that the bride is not literally Magdalene and the bridegroom is not literally Yeshua, we also come to a deeper understanding of an internal bridal chamber where this bride and groom are as one, where the feminine and masculine embrace in unity through trust and consciousness. There is a story in the Sophian tradition where a disciple inquires of Mary Magdalene, some years after Yeshua's death, as to the nature of her sorrow and missing communion with him. She replies that her communion is even stronger than when he was alive. We may interpret this in a very obvious way of her ongoing connection with him in spirit, but also there is a deeper meaning she is conveying here. As Yeshua himself spoke before his death, it was necessary for him to leave in order that the disciples come into their own full power (John 16:7). Even though she came into her power while with Yeshua, Magdalene continued to develop her spiritual capacity after he was no longer physically present, thus aiding an even deeper spiritual connection between them. Certainly there was the natural human mourning after his death; however, there was not an unhealthy reliance on him for her spiritual advancement. She knew her own power within. Such maturity requires a stepping into both the bride and bridegroom of self, with the receiver and the giver dissolving in the bridal chamber, where the incomprehensible silence of union is known. It is the Virgin of the Clear Light who is this utter silence.

Our aloneness can be the greatest spiritual gift if we are willing to stay with it, to sit and walk through the uncomfortable nature of its smallness and reach into the greatness of our aloneness, our all-oneness, or our alpha and omega. Can we sit in the incomprehensible silence or does it frighten us? Do we want to fill it back up with the familiar noise of our life? It is odd what we can find falsely comforting, turning our back on true peace.

While playing in a river and enjoying the elements of the water and sun, and connecting with the rocks and the trees, I was aware that in that moment I needed to enter into a spontaneous ritual of self-baptism. And so I did, submerging myself three times. As I rose from the third submersion I was gifted with the blessing of the joy and perfection of being alone. I felt immense freedom, joy, and exhilaration, and I knew this was opening the way for a much greater love to be experienced in my life. And so it did, not only with myself but also with others, in such a pure and rich way of connection, without wanting or needing anything from them. This opens the way to pure enjoyment of another just as they are, finding the deepest connection through the most alive and unified place of being.

This aloneness is life and it is death, which is no death at all, for through it we enter into the eternity of our nature. Knowing the aloneness is the key to knowing this nature, our alpha and omega, our beginning and our end. May we befriend it now and know the truth of our resurrected Clear Light Being before we die.

Prayer for Eternal Silence of My Nature

    Magdalene, you who knew intimate union

    With the depth of your aloneness

    With the source of your power

    May you assist me now with this same journey

    May I step into my spiritual maturity

    Into my bridal chamber

    Embracing trust and consciousness

    And the light of my soul

    May I not pull back or cover over

    Fill up or ignore the greater

    Eternal nature that lies in wait for me

    May I know the truth of life

    The truth of death

    My beginning and my end

    My bride and my bridegroom

    May I know the incomprehensible silence of

    My virgin being.

Chant

Eheieh (ah-hi-yah)

I am and I am becoming

Affirmations

I am bride and bridegroom (for seeking unity of feminine and masculine self in your inner bridal chamber).

I am alpha and omega (for seeking your beginning and end).

I am the eternal silence of being (for seeking your incomprehensible virgin silence).

Meditation

Begin with the chant and then take up the bride and bridegroom affirmation. Speak the affirmation softly out loud; say it over and over as a mantra. Feel the sounds and vibrations on your lips and in your throat, letting these vibrations fall through the whole of your mind and body, losing yourself in the speaking chant. Continue until you fall into silence and simply be in your eternal nature.

The next day come and take up the chant and the alpha and omega affirmation and follow as above.

The following day take up the chant and eternal silence of being affirmation and repeat as above.

Journal each affirmation experience.

Playing in the Spirit

*The playing adult steps sideward into
another reality; the playing child advances
forward to new stages of mastery.*
Erik H. Erikson

In Kabbalistic teachings it is spoken that the Shekinah rests upon the joyful spirit, showing her wisdom and ways to the one who knows how to play in the spirit. As we immerse ourselves deeper into the mysteries we begin to realize that the whole of life is at play. The wind is playing with the leaves in the trees, the sun is playing with the flowers, the water is playing with the rocks, human beings are playing with one another, and the angels are playing with those humans who are willing to play back. It all becomes a grand swirl of different energies playing together. And so it can be with our own relationship with the Shekinah, the indwelling spirit of wisdom.

When I speak of playing in the spirit with those I work with, I watch as their mind immediately scours their memory for some childhood activity where they experienced play and joy. This is a good beginning; however, what I speak of is a maturity of spiritual play where we can consciously enter into and be taken up by the spirit. It is a prayerful place of play, where one first opens to and invites the connection with one's indwelling Shekinah and then simply follows where this may lead. It is a form of energetic play where angels will respond and recognize your presence, whether it is the earth angels in nature or the heavenly angels coming to join you. As part of this play, if we choose to invite and are able to feel or recognize these angels, then so much the better.

As children we take on play in an instinctual way; as adults we take on play in a conscious way. Trusting as a child can be tantamount to having blind faith. Trusting as an adult is rooted in clear and mature consciousness. Embracing both faith and consciousness through play can be a very real opening of the portal into the bridal chamber. As

Erikson says in the quote above, "The playing adult steps sideward into another reality." Beautifully said!

I have a power stick that was specifically made with the intention of uniting feminine and masculine energies, and communing with the different realms and universes. Most of my work with this power stick has been through play, drawing and sending blessings through playful dance. And I must say, the energy generated from such prayerful play is ripe with the Shekinah. There is no mistaking her presence as she moves through the space that my body and power stick inhabit. Sometimes I cannot even say exactly what happened, but I do know that something very real did occur. At other times very specific prayers come through me, prayers for others and myself that I would not otherwise think to utter. Whatever the outcome, I do know of her visitation through the feeling in my body and soul. I have been energetically charged and changed through the conscious awareness and playful exchange with this indwelling Presence.

There are many ways we can invite the spirit playfully into our lives, and sometimes our own earnestness works against us. With earnestness usually comes expectation of some result, and if this result is not forthcoming in the way we think it should be, discouragement can set in. Discouragement is a stranger to joy and play. Best we come with an innocent desire to commune, initiating a connection of sacredness and opening our bodies and souls to how and where they wish to be. And most of all, enjoy! Feel once more the freedom of enjoyment, the true joy of your spirit, your indwelling Presence. Let yourself be truly free for a time in your own sacred space and way.

Prayer for Sacred Play

Indwelling Shekinah
My inner Presence
I come to invite you to the
Sacredness of our play
Show me where and how

I can free myself
So that I may join this wondrous
Dance of life
Show me how I can free myself
From cares and worries
And spiritual expectation
And fall into faith and consciousness
Let me know that our communion
Will bring much more than I can know
Let me dwell with you
And you with me
In this eternal and internal embrace.

Chant

Eheieh (ah-hi-yah)
I am and I am becoming

Affirmation

I am the playfulness of the Shekinah.

Meditation

Feel into your heart and pray to be shown what place or activity will best support your sacredness of joy and play. Go with what first comes to you. Following your guidance, openly invite the Shekinah to be present, expressing your desire for communion. If you are in nature, connect with the spirits of nature; invite any angels or beings you wish to be present, and then simply let your dance of play unfold. Let blessings and prayers flow through your being or simply play in the silence of it all. When complete, give thanks. Feel into a deepening of faith and consciousness, and walk in the world in this way.

Journal your feeling of playing in the spirit.

Mystic Self-Knowledge

Those whom the Beloved brings to a certain
clear knowledge love very differently.

Teresa of Avila

Self-knowledge implies a mystic journey toward and into familiarity, friendship, and finally intimacy with All That Is. With this intimacy we move from the conceptual to the experiential, from outer words to inner sounds and knowing, and from disconnection to wholeness of substance. This wholeness then leads us to full embodiment.

Clare of Assisi, who has been a drastically reduced feminine figure by falling into the shadow of Francis of Assisi's light, brought forth great wisdom of embodiment. Feel her words as she speaks:

Place your mind before the mirror of eternity
Place your heart in the body of glory
Place your soul in the figure of the divine substance
And through contemplation
Transform your entire being into the image of
The Godhead itself.

She leaves nothing out. She speaks to mental consciousness and knowing one's mind as the eternal mind; knowing one's heart consciousness as the resurrected heart, raying out in all directions and revealing the Body of Light or Body of Glory; knowing one's soul consciousness as made up of the divine substance or eternal nature; and, through contemplating all of this, transforming your entire being into that image and likeness of the Godhead.

Contemplation is different from meditation. We meditate in order to know the contemplative state, where there is a quiet spaciousness of soul, free of our thinking and distraction. It is in this state where transformation can occur, taking us beyond "aha" moments and inspiring thoughts to experiencing a place of eternity, a space of something wholly other, a place of true self-knowledge or knowing.

Translating our eternal moments into moments in time is where embodiment happens. We must now, says St. Clare, give shape and form, sound and color, to what has none. The body, the soul, and the earth become the meeting place of the different worlds and experiences we can inhabit. Some can be spoken about, others remain in the intimate embrace, but they all contribute to the knowledge and the utterance of our being, the knowledge and utterance of our true name. May we join with Clare of Assisi and the many mystics who have walked before us, and those walking with us now, to come into this mystic self-knowledge, to embrace and embody it. May we dare to sit in the empty desert of our soul and allow the Godhead, or the light without end, to completely transform who we are, and especially allow it to spill over into our bodies. For the prefix "em" means to put into or within—that is, we can put our experiences within our bodies, allowing transformation of our entire being. You will know when this occurs, for the body feels distinctly different as it also evolves. And as Teresa of Avila so wisely said, the body can affect the soul, just as the soul can affect the body.

Our inner body experiences and our outer body experiences are long overdue for collaboration and union. This is what the feminine brings. May we rise to her grand wisdom and ways.

Prayer for Mystic Self-Knowing

I call upon all women mystics of the past
    the present, and the future
May your wisdom of wholeness set my
    disconnected self free
May I marvel at the fullness of my
    own created being
    my own substance of glory
Knowing I am the image and likeness.
May this feminine wisdom reveal
The divine sound of my name

The truth that it whispers.
May I become the
Utterance of my own name.

Chant

Eheieh (ah-hi-yah)
I am and I am becoming

Affirmations

(1) I am the utterance of my own name.
(2) My mind is the mirror of eternity.
(3) My soul is the divine substance.
(4) My heart is the body of glory.
(5) My entire being is the Godhead itself.

Meditation

Begin with the chant and then take up the first affirmation.

Speak the affirmation softly out loud, saying it over and over as a mantra. Feel the sounds and vibrations on your lips and in your throat, letting these vibrations fall through the whole of your mind and body, losing yourself in the speaking chant. Continue until you fall into your own name.

The next day take up the second affirmation and repeat as above. Continue until you fall into your own mind as the mirror of eternity.

The next day take up the third affirmation, with your soul falling into your divine substance.

The following day, take up the fourth affirmation of your heart and the body of glory becoming as one, and on the last day, your entire being as the Godhead itself.

After each meditative affirmation, give thanks and ask to be shown how to live this in the world.

Journal what you are shown, and ask to be assisted in living it.

Living the Fullness of Being

Mary said, "The essence of the Light is
transparent, it is the Holy Virgin; when you
become transparent, you will be united with her
and attain the perfection of your freedom."

*Tau Malachi, The Secret Gospel of St.
Mary Magdalene, saying 243*

The greatest contribution the feminine presence can make to humanity at this time is through bringing forward a grounded consciousness, where the soulful valleys meet the spiritual mountaintops and where heaven touches earth. We are called to enter into life in a fully engaged way of being and to let shine through a transparency of Light, a fullness of being. This is where we no longer seek any form of spiritual escapism or become bound by our emotional reality but skillfully navigate our inner and outer world as one reality.

The prefix "trans" indicates going beyond. When paired with "parent," we can understand it to mean going beyond any outer authority and also beyond any one gender. We step into our maturity, our inner authority, with our transparency leading to no-form or no-body. In order to do this, we must be willing to let go of any form, even the feminine one, knowing she will return with even greater presence and strength. A very literal example of this was when I experienced the actual dissolution of my physical body. I was energetically engaged with another at the time, and we both simply dissolved and disappeared, and yet our consciousness remained in full awareness and communion with one another. There was no fear, no grasping at the form of the body or who I thought I was or wanted to be. There was not any thought of whether my body would return or not. It was pure ecstasy! It was a wonderful, delight-filled experience that showed me the many possibilities of existing as this wondrous human being. When we can dissolve the self and/or body in such a way, then the ability for all forms to be manifested and expressed becomes a palpable reality, as Magdalene clearly showed her close companions in her transfiguration display. In being willing to walk into her formlessness, she resurrected into an even greater feminine form and was then able to share it with others through her healing, teaching, and guiding souls, calling upon the daughter, mother, and crone energies as they were needed. Through her ability to transfigure, Magdalene gives us a very clear example of losing oneself to find oneself, joining the heavenly realities with the earthly, and living them daily.

We are also called to know this no-form and all-forms, and are asked to enter into the willingness to know all of who we are. In becoming completely transparent, the inside becomes like the outside and the outside like the inside, as spoken of earlier in the Gospel of Thomas, verse 22. This is not just an emotional revealing but also a soulful reality of our true nature. We must know this true nature before we can reveal it. In knowing it, we then know the perfection of our freedom. And yet, most of us still cower and hide on the inside, whether it be our shadow or our light we are attempting to hide—even though, ironically, this attempt at hiding is obvious to others who watch on. To be transparent means no more hiding of our light or our darkness but understanding them as coming from one and the same source and thus bringing them into a union where they are transformed into something wholly other.

We have many women figures rising in our world, whether it be in politics, leadership, or teaching, all contributing their wisdom in ways that were previously not accepted. We have women still working in old patriarchal paradigms or in completely matriarchal ways. We have those who are bridges between the mountaintops and the valleys, and those who are muddling along anywhere in between, still trying to find their place. Some are still too earthbound, some too spiritbound, and some flying in both. Many are far too busy in their lives, still being dictated by the ways and expectations of this world, and do not give themselves the opportunity to enter into the fullness of their capacity, much less be aware of the greater capacity available. How can we live our nature of pure radiant awareness when we do not make room or time for it to be known?

If we bind ourselves with a story of "this is who I am," and name our better or worse characteristics as proof of that person, then we do not know ourselves. If we repeat our "I am" affirmations and still cry our victim woes in the night, then we are still bound in our divine conceptual fairyland. When we can sit in the richness of it all and have the ability to transfigure it at will, moving effortlessly from form to no-form to form, from mountaintop to valley, all as the moment asks of us, then we are beginning to live, to really live the truth of our nature. And when we can begin to do this collectively, then we will begin to understand the words of Yeshua when he said that we would do even greater works than he (John 14:12). This is the manifestation of the feminine in the form of the many, joining our collective energies to bring about the grounded consciousness of aware action and powerful love.

Prayer for Pure Radiant Awareness

Mother Virgin
Magdalene of the many faces
I come seeking my transparency
The essence of my pure radiant awareness
May I be willing to release all thought
Of who I think I am
And open to my greater capacity
May I be this in the world
Live this in the world
Joining my energies with others
Helping those still bound
In pain
May we rise, Holy Virgin
We as the many
And may the power of love reign.

Chant

Eheieh (ah-hi-yah)
I am and I am becoming

Affirmation

I am pure radiant awareness.

Meditation

Bring yourself into a quiet rhythmic breathing. Then, placing your attention at the top of your head, envision or feel your head and face slowly dissolving. Let this gentle dissolution continue down through the neck and shoulders, collarbone and arms and hands and fingers, allowing the very bones to dissolve. Continue down through the ribcage and chest, upper abdomen and belly, the whole of your back, moving down through the groin area and buttocks. Let the dissolution continue down through the thighs and lower legs, feet and toes. Feel the lightness and consciousness of your being.

When ready, envision a pure, radiant light beginning at your feet, coming up your legs and thighs, groin and buttocks. Let it come up the whole of your back and the whole of your torso, spreading into your heart and chest and across to your arms and hands and fingers. Feel it come up the neck and head and face. Feel the very bones and your blood also made of this radiance. Feel or see the beautiful radiant transparency of your being, and know you are made anew in the true light of your being.

Ground yourself through your breath and feel your feet upon the ground. Feel your body becoming more solid. Enter into a gentle physical swaying/dancing of the body and feel yourself becoming more and more grounded upon this earth but still emitting your radiant light. Take a walk in nature and continue to ground yourself in this existence, in perfect balance and harmony of dark and light, physical and spiritual, earth and sky, knowing the inside to be like the outside and the outside like the inside.

Amen and amen! Journal your dissolving and re-arising.

The Crown Star

*I am the forethought of pure light, I am the
thought of the virgin spirit...Arise, remember
that you have heard and trace your root.*

The Secret Book of John

Once we become more adept at coming into the stillness of mind, we open the gateway to experience the crown star. This star is where our small thoughts are transcended and we enter into a state of pure radiant awareness. From this awareness, knowledge and thoughts of Sophia Wisdom are transmitted to us, revealing the truth of our nature and the universe.

"I am the forethought of pure light." This tells us that divine thought precedes the light and that there is indeed a cosmic plan, as forethought implies a forward planning of some kind. As we read in Genesis, speaking the word of light into existence was the beginning of the first day of creation (Genesis 1:3–5), and to speak a word into manifestation first requires a thought. Creation continued to unfold from that initial and ongoing divine thought.

"I am the thought of the virgin spirit." This virgin spirit, as we have seen, is the purity of our being, the one who knows its spiritual root and the one who reveals the divine will. It is not immersed in or affected by our emotional experiences or traumas upon this earth. It witnesses all of this merely like a dream, and it beckons us to awaken to another reality in and behind this relative reality. Its thought is pure, coming directly from the radiant awareness of our being, and its knowledge is not of this world but draws us deeply into the mystery of creation.

We can experience this interior crown star through unification with the greater mind of the divine persona and seeking to know the very Virgin of Clear Light of our being, or also as witnessing ourselves as part of the great cosmic geometric design, if you will. This star can also be understood as coming into direct experience of the cosmic Christ consciousness. We can describe this consciousness as experiencing the intimate oneness of our being with this cosmic Christ, with the universal life force, and with all beings of creation. It is a deeply blissful experience where the underlying nature of infinite love is felt and known, and we experience that we are created from this light and love, with pure radiant awareness shining in and as our being. There is awareness that you are the divine names and every divine quality, archangel, and angel, with no longer any sense of separation or distinction, only unification. Teresa of Avila wrote that

> [T]he union is like…when rain falls from the sky into a river…
> all is water, for the rain that fell from heaven cannot be divided or
> separated from the water or the river.

The experience of unification, of which there are many gradations, goes beyond the escapist fantasy of a perfect world only filled with love and light. It reaches much deeper into our spiritual root and has a profound effect on both soul and body. It is a gateway to our true nature not as we perceive it to be or want it to be but far beyond our dreams, thoughts, or spiritual concepts. It is difficult to convey such experiences in words, but mystics have been trying for centuries to open the gateway for others to walk through. When you have been fortunate to experience such a gift, then you must "arise, remember that you have heard, and trace your root." In other words, you must now live from this root. In my own experience, it is the living of this that proves to be far more difficult than the experiencing of it!

There is never one prescriptive experience that describes these interior stars. To prepare ourselves for such experiences, it does require training, and especially that of the mind. We must become vigilant as to where our attention is being placed throughout the day. What are our minds absorbed in? Also, what aids us in focus and concentration? Like Teresa of Avila, if my mind is running rampant, I turn to the sacred texts and scriptures or immerse myself in one of the Gospel stories, feeling myself as part of the story and thus breaking whatever thoughts are seeking to dominate me. If I am in negativity, I seek a practice to help with this or I take up something I love to do; both of these help. Ultimately, we must train the mind out of its obsessiveness and learn to go beyond, to the expansiveness of the crown star. When we do this we can then open and become receptive to what is waiting to be given, as the forethought of pure light—the thought of the virgin spirit or the divine intelligence—seeks its expression through us, each in our own unique way.

A good example of this interior crown star is the story where the women and men disciples gathered to pray and meditate after Yeshua's death. They were in the Upper Room, which indicates they were in another realm or altered state of being. There came upon Magdalene's head, or crown, a great fiery light, and it then divided into many tongues of fire and went out to all present, also resting upon their crowns. *Ruach Ha-Khodesh,* the Spirit of Fiery Holiness, then inspired the men to go out and speak to others of this great gift of the Spirit. We are told they were able to speak many languages previously unknown, which esoterically means they could now access divine knowledge and read and speak the language of each person's soul. Meanwhile, the women remained in the Upper Room, in the greater realms, praying and dancing and chanting, generating the force field, or matrix of light, for the world.

Magdalene, known for her great spiritual intelligence and wisdom, readily engaged with Yeshua, drawing forth very advanced spiritual teachings through her questions and reflections. These reflections served to draw Yeshua into the fullness of who he was to become on earth, and they also proved to be a source of great consternation for many of the male disciples, as they could not match her great wisdom-mind. As a mentor and guide, I can speak affirmatively to this experience of being asked questions, as it can draw forth wisdom that I do not know or I might hear it in a new light in the speaking. It therefore helps my own evolution as well.

Let us, like Magdalene, open inward and upward toward our great feminine wisdom nature that is seeking to be known through this crown star and contribute to the intelligent advancement of our spiritual evolution.

Meditation

The color of the interior crown star is white. Envision a crystal cave filled with light. This cave is in the field of Machpelah, the cave of the ancestors (Genesis 49:29–33). When you are ready, enter the cave and see the reflections and the sparkling crystal points, and imagine that every point is filled with divine knowledge and wisdom. Sit in meditation, focusing on your crown star. Open to the wisdom that surrounds you and ask what is yours to be given. Stay as long as you feel. When complete, give thanks and leave the cave, drawing into your body the wisdom given.

Pentecost Meditation

See yourself in the Upper Room with many women and men disciples. See Magdalene also present. You are all in prayer and meditation. Then you become aware of a great fiery white light, and you see it alight upon the crown of Magdalene. She is radiant and on fire with this light. Then witness it dividing into tongues and feel it come to rest upon your own crown. Everything changes. Your mind opens. Your spirit is alive and on fire. You dance and rejoice, you chant and pray, joining with all the women present. When complete, you kneel and bow in gratitude, and you ask that this Spirit of the Shekinah make its home in you now and always.

Journal your experiences.

Further Practice

Come back to all of your journal entries of the Virgin of the Clear Light and see how your experiences may be opening to greater expansiveness of being. See how you may increase your focus and concentration, and ask to know your greater spiritual intelligence. Honor your own virgin being. When ready, continue onward.

The Weaving and Continuation
of the Interior Stars

I shall pour out my spirit on all humanity. Your sons
and daughters shall prophesy, your old people shall
dream dreams, and your young people see visions.
The Book of Joel 3:1

As we saw, divine thought preceded and brought about creation, which tells us where our creations can and ultimately must begin. Our task is to move from creating from the small mind to that of our divine mind, for in truth we are always creating—that is our nature, just as it is the nature of the Creative Intelligence from which we are formed in the image and likeness.

Our creation process in its purest form looks like this: we begin with thought, the crown star; we then have a vision of what this looks like through the brow star and the speaking of this with the throat star. Imbued with love and feeling, it enters the heart star, manifesting in its power through the solar plexus star, reaching into the navel star of desire to come into being, and finally finding its ground and manifestation through the root star on this earth. And so the pure light finds its home in us, in our entire being (as Clare of Assisi wrote) and our creations. Though spoken of in a linear way for purposes of clarification, the process is not linear at all. The interior stars are constantly interpenetrating one another, weaving their energies back and forth— that is, if they are opened and energetically flowing freely. Often there is an imbalance as we tend to lean toward either the upper or lower stars, or perhaps certain stars are closed or weak due to unhealed trauma. The preceding chapters will give you an indication of where your strengths and weaknesses lie.

Many mistake the interior crown star for the end of the journey, so to speak; however, that is not the case. In fact, as with any path of realization, we are always just beginning, no matter where we find ourselves. And so it is with the interior stars. In opening to our crown star, we move from white to a crystalline white reflecting all the colors of the rainbow, and we open another gateway to the eighth or transcendent star (located above the crown). This can be called the Primordial Sophia or the Primordial Christ Wisdom, going beyond mental conscious awareness and entering into an even greater form of realization and wisdom. It is here where the most intimate of journeys with the Beloved unfolds—where unification brings about our unique being as intended and destined to be known and lived in its glory.

A sighting of this was given many years ago when one evening as I was reading a tremendous force of energy came upon me, as if I was being swept up. I immediately went to my meditation chair, knowing something was happening, though I was unsure what. I was a little fearful of this unknown energy, but there was little time for this fear to take hold, as the Spirit took hold of me first. And then I saw Yeshua in pure golden form and as I looked upon myself, I saw that I also was in this same pure golden form. He took me far beyond this earthly plane into a space of pure nothingness. We were standing side by side but with quite a wide space in between. We then began moving toward one another and came together in complete oneness. And then we moved apart again, this time I moving to where he had come from and he to where I had come from. I became him and he became me. And then we moved and joined as one again. Once more we moved, with me returning to my original position, my being, and he to his. This continual exchange and joining happened many times, experiencing my own feminine being and then Yeshua's masculine being. When the uniting happened, no words can describe the sensation, only to say that in that moment I was completely and utterly my own unique golden being and the Christ being at the same time, with no gender or perhaps all genders. It was not an experience of merging and losing oneself but one of unifying and finding oneself, the true self.

Such was the nature of this experience that I found myself upon my bed (not knowing how I got there) six hours later, as though paralyzed. I could not move a muscle but was aware of every cell in my body seemingly being rearranged and alive in a way that they had not known before. It was deeply profound and affected every level of my being. Even my smaller self was bowed down in complete awe and humility, and had no need to try and take over and return to its false notion of leadership. It too had been touched and brought into true alignment. Nothing was excluded, and everything was expanded. What this speaks of are the very real possibilities for the ongoing expansion and evolution of humanity if we care to open to this and then seek to live it.

When our interior stars can know their true alignment, each within their own sphere and in relationship to one another, then we can continue opening to the transcendent star and to the rainbow body of crystalline light. For all the colors of the stars are as the rainbow, and a transparent crystal reflects ever so subtly these colors. In our pure transparency of being we can become this rainbow body, which can provide the bridge, if you like, not only to other realms and experiences but also to our inner nature and innate power.

The story of the Samaritan woman at the well (John 4:1–39) gives us an example of the opening and expanding of these stars. It has been commonly interpreted that this woman was of ill repute, as she had had five previous husbands and was with another man at that present time. However, if she was indeed held in such low regard in her community, they would not have believed in Yeshua upon the woman's words of testimony. Clearly she was a woman of great spiritual influence, a teacher known for her wisdom, which Yeshua also confirmed by addressing her as "woman." You may remember this is recognition of the wisdom of the Shekinah residing in one's being as spoken of in chapter 4, Our Mother of Light. Esoterically speaking, the six husbands of the Samaritan woman may be understood to be the six interior stars, and through her conversation with Yeshua her seventh star was activated and brought into alignment, opening the way for the eighth transcendent star and greater wisdom to be known. And this opening results in Yeshua revealing himself as *Mashiach*, the Messiah, as the one who is embodying the fullness of the Living Presence upon the earth—his first revealing of such a thing.

We can only marvel at the exchange of energy that transpired in this conversation. Clearly it was something his disciples were unable to enter, as we read of their jealous questions put forward to Yeshua as they arrived on the scene when they ask, "What do you want from her?" and "What are you talking about to her?" And when they try to ply him with food they have brought, Yeshua, still transmitting the Spirit, speaks of his food as doing the will of the One who sent him. Poor disciples; they were obviously not ready to receive what this woman was capable of receiving.

Similarly, the story of Yeshua expelling the seven demons, or seven forces of darkness, from Magdalene (Mark 16:9) speaks directly to the purification of the seven interior stars as opening the way for the transcendent star and its clear light source to be known. Magdalene was renowned, in turn, for healing many women and some men who acknowledged her, opening the way for each to encounter the wisdom of Sophia as their soul was capable. Let us open to our capacity in this moment and ask the bride, as the wisdom of Sophia, to reveal to us what healing and alignment we require with our interior stars, and thus help to heal the soul of the world.

Chant

Adonai Kallah Mashiach (a-doe-nigh kal-lah ma-shee-ach)

Meditation

Bring yourself into your mother-ground of being, opening to your ground of peace and pure radiant awareness. Ask for the bride to be with you and envision her as emitting a rainbow light. Let this rainbow light ignite your interior stars. Allow the bride to guide you in this exploration and experience. When complete, give thanks and take these blessings into the world, walking as your own holy bride, your own sacred woman and daughter of Sophia.

Journal all that was revealed.

Returning to all of your journal entries for all of the faces and the interior stars, see which stars flowed more easily than others. Spend time strengthening those interior stars in need, and ask to know an alignment of them all. Contemplate the interrelationship between the faces and the interior stars, and open to their eternal evolution in and through you.

Afterword

> But look, I am going to seduce her and lead her
> into the desert and speak to her heart. There
> I shall give her back her vineyards, and make
> the Vale of Achor a gateway of hope. There
> she will respond as when she was young, as
> on the day when she came up from Egypt.
> *The Book of Hosea 2:16–17*

Just as the interior stars weave in and out of each other, so too do all the faces of the feminine. Circumstances arise daily that invite us to take on different energies as called for, whether it is daughter, mother, or crone. Ultimately, that is what this book is about: learning how to actively engage with our many varied cosmic and human energies, and joining them through our earthly walk and embodiment, constantly reminding ourselves that our human potential is far beyond what we think we are capable of. Let us, in closing, return to the daughter.

Saintes-Maries-de-la-Mer, in Southern France, is believed to be the place where Mary Magdalene and those who traveled with her from the Holy Land first landed in their boat. There is a magnificent church in honor of the purported three Marys who came there, with much speculation as to who these three actually were. What we do know is one of them was definitely Mary Magdalene, and perhaps Jean-Yves

263

Leloup gives us a clue that goes beyond the physicality of the other two Marys when he writes:

> There were three who always walked with the Lord. Mary, his mother; Mary, her sister; and Miriam of Magdala, who was called his companion; for Miriam is his sister, his mother, and his companion.

We could also understand the three Marys as daughter, mother, and grandmother/crone. This does not negate the fact that there could have been (and most likely were) three physical Marys; it simply opens us to other dimensional understandings.

Whatever the case or cases may be regarding the three Marys, the church itself I can only describe as akin to the mother's womb. It is large, dark, moist with the ocean air, and overflowing with the feminine presence. In the crypt within the church there is a magnificent statue of a radiantly black St. Sarah, and she is perpetually basking in the light of the hundreds of candles brought by pilgrims. Legends surround St. Sarah as to who she actually was or is. One such legend tells that she was a young Egyptian midwife, brought with Magdalene from the Holy Land; another speaks that she is Mary Magdalene's daughter. I visited many times, praying and meditating, communing and honoring this feminine shrine of power. I was intrigued to know who she was, this Sarah. When we inquire into the meaning of the name Sarah in Hebrew, we are given the meaning of "princess." This title takes us immediately to an image of royalty, and in this instance it indicates a divine royalty of spiritual heritage. Digging deeper into the etymology of the linguistic roots of Sarah, we come across "to rise in splendor" or "ruler of righteousness." This opens the door even wider.

My own experiences with St. Sarah in the crypt were very powerful. In contemplating whether she truly was the daughter of Magdalene, it was revealed that, in itself, this did not matter. As spiritual teacher or mother, Magdalene had many daughters, whether by spiritual or physical birth. What mattered in St. Sarah's revealing was it was time for her mother's work to be completed. I felt the charge, the urgency for this to be so, and understood that it now rested with those of us in woman's form in particular to undertake and complete this work, the great work of the feminine pathway of realization.

On another occasion while in communion with St. Sarah I felt her ignite all of my interior stars, with light streaming from her interior stars to mine. This continued for a long time—in fact, so long that I was concerned for the other pilgrims entering as I was unable to move or leave off this transmission. The pilgrims were aware that something was occurring and very sensitively flowed behind me to give their offerings and prayers, honoring and not disturbing this communion. I was deeply humbled and grateful for their awareness, and felt the blessings of St. Sarah extending out to all.

What St. Sarah represents to us today is the daughter who rises in her splendor, into the fullness of her realized being. It is she who takes her place as a ruler of righteousness, offering and living a life of right ways and right wisdom. In the Gnostic text *The Reality of the Rulers* we previously saw Eve (as mother) and Norea (as daughter) contending with the rulers of unrighteousness seeking to defile or enslave them; Eve tricks them and Norea frightens them with her voice of sovereignty and sends them packing. The text then continues with another daughter, Zoe Sophia, who ultimately defeats these rulers of unrighteousness, or those who seek to enslave and control others. *Zoe* means "life" and represents the Daughter of Life, the living reality of wisdom (Sophia), and the realization of our sacred womanhood.

Magdalene was the Way-Shower for the realized woman, and each of us must find our uniqueness in the recognition, realization, and expression of this. The journey is not always an easy one, as it most certainly was not for her or Mother Mary or any of the women at that time, just as it is not in our time. Each age lives with its heartbreaks of humanity, and we are also asked to live these heartbreaks, personally and collectively, each as we are called, ever reaching into our faith wisdom, knowing that love will prevail even if—and especially when—the outer world does not portray this. We are being asked to join our Lilith and Eve, our darkness and our light, in order to complete Magdalene's work here on earth. May we be grateful to be brought up from the land of ignorance and to come back from our desert wastelands, returning to plant and tend to our renewed vineyards. May we do so with joy in our souls and with hearts on fire with love, bringing forth the fruits for all beings, bringing to fruition the Second Coming. Jean-Yves Leloup in *The Gospel of Mary Magdalene* seems to summarize this beautifully when he writes:

> We ourselves must live the love-filled, waking dream of the Magdalene, where death is met, passed through, and finally understood within the space of the Resurrection.

I leave you with two separate meditations and a last chant.

Meditation 1

You may wish to make a connection with St. Sarah. If so, I suggest finding an image of her and asking to enter into communion with her. You may feel compelled to speak your desire to help bring her mother's work to fruition on this earth. Ask for her blessings, and follow where she leads. Know you are a blessing for the people and the land.

Chant

> *Kallah Mashiach Ta-La Ta-La Talithael* (kal-lah ma-shee-ach ta-la
>   ta-la ta-lee-tee-el)
> Anointed daughter-bride, rise!

Archangel Talithael, which means "Rise! Daughter/Maiden of God," is the one we invoke and pray to for the realization of the feminine embodiment and the Second Coming. She is the keeper of the evolutionary women's lineage and traditions. Through communing with her, we commune with all those feminine beings of light who have paved the pathway for us to now walk and dance upon.

Her name is inspired by the story in the Gospel of Mark 5:35–43, where Yeshua raises the young girl to life. By invoking Talithael, we are also evoking our own daughter to rise into new life.

Meditation 2

Imagine you are the daughter who has died in story of the Mark Gospel. You are lying on the bed; your family and friends are crying. Then there come into the room beings of great light. It is Magdalene and Yeshua, and they are accompanied by both women and men companions. Magdalene and Yeshua stand on either side of you by your head, and the women stand on the same side as Magdalene, the men on the opposite side with Yeshua. The companions take up the chant of Talithael (as given above), and Magdalene and Yeshua take up prayers of the divine names. All of them have their hands outstretched over your body.

After some time you feel an incredible life force entering your body, and as Magdalene and Yeshua both command you to rise, you instantly rise up from the bed, drawing in a long breath of life and soul.

All the companions break out in prayer of thanksgiving, your family and friends now cry with gratitude, and Magdalene looks deeply into your eyes and says, "Now, go with this new life. Go and live for the restoring of the feminine and the soul of the world to their rightful place."

You offer your own thanksgiving and have a deep feeling of awe and wonder at this miracle of life and soul.

Appendix I

Hebrew Letters

Each Hebrew letter has many different nuances and meanings, depending upon the word it is used in and the letter it sits next to. It is all about relationship. I have therefore given various meanings. There are three Mother Letters that bring through the spiritual nature of the elements of air, fire, and water. All words in italics are Hebrew words. These letters are understood to have created the world and all the energies contained therein.

The Aramaic alphabet corresponds to the Hebrew alphabet in both symbolic form and meaning.

א *Aleph: Oneness*

The first letter; the letter that begins the many names of the Holy One, though spelled with an E in English: for example, Elohim begins with aleph; coming into *ain* (the cosmic womb of eternal spaciousness or the mother-ground of being) and *ani*, the true self; the Mother Letter of air and the letter of the primordial fire; all is contained in this no-thingness of aleph, the unification of all realms and universes.

ב *Beit: Home*

The dwelling place of the Holy One; the human one as this dwelling place; showing how to be at home in all realms; receiving or sending out the blessing, *brakha,* that is needed.

ג *Gimmel: Camel*

Giving to others in spiritual and material need, not from a place of superiority but from a place of knowing all your riches come from the mother; to lift up or be lifted, as a camel raises itself and the one who is upon it; the beginning of action, bringing the greatness, *gadol,* of the Holy One into embodiment.

ד *Dalet: Door*

The doors of our initiatory journey back into conscious love and unification; knock and the door will be opened; there are many doors we must knock on, and just as many that we are invited to walk through, leaving behind all from where we have come. Associated with the number four, the four directions of east, west, south, and north, and air, water, fire, and earth, respectively. Opening these gateways, or doors, we open to the spiritual dimensions in and behind these directions.

ה *Hei: Window/Transparency*

The letter that created this world; the feminine aspect of the Holy One; when we whisper *hei* we stand very close to the Divine. *Hineini,* "Here I am"; when hei occurs twice in a word, the first hei represents the mother and the second, the daughter. The window of the soul, the transparency of pure Presence; opening the window to your embodied feminine realized being.

ו *Vau: Linking*

Connecting heaven and earth; joining you to what is real; the ultimate truth; creating a spiritual link to your holy soul and to the one who watches over and protects; coming into unification, yet still retaining your uniqueness; the continuity of past, present, and future; spiritual continuum.

ז Zayin: Sword

The sword of truth that cuts through the small mind and all ignorance; the struggles we enter into for the sake of our evolution and healing; the spirit of sustenance; what truly sustains us on the journey.

ח Chet: Fence

A fence partitions and divides; the letter of polarities and opposites; challenges us to go beyond the ego-mind of separation; a letter of life; in bringing polarities into balance and completion, we enter true life; associated with the number eight; new realities and new beginnings; a soul no longer torn apart.

ט Tet: Serpent

The letter of absolute goodness, containing the power and potential of life; the primal energy of the feminine; the power of the kundalini; revealing that we were created with the benevolent wisdom and life force of the great mother and great father.

י Yod: Hand of God

A powerful and primal force, creative and transformative, yod is the letter that is to create the world to come. It is the smallest of all the letters but comprises the greatest power and contains infinity; we are asked to know that we also contain this. The dove is *yona*, flying out to find new life, a new earth, a new consciousness for the human one.

כ Kaph: Palm of Hand, Sole of Foot

Kaph is a sign of receiving our royalty and majesty; queenship and kingship, related to both the daughter-bride and the crown of the Tree of Life; sole of the foot; we are asked to walk this royal power on earth, within and through our true spiritual inheritance as being a divine child of the mother.

ל Lamed: Teaching and Purpose

To learn, to choose, to move forward; it is the first letter of the word heart, *lev*; we must therefore learn, choose, and move forward from the stirrings of our spiritual heart, learning how to discern, how to say yes, how to say no. Lamed is the tallest of all the letters, asking us to ever reach beyond, to evolve into the grandest human being that we can be; come to know your purpose as this.

מ Mem: Water

The Mother Letter of the compassionate womb-waters; to drink from the mother's living well, the living waters of life. Are we willing to walk in the *midbar*, in the wilderness of our soul, to bring all parts of ourselves home? We rest, *minucha*, in our mother-ground of being.

נ Nun: Fish

The mystical death, dying over and over again to who we think we are, to become who we are in our true radiant awareness. When at the end of a word, nun stands tall in her fertile nature, allowing the Shekinah to raise her into her full height and wisdom. In the beginning or middle of a word Nun is bent over in pure faithfulness to its own soul and to the Holy One. The Holy One's faithfulness to us can be trusted; do we trust in this divine faithfulness?

ס Samech: Circle

The enclosed dwelling of the mother, surrounding and supporting all souls and all of life; it is the circle or vessel of love that we live in, sealing the sacred circle with and within the feminine mystery.

ע Ayin: Eye

Seeing with the mystical vision into different realms and universes; seeing into and behind this reality into the nature of truth, into the no-thingness of reality and self; seeing divine light with the spiritual eye. The eye is the light of the body; do we see with the eye of God or with the judging eye?

כ Pei: Mouth

The power of speech: knowing when to speak and when to be silent, letting the spirit of the Shekinah speak through you and trusting that she will. We speak our world into existence, both small and large; the power of creation through our expression.

צ Tzaddi: Hook

When the mother's hook is in our soul and when our soul is hooked on the mother, there is nowhere else for us to go; in true humility we come to the Creator for everything. In this way true righteousness and justice are lived and fulfilled, dispelling the negative forces. Tzaddi can be known as the bride marrying the oneness of aleph.

ק Koph: Eye of the Needle/Back of the Head

Koph denotes absolute holiness and the cycles we move through in order to have this revealed in our being, or coming into our true sacred image. The back of the head is traditionally where negative forces enter, subverting our sacred image; the eye of the needle is the narrow path.

ר Resh: Head

A leader showing the way; the head of the year; renewal; the end of pretending, the end of illusion; returning to the true spirit of love to receive healing, *refuah*; returning to the sanctuary of grace.

ש Shin: Fiery Spirit

The *Shekinah* is the shining glory of the divine feminine presence; the Holy Spirit. The Mother Letter of fire, it is the holy fire that burns with passion, with a fiery intelligence, letting the holy fire liberate us from what is binding, thus bringing ultimate peace and completeness, or *shalom*.

ת *Tau: Fulfilled Perfected One*

The last letter, tau brings fulfillment—the return, *teshuvah*, to true wholeness and blessed healing, *tikkune*, repairing the ways that led you away from your queendom. The seal and fulfillment of the cross, the unification of all, tau is the return of humanity to its destined place in cosmic existence.

Appendix II

Spiritual Practices for Difficult Times

All of these practices can be taken up for yourself or others needing assistance. At the end of every practice pray that all beings in the same need will also benefit.

Negative Thoughts

When judgmental, self-critical, or other negative thoughts arise about oneself or others, very firmly say *no, I am not thinking that; no, I choose the light*.

And then, seeing yourself turning the other way, pray that the light of the mother will fill you. Choose an affirmation that is the opposite to the negative thought, such as *I am a daughter of Light; I am the heart of goodness*.

Chant *Adonai Kallah Mashiach* (a-doe-nigh kal-lah ma-shee-ach).

Painful Feelings

Let them arise and feel them. Then take your heart to the Dark Mother and ask for her healing balm.

Take up the chant *Kali Imma* (ka-lee ee-ma), *Ah-yah-mah Ah-yah-ma Ah-yah-ma*. Allow the pain to dissolve and the peace to come.

Stubborn Patterns and Obstructions

For those very stubborn patterns that keep returning, compassionately invoke and take up this chant to the Red Maiden. Akin to Tibetan dakinis, she is a wild young woman with a ruby red heart/energy body and long black hair who dances upon your negative patterns. Let her bless you with purified grace from her blessing bowl.

Chant *Ma-ah-sha Ma-ah-sha Ma-ah-sha Shekinah Ha-Mashiach*.

Protection from Negativity

By taking up our practices regularly, we can seal the light within. This Woman of Light chant is good for keeping negativity at bay.

Chant *Ha Isha Ha Elyona Amma Israel* (ha eesha ha el-ee-oh-na ah-ma is-ray-el), meaning "the Woman of Light, Mother of all humanity."

Envisioning the Light

Come into a place of quiet strength. Feel the light of Christ within your heart. Envision this light shooting out in front of you; speak or chant *Adonai Yeshua Mashiach, Adonai Kallah Mashiach*. Then envision the light shooting out behind you with the same chant, and then to your right side and to your left, above and below you.

Know this light of the unified Christ is within and all around you. And remember the holy bridegroom and holy bride are only personified through Yeshua and Magdalene, and both are contained within each one of us. *Adonai* means "my beloved" or "my foundation."

Archangels of Protection

ARCHANGEL MICHAEL: *Ya-mee-ha Mick-ee-el*

A being of great strength with a sword of fire. You may also envision the face of the lion and the roar of protection shattering all that is disturbing you.

Forcefully chant *Elohim Givor* (el-oh-heem give-or), *Ah-ya-ko-ma Kamael* (ka-mee-el).

Envisioning Kamael as a great being of fire burning through the darkness or negativity assailing you. Also envision yourself surrounded by a ring of fire.

Finding Comfort in Difficult Times

Sometimes when we have been through troublesome times and emotions, we need to feel comforted. It is good then to ask for this and let yourself be enfolded in the womb of the Mother or the Archangel Mumiah.

Chant *Ma-ya Ma-ya Moom-ee-ah*.

Keeping Faith in Dark Times

Sometimes our lives or the world can overwhelm us with their dark bleakness, violent means, and lack of love. More than ever, we need to keep our faith strong in these times, which really means to hope—keeping the faith alive even when everything else points the other way. Our world needs this more than ever right now.

Archangel Dahariel can restore and strengthen our faith and the faith of others in need. Chant *Adonai Da-ha Da-ha Da-ha-ree-el*.

For Inner Strength

When we can realize our inner strength, beauty, and intelligence, then very little can disturb us. Welcome Na'amah into your being for this realization. Chant *Nay-ah Nay-ah Nay-ah-mah*.

Glossary

Adonai: My beloved; my foundation; the divine name for the daughter-bride branch, *sefirot*, on the Tree of Life.

All That Is: The entirety of all realms of creation, creator, and the created.

Amma: "Mother" in Aramaic.

Anima Mundi: The soul of the world; the feminine principle and energy; the one who births forth the creative life force of all beings. She dwells within us and every living creature. She is the very matrix itself in which life was created and continues to be created.

Anointed: One who is embodying the fullness of the light; the enlightened state of body, mind, and soul, female and male energies together. *Mashiach* in Hebrew, *Christos* in Greek, in the form of Magdalene and Yeshua, bride and bridegroom, all of humanity has this potential.

Asherah: The divine name for the goddess of Canaan; the wife or divine consort of Yahweh. Archaeological evidence has been found giving blessings from Yahweh and Asherah; she was represented as a tree or wooden pillar. In Sophian tradition Asherah is known as the joining of the mother and the daughter.

Bardos: In Buddhist terminology, bardos are the transitional states of consciousness we enter into during our death process. In Gnostic terminology these bardos are called the heaven and hell realms and are also recognized as states of consciousness; we are living in these states or realms daily and will experience them in greater vividness at our death.

Beloved: The Living Presence within every being and creature.

Black Path: The primordial space or great no-thingness that we enter into at our death before we begin our journey through the *bardos,* or transitional states of consciousness.

Cathars: The Christian Gnostic/mystics who were ruthlessly persecuted by the Roman Catholic Church in the early eleventh century. The Cathars practiced nonviolence and sacred sexuality, had women leaders and priestesses, and honored the union of the feminine and masculine.

Clare of Assisi: Thirteenth-century saint called *Chiara* in Italian, meaning "light," she was sought out by many, including Francis of Assisi and popes and bishops for spiritual guidance. She brought a purity of the light forward with deep understanding of the way of embodiment.

Cosmic Womb: From where all life is born and to where all life returns; the womb of eternity and eternal love.

Dahariel: The archangel who helps souls restore faith. Dahariel can take on any form to assist souls in need and is a gentle presence who leads souls back to the original love.

Daughter of Light: Daughter of the Day, daughter Sophia, the maiden, Kallah Mashiach, the holy bride; the aspect of vitality and life; one who embodies the light and life itself walking upon this earth realm.

Daughter of the Dark: Lilith or Lilatu; Kali Kallah; embodies the wild boldness of the feminine, whom no one can tame or contain; she represents both our shadow self and the energy that liberates.

Elizabeth: The wise crone who teaches the young Mother Miriam (Mother Mary) and learns from her at the same time; the mother of John the Baptist.

Eve: *Havah* in Hebrew, meaning "to be and become life." The daughter/mother who set humanity on its course of conscious unification while walking in the land of duality.

Gnosis: The mystic knowledge that reaches into the ultimate reality and truth. Going beyond the small mind, it enters into the wisdom mind of Sophia, revealing divine mysteries and direct experience of this.

Havah: See Eve.

Holy Bride: Embodied in the persona of Mary Magdalene; the inner royal feminine soul of every woman and man.

Iggaret: The great cosmic grandmother or crone; Ancient One of Knowledge; the very Soul of Creation; also known as the Hag of Chaos, the Void, and End of Days; the creative and destructive force of creation itself respectively.

Imma: "Mother" in Hebrew.

Incubi: Demons taking on the form of a male said to have sexual intercourse with women in their dreams or nightmares; from the Old Latin word meaning "to lie on top of" or the Latin word meaning "nightmare."

Kabbalah: The Jewish mystical system revealing the universal pattern of creation and the relationship between creator, creation, and the created, including human and all beings, angelic, elemental, and the myriad other beings that populate the many universes and realms.

Kali: "Origins" in Sanskrit; in Hebrew it means "to be toasted or parched," that is, one that is darkened or one who thirsts for the hidden light.

Kali Kallah: Dark or Black Bride; see Daughter of the Dark.

Kallah Mashiach: The anointed bride; see Daughter of Light.

Klippot: Energetic influences that keep us bound, or protective influences that cover our soul until we are ready to let them go; singular is klippah.

Korbanot: In the Hebrew tradition, the many laws pertaining to sacrifices and offerings to God. Korban is singular.

Kundalini: See Serpent.

Land of the Living: Those souls who are in the enlightened state.

Lilith: See Daughter of the Dark.

Living Presence: The Indwelling Spirit.

Machpelah: The cave of the ancestors where Abraham and Sarah, Isaac and Rebekah, and Leah and Jacob were buried; a cave of great wisdom (see Genesis 49:29–33).

Maitreya: The one who is to come as the second Buddha, restoring the *dharma*, the teachings, when people and the earth are in much darkness.

Mashiach: See Anointed.

Mater: Latin for "mother"; the material nature of our being.

Michael: The archangel who burns the dross of the soul in the purifying flame and fire; the protector of souls who guides souls into and through the *bardos*, or heavens, of the afterlife.

Midrashim: Ongoing revealed spiritual teachings and commentaries made accessible and relevant to the contemporary needs of the people.

Mochin d'gadlut: Aramaic for "expanded consciousness" or "radiant spacious awareness"; the ability to enter into the higher branches on the Tree of Life, leading to ever-greater compassion.

Mother-Ground of Being: The eternal being from which all of who we are arises from; the eternal being that is the very nature of our soul and ever beyond it at the same time.

Mother Miriam: Mother Mary, the mother of Yeshua; an advanced soul.

Mother of the Dark: The Black Madonna, the Dark Mother, Na'amah, Queen of the Night; the strength and intelligence of the feminine nature; the compassion of knowing all beings and spirits are born from her; feminine justice; the great liberator from negative influences.

Mumiah: The archangel bringing the energy of the womb of the mother; a very nourishing, protective energy; all-enfolding.

Na'amah: See Mother of the Dark.

Norea: Eve's virgin daughter, the one knowing her divine image and consciousness; the one who speaks loudly and repels the negative forces seeking to bind her.

Ouroboros: The alchemical image of the serpent eating its own tail, creating an unending circle and representing the eternal nature of life and the soul.

Pistis Sophia: Literally "faith wisdom"—the daughter of Sophia.

Rechabiya: The archangel who brings great expansiveness to one's soul; she will open your mind and soul to other realms and ways of being.

Red Maiden: An aspect of the dark daughter envisioned as a wild, strong young woman with long black hair and a ruby red heart energy, carrying a sword to cut away all falsity and ignorance, false pride and arrogance, lack and other soul lies. She also carries a blessing bowl from where she pours her blessings upon you. These blessings are the transformed energies of your being.

Ruach Elohim: In Hebrew, the very spirit of creation; in the Book of Genesis and the creation story it is Ruach Elohim who breathes upon the waters to bring this material world into being.

Ruach-Ha-Khodesh: In Hebrew, the "Holy Spirit" or "the Breath of the Spirit."

Saint Sarah: The black daughter whose original image resides in the Church of the Three Marys at Saintes-Maries-de-la-Mer, Southern France. She is known as the daughter of Magdalene, spiritual and earthly midwife, and patron saint of the gypsies.

Sandalphon: The archangel associated with Magdalene/the daughter-bride; the shoe angel who will teach you to walk upon this earth in sacredness. Sandalphon reveals the feminine mysteries and is the guardian of the sacred circle who seals the directions accordingly.

Second Coming: The time when the many will experience the radiant awareness of their being; the rising and embodiment of the Feminine Realized Being in all.

Secret Gospel of Mary Magdalene: An additional collection of secret sayings of the bride as given in *St. Mary Magdalene: The Gnostic Tradition of the Holy Bride.*

Serpent: The kundalini energy; the life force of the human one. Lilith in the Garden of Eden initiated this life force, which eventually transferred into negative connotations of the feminine and/or the force of evil.

Shekinah: The indwelling feminine presence of the Holy One; the immanent one who guides all on earth.

Sheol: The realms where the Holy One and the archangels and angels cannot be seen, heard, or felt.

Snake: See Serpent.

Sophia Nigrans: See Mother of the Dark.

Sophia Stellarum: Our Wisdom Mother of the Stars; the Cosmic Nature of the Mother.

Soul of the World: See *Anima Mundi.*

Succubi: Demons taking on female form said to seduce and have sexual intercourse with men in their night dreams, responsible for male nocturnal emissions; *succubi* means "to lie beneath."

Talithael: The archangel who brings forward feminine lineages and wisdom and the Second Coming; the movement and energy of rising into renewed life, based on the healing resurrection of the young girl by Magdalene and Yeshua and the disciples. The name Talithael alludes to the meaning "Rise, Daughter!" as referred to in Mark 5:41.

Teresa of Avila: Sixteenth-century Spanish mystic who overcame extraordinary opposition by male clerics and who, by following her own inner voice, created a new Carmelite Order. She is renowned for exceptional insight into the workings of the human soul and for her humor in dealing with the ego.

Tikkune: Means "to restore or repair" in Hebrew; to heal the personal wounds for the sake of the universal soul of the world.

Thunder, Perfect Mind: A text in Coptic discovered as part of the Nag Hammadi Library, dated around second or third century. A remarkable paradoxical text attributed to the voice of Sophia, that of the feminine nature who has gone beyond and yet includes all duality. She is the voice of pure radiant awareness in the fullness of her strength, willing to every experience and feeling in life.

Tree of Life: See Kabbalah.

Virgin of the Clear Light: The aspect of soul that cannot be touched or defiled—the pure essence or radiant being.

Zoe Sophia: The Daughter of Life; the living reality of wisdom and realization of sacred womanhood; the one who defeated the rulers of unrighteousness.

Bibliography

Andrews, Ted. *Animal Speak: The Spiritual & Magical Powers of Creatures Great and Small.* St. Paul, MN: Llewellyn, 1997.

Armstrong, Regis J., translator. *Clare of Assisi: Early Documents— The Lady.* New City Press, 2006.

Barnstone, Willis, and Marvin Meyer, editors. *The Gnostic Bible.* Boston & London: Shambhala, 2009.

Don, Meghan. *Meditations with Teresa of Avila: A Journey into the Sacred.* Novato, CA: New World Library, 2011.

———. *Sacred Companions Sacred Community: Reflections with Clare of Assisi.* Bloomington, IN: iUniverse, 2008.

Freeman, Mara. *Kindling the Celtic Spirit.* San Francisco: HarperSanFrancisco, 2001.

George, Demetra. *Mysteries of the Dark Moon: The Healing Power of the Dark Goddess.* New York: Harper One, 1992.

Haas, Michaela. *Dakini Power.* Boston & London: Snow Lion, 2013.

Hall, Nor. *The Moon and the Virgin.* New York: Harper & Row, 1980.

Hurtak, J. J. *Pistis Sophia: A Coptic Text of Gnosis with Commentary.* Los Gatos, CA: The Academy for Future Science, 1999.

Judith, Anodea. *Wheels of Life: A User's Guide to the Chakra System*. St. Paul, MN: Llewellyn, 2002.

Jung, C. G. *Mysterium Coniunctionis*. Princeton, NJ: Princeton UP, 1989.

Kaplan, Aryeh. *Sefer Yetzirah: The Book of Creation*. Boston, MA/York Beach, ME: Weiser Books, 1997.

Kushner, Lawrence. *The Book of Letters: A Mystical Alef-bait*. VT: Jewish Lights Publishing, 1990.

Ladinsky, Daniel. *I Heard God Laughing: Renderings of Hafiz*. Walnut Creek, CA: Sufism Reoriented, 1996.

Leloup, Jean-Yves. *The Gospel of Philip*. Translated by Joseph Rowe. Rochester, VT: Inner Traditions, 2004.

————. *The Gospel of Mary Magdalene*. Translated and notes by Joseph Rowe. Rochester, VT: Inner Traditions, 2002.

Malachi, Tau. *Gnosis of the Cosmic Christ: A Gnostic Christian Kabbalah*. Woodbury, MN: Llewellyn, 2005.

————. *The Gnostic Gospel of St. Thomas: Meditations on the Mystical Teachings*. St. Paul, MN: Llewellyn, 2004.

————. *St. Mary Magdalene: The Gnostic Tradition of the Holy Bride*. Woodbury, MN: Llewellyn, 2006.

Markale, Jean. *Cathedral of the Black Madonna: The Druids and the Mysteries of Chartres*. Translated by Jon Graham. Rochester, VT: Inner Traditions, 2004.

Matt, Daniel, C. *The Essential Kabbalah: The Heart of Jewish Mysticism*. Palo Alto: Harper San Francisco, 1996.

————, translator. *The Zohar: Pritzker Edition, Vols. 1 & 2*. Stanford University Press, 2003.

McDermott, Violet, translator. *The Fall of Sophia*. Lindisfarne Books, 2001.

McGuire, Anne, translator. *Thunder, Perfect Mind*. Diotima, 2000.

Meyer, Marvin W., translator. *The Secret Teachings of Jesus: Four Gnostic Gospels*. New York: Random House, 1984.

Munk, Rabbi Michael L. *The Wisdom in the Hebrew Alphabet*. New York: Mesorah Publications, 1998.

Nachman, Rebbe. *Anatomy of the Soul*. Collated by Chaim Kramer. 2nd Edition. Jerusalem, New York: Breslov Research Institute, 2014.

The New Jerusalem Bible: Standard Edition. New York: Doubleday, 1999.

O'Donohue, John. *To Bless the Space Between Us: A Book of Blessings*. New York: Doubleday, 2008.

Patai, Raphael. *The Hebrew Goddess*. Detroit: Wayne State UP, 1990.

Prophet, Elizabeth Clare. *Mary Magdalene and the Divine Feminine: Jesus' Lost Teachings on Woman*. Gardiner, MT: Summit University Press, 2005.

Ray, Reginald. *Touching Enlightenment: Finding Realization in the Body*. Boulder, CO: Sounds True, 2008.

Roob, Alexander. *Alchemy & Mysticism*. Cologne, Germany: Taschen, 2001.

Seidman, Richard. *The Oracle of Kabbalah*. New York: Thomas Dunne Books, St. Martin's Press, 1999.

Stone, Sidra. *The Shadow King: The Invisible Force That Holds Women Back*. Lincoln, NE: iUniverse, 2000.

Tweedie, Irina. *Daughter of Fire: A Diary of a Spiritual Training with a Sufi Master*. Nevada City, CA: Blue Dolphin Publishing, 1986.

Underhill, Evelyn. *Mysticism: The Nature and Development of Spiritual Consciousness*. Oxford, England: Oneworld Publications, 1999.

Vaughan Lee, Llewellyn. *The Return of the Feminine and the World Soul*. Inverness, CA: The Golden Sufi Center, 2009.

Index

To Write to the Author

If you wish to contact the author or would like more information about this book, please write to the author in care of Llewellyn Worldwide Ltd. and we will forward your request. Both the author and the publisher appreciate hearing from you and learning of your enjoyment of this book and how it has helped you. Llewellyn Worldwide Ltd. cannot guarantee that every letter written to the author can be answered, but all will be forwarded. Please write to:

Meghan Don
c/o Llewellyn Worldwide
2143 Wooddale Drive
Woodbury, MN 55125-2989

Please enclose a self-addressed stamped envelope for reply or $1.00 to cover costs. If outside the USA, enclose an international postal reply coupon.

Many of Llewellyn's authors have websites with additional information and resources. For more information, please visit our website at

www.llewellyn.com